SCHOOL COUNSELING PRINCIPLES

REMEMBERING THE PAST, SHAPING THE FUTURE

A History of School Counseling

BY NORMAN C. GYSBERS, PH.D.

AMERICAN
SCHOOL
COUNSELOR
ASSOCIATION

The American School Counselor Association (ASCA)
supports school counselors' efforts to help students focus on
academic, personal/social and career development so they
achieve success in school and are prepared to lead fulfilling lives
as responsible members of society. ASCA, which is the school
counseling division of the American Counseling Association,
provides professional development, publications and other
resources, research and advocacy to professional school
counselors around the globe. For more information, visit
www.schoolcounselor.org.

1101 King St., Suite 625, Alexandria, VA 22314
(703) 683-ASCA, (800) 306-4722, fax: (703) 683-1619
www.schoolcounselor.org

ISBN 978-1-929289-24-0

Dedication

To Professional School Counselors:
With Respect, Admiration, and Deep
and Lasting Appreciation

Acknowledgements

The field of school counseling has a deep and rich history. Thus, any book that attempts to provide an overview of this history must acknowledge the substantial and long-lasting contributions of many individuals over the past 100-plus years. No attempt is made here to name these individuals. Instead, you will find the names of these individuals and descriptions of their contributions in the pages of this history as the decades unfold. New entrants to the field of school counseling need to understand that they are standing on the shoulders of many individuals who have come before them.

Particular acknowledgement is due to the American School Counselor Association, its executive director Kwok-Sze Wong, Ed.D., and Kathleen Rakestraw, director of communications, for their willingness to take on a project of this type, firm in their belief that an understanding of our history is critical to our success today and in the future.

Finally, and most importantly, I gratefully acknowledge all of the work that Linda Coats, administrative associate at the University of Missouri Career Center, did to bring the book to print. Without her assistance this book would not have happened.

Preface

The field of school counseling as we know it today is just over 100 years old. During these 100-plus years, school counseling evolved from a focus on vocational guidance being delivered mainly by teachers and administrators to a comprehensive program focusing on the academic, career and personal-social development of all students being delivered by school counselors working closely and collaboratively with teachers, parents and administrators. These 100-plus years witnessed wide-ranging and sometimes spirited discussions and debates about school counseling purposes; the terminology to describe and label school counseling; the school counselor's role and functions; and the appropriate structures to organize, implement, manage and evaluate school counseling. Discussion and debates about school counselor selection, training, leadership and supervision also occurred over the decades.

It is clear that school counseling did not evolve in a vacuum. It evolved as a result of the interaction of myriad changing and challenging social, educational and economic forces at work over the past 100-plus years. The progressive movement of the early 1900s sought to change conditions brought about by the Industrial Revolution by reforming education. The social justice issue for vocational guidance then was child labor. World War I followed and had an impact as did the various social and educational movements of the 1910s and 1920s, including the mental hygiene, progressive education, child study/development and psychometric movements. The 1930s witnessed turbulent times due to the Great Depression. World War II in the 1940s, the Korean War of the early 1950s, the cold war of the late 1940s to the early 1990s, the Vietnam War of the late 1960s and early 1970s and the conflicts in Iraq and Afghanistan all have had an impact on our society and our educational and economic systems. At home, during this time period, the civil rights movement, school reform, the issues of gender equity and sexual orientation as well as increasing concern about multiculturalism and diversity were having an impact too. In the late 1990s and during the first decade of 2000, academic achievement became a national priority, particularly the academic achievement of low-income students and minority students. The term "academic achievement gap" was used to label this issue. As a result of these issues and concerns, school counselors were being asked to take on leadership, evaluation and advocacy roles and to become actively involved in social justice issues.

At the same time our economy was changing rapidly. Occupational and industrial specialization continued to increase dramatically. Increasing size, globalization and complexity were and are the rule rather than the exception, often creating job invisibility and making the transition from school to work and from work to further education and back again more complex and difficult.

It is important to acknowledge as well the contributions of many individuals to school counseling's growth and development. They contributed their knowledge and expertise to this effort. Legislation also played a part at the state and national levels by focusing attention on specific societal concerns and economic issues. Examples include vocational education (career and technical education) legislation and educational reform legislation such as the National Defense Education Act and the No Child Left Behind Act. Finally, projects such as Education Trust's Transforming School Counseling Initiative and the development of standards for school counselor preparation by the American School Counselor Association, the Association for Counselor Education and Supervision and the Council for the Accreditation of Counseling and Related Programs have had and continue to have an impact on the nature and structure of school counselor education as well as on the practice of school counseling.

Several books have traced the history of the field including ones by Brewer (1922, 1942), Davis (1956), Picchioni and Bonk (1983), Reed (1947) and Stephens (1972). A number of dissertations also added to our understanding of the evolution of our field including ones by Johnson (1972) and Odell (1971). Other books have chapters that traced our history too, but there has not been a recent book that has focused on our history over the full 100-plus years.

Why is a book about the history of school counseling important?
Picchioni and Bonk (1983) answered this question as follows:

"Every field of knowledge has a history. Ideas and institutions which are
now accepted as commonplace all had their origins in the past. Present
identity results from innumerable historical antecedents. No one can succeed in being ahistorical ... Modern guidance grew from the discoveries,
inventions and mistakes of yesterday. Out of the search for guidance's
past it is possible to apply what is learned to the future – this is ultimate
use of historical knowledge. History does not cheat us: indeed, if those in
guidance do not think about its past, then surely guidance will have no
future" (p. 1).

Purpose and Organization of the Book

The purpose of the book is to trace the development of school counseling from its beginnings in the early 1900s to the present time. To accomplish this the book is organized by decades.

The sources of information for the book were the early histories, articles in many journals, and many books and book chapters. No preconceived organizer was used to select and group the contents of each of the chapters. Instead, the contents to be included in the chapters flowed from the material available in these sources for the decades in question. The goal was to let the literature of the decades tell the story of U.S. school counseling's history. As a result, while I use the term school counseling to label the program, others over the decades and even today use terms such as guidance or guidance and counseling to label the program.

It was not possible to use all of the available sources, so they were carefully reviewed and ones were chosen to reflect as accurately as possible the story of school counseling as it unfolded over the past 100-plus years. You also will find numerous direct quotes used in the book. This was done to allow you to read the exact words that authors used in their debates and discussions that occurred over the decades.

WHO SHOULD READ THIS BOOK?

This book is designed for a variety of readers. First, it is designed for school counselors in training and practicing school counselors to help them gain an appreciation of their rich professional heritage. It guides them through the 100-plus years of school counseling, decade by decade, providing them with the actual discussion and debates about what school counseling should look like and how it should be practiced. It also helps them understand how school counseling has responded to turbulent economic times and the many changing and challenging social and economic forces that have been at work in our society over the past 100-plus years. Second, this book is designed for school administrators to help them understand the evolution of school counseling with the goal that they will understand how school counseling is practiced today rather than relying on past traditions and practices. Third, this book is designed for individuals generally interested in the history of a field in education who may wish to learn more about how school counseling has evolved.

References

Brewer, J. M. (1922). *The vocational-guidance movement: Its problems and possibilities*. New York: The Macmillan Company.

Brewer, J. M. (1942). *History of vocational guidance: Origins and early development*. New York, NY: Harper & Brothers.

Davis, J. B. (1956). *The saga of a school master*. Boston, MA: Boston University Press.

Johnson, A. H. (1972). *Changing conceptions of vocational guidance and concomitant value-orientations, 1920-1930*. Unpublished doctoral dissertation. Indiana State University, Terre Haute, Indiana.

Odell, L. (1971). *American School Counselor Association: The historical growth and development of a professional organization*. Unpublished doctoral dissertation. George Washington University.

Picchioni, A. P., & Bonk, E. C. (1983). *A comprehensive history of guidance in the United States*. Austin, TX: Texas Personnel and Guidance Association.

Reed, A. Y. (1947). *Guidance and personnel services in education*. Ithaca, NY: Cornell University Press.

Stephens, W. R. (1970). *Social reform and the origins of vocational guidance*. Washington, DC: National Vocational Guidance Association.

Table of Contents

CHAPTER I

The Genesis and Early Beginnings of School Counseling: Vocational Guidance

By 1900, the United States was deeply involved in the Industrial Revolution. It was a time of rapid industrial growth, social protest, social reform and utopian idealism. Social protest and social reform were being carried out under the banner of the Progressive Movement, a movement that sought to change negative social conditions associated with the Industrial Revolution.

"These conditions were the unanticipated effects of industrial growth. They included the emergence of cities with slums and immigrant-filled ghettos, the decline of puritan morality, the eclipse of the individual by organizations, corrupt political bossism and the demise of the apprenticeship method of learning a vocation" (Stephens, 1970, pp. 148-149).

School counseling as we know it today was born during these turbulent times as vocational guidance. According to Reed (1947) the first wave of interest in vocational guidance began in the early 1900s, reaching its peak just before the United States entered World War I.

"Thus it is justifiable to assign the beginnings of organized guidance to the years 1900–1916 and to consider these years a logical first period in the history of the organized guidance movement" (p. 86).

Brewer (1942) suggested that four conditions, acting together, led to the development of vocational guidance. He identified these conditions as the division of labor, the growth of technology, the extension of vocational education and the spread of modern forms of democracy. He stated that none of these conditions alone were causative but were all necessary for the rise of vocational guidance during this time period. To these conditions, Davis (1956) added the introduction of commercial curriculums, the increase in enrollment in secondary schools leading to the introduction of coursework such as practical arts, manual training, and home economics and child labor problems.

Chapter 1 explores in detail the conditions, organizations and individuals involved in the beginning of vocational guidance during the late 1800s and the first two decades of the 1900s. The chapter opens with a presentation of some of the early pioneers of vocational guidance. Then the focus shifts to discussion of the conditions, issues and organizations involved in the development and spread of vocational guidance in the K-12 educational system between 1910 and 1920. Descriptions of vocational guidance activities in Grand Rapids, Mich., and Boston, Mass., are provided to illustrate the nature and structure of this work during this time period. The chapter closes with a review of the major trends and issues for this time period.

Early Pioneers of Vocational Guidance

"Social movements as a rule do not originate; they evolve. They are not set down full-fledged among us, even though such may appear to be the case. Rather, from very small and unimportant beginnings, modified as they progress by social and economic conditions and in their tangible form adapted to the cultural milieu in which they find their expression, they evolve very slowly until eventually there are observable evidences that a new movement has come into being" (Reed, 1947, p. 1).

Reed's statement that social movements don't originate but evolve is true for vocational guidance. Prior to 1908 the term vocational guidance was not used. Concern about what vocational guidance came to represent, however, helping an individual answer the question, "What should I do with my life?" was evident in literature throughout the ages. For example, Brewer (1942) described literature from as early as 1673 that spoke to this question.

By the late 1880s and early 1900s, a number of individuals were beginning to describe and initiate activities that would later be labeled as vocational guidance. Who were some of these early pioneers? Histories of vocational guidance written by Brewer (1942) and Reed (1947) identified individuals such as Lysander Richards, George A. Merrill and Eli W. Weaver as early pioneers before 1900 and Frank Parsons and Jessie B. Davis as early pioneers in the first decade of 1900.

THE WORK OF LYSANDER RICHARDS

In 1881, a book by Lysander Richards titled "Vocophy: The New Profession" was published. In it Richards (1881) described a new profession to help individuals find a vocation. His goal was to bring order out of chance.

"All we claim to perform is to bring order out of chance and chaos, and form or establish a system to enable a person to find the most fitting pursuit in which he can reap the greatest success that is possible for him individually to gain" (p. iv).

Richards' goal was to have counselors or vocophers as he called them in every town and city. He wanted to establish a professorship of vocophy in colleges and universities where attention could be given to the study of vocophy and the work of vocophers. He also suggested establishing an institution with the sole purpose of teaching individuals how to become vocophers.

What would be the work of vocophers? Richards recommended that vocophers would help "to discover the gift or genius latent in an individual, favorable conditions and circumstances must be brought to bear upon him, after looking into the physiological, phrenological and physiognomical indications of his powers and abilities, recount to him thoughtfully and carefully the leading features of every trade, profession or occupation, the results, operation and their requirements; gain from him in passing from the description of one pursuit to another the measure of his dislike or like for each, and note it down, also gain the measure of his mental and physical ability for each and all" (p. 32).

THE WORK OF GEORGE A. MERRILL

In 1894 Merrill organized a high school in California called the California School of Mechanic Arts. In it he proposed that the first two years should focus on exploratory activities along with academic subjects while the last two years should be devoted to specialized trade preparation. According to Brewer (1942) the plan was put into practice in January 1895 as follows:

- Two years of sample exercises drawn from simple work in each of the trades taught by the school, with about half of the time given to such studies as English, civics, mathematics and science
- Study of the individual and counseling
- Choice by the pupil of a specific trade
- Two years of preparation for a trade, including related technical studies
- Placement at work, and follow-up (p. 49).

THE EARLY WORK OF JESSE B. DAVIS

Davis began his career in education as a high school teacher of beginning algebra in Detroit, Mich., in 1895. Two years later he became a history teacher. Then he became principal of the 11th grade. Davis (1956) stated that he "… was responsible for their [students] attendance and issued permits to re-enter classes after absence, the planning of their individual programs of study, and for handling all matters of discipline" (p. 114).

In the fall of 1907, Davis moved to Grand Rapids, Michigan to begin work as principal of Grand Rapids Central High School. Being in this position gave him the opportunity to "organize an entire school for systematic guidance" (p. 176) using grade level principals. They did little teaching so they could "devote their time as counselors to about three hundred pupils each" (p. 177).

THE WORK OF ELI W. WEAVER

Eli W. Weaver was principal of the Boys' High School in Brooklyn, New York. He was very interested in placement activities, helping boys find placement for summer work and for part-time work related to their educational plans. He also published early materials on occupational information.

THE WORK OF FRANK PARSONS

Frank Parsons was a teacher, lawyer, social reformer, and prolific author. According to Brewer (1942) Parsons was concerned about the industrial system. He was concerned about the lack of training provided, the methods for selection and the waste of human effort. As a result he became involved in the Breadwinner's College in 1905, which was part of the Civic Service House that had been established in 1901.

On Jan. 13, 1908, Parsons opened the Vocation Bureau of Boston in the Civic Service House. He issued his first report of the bureau on May 1, 1908, and according to Davis (1969), "This was an important report because the term vocational guidance apparently appeared for the first time in print as the designation of an organized service" (p. 113).

Parson's conception of vocational guidance stressed the scientific approach to choosing an occupation. The first paragraph in the first chapter of his book, "Choosing a Vocation" (1909), illustrated his concern:

"No step in life, unless it may be the choice of a husband or wife, is more important than the choice of a vocation. The wise selection of the business, profession, trade or occupation to which one's life is to be devoted and the development of full efficiency in the chosen field are matters of deepest movement to young men and to the public. These vital problems should be solved in a careful, scientific say, with due regard to each person's aptitudes, abilities, ambitions, resources and limitations and the relations of these elements to the conditions of success in different industries" (p. 3).

The basis for Parson's conceptualization of guidance, stressing the scientific approach, was his concern about society's general lack of attention to the development of human resources.

"It trains its horses, as a rule, better than men. It spends unlimited money to perfect the inanimate machinery of production but pays very little attention to the business of perfecting the human machinery though it is by far the most important in production" (p. 160).

Parsons also was concerned about assisting young people in making the transition from school to work: "Yet there is no part of life where the need for guidance is more emphatic than in the transition from school to work – the choice of a vocation, adequate preparation for it and the attainment of efficiency and success" (p. 4).

In "Choosing a Vocation" Parsons described his three-step approach, giving vocational guidance "its status as a science" (Savickas & Baker, 2005, p. 24).

"In the wise choice of a vocation there are three broad factors: (1) a clear understanding of yourself, your aptitudes, abilities, interests, ambitions, resources, limitations and their causes; (2) a knowledge of the requirements and conditions of success, advantages and disadvantages, compensation, opportunities and prospects in different lines of work; (3) true reasoning on the relations of these two groups of facts.

Every young person needs help on all three of these points. He needs all the information and assistance he can get. He needs counsel. He needs a vocational counselor. He needs careful and systematic help by experienced minds in making this greatest decision of his life" (p. 5).

To carry out his three-step approach, Parsons depended "on self-analysis by the candidate himself, shrewd intuition on the part of the counselor and even physiognomatic observations" (Hale, 1980, p. 122). His method involved seven steps including personal data, self-analysis, the person's own choice and decision, counselor's analysis, outlook on the vocational field, induction and advice, and general helpfulness in fitting in the chosen work (Parsons, 1909). He also began relying on the new field of testing to measure mental capacities. He called on Hugo Munsterberg, director of the Harvard Psychology Laboratory, to test Vocational Bureau clients using mental tests (Hale, 1980).

The Impact of the Progressive Movement on Education

One of the goals of the Progressive Movement in the early 1900s was to change education, making it more relevant. According to Rudy (1965) individuals such as John Dewey, Felix Adler, Edward L. Thorndike and G. Stanley Hall joined together in an effort to modernize the educational system.

"It was the hope of these bold innovators that American education could be made more socially responsive, more helpful in the meaningful reconstruction of the modern social order, more cognizant of the needs of the individual child, more solidly based on an objectively established science of learning" (p. 11).

What concerns were being expressed about education during this time period? Wirth (1980) stated that during this time period public schools were "too exclusively literary in their spirit, scope and methods" (p. 77). What was needed was education to meet "modern industrial and social conditions" (p. 77). What was needed was industrial education.

One outcome of the expression of the need for industrial education was the formation of The National Society for the Promotion of Industrial Education (NSPIE) in 1906. NSPIE's formation was "a result of the findings of dropout studies and in answer to the sentiment of reformers to vocationalize the schools" (Stephens, 1970, p. 56). NSPIE's goals were:

- To provide men capable of meeting modern demands of manufacture and to enable the United States to compete in the markets of the world
- To provide training under the specialized conditions of modern manufacture, which will be the equivalent to training formerly given by apprenticeship
- To give boys and girls a broad familiarity with industrial processes, which will open to them a wide range of useful employments (quoted in Stephens, 1970, p. 60).

Various individuals and organizations such as NSPIE came together under the Progressive Movement to change education. It is important to understand that the Progressive Movement was not monolithic; rather it consisted of different organizations and individuals with differing viewpoints. Wiebe (1967) separated the organizations and individuals involved into two groups. One group focused on reform that emphasized social efficiency and social control because they were concerned about financial and educational waste. The other group was concerned about humanitarian social reform focusing more on human waste, the waste of human potential. This difference of values had and continues to have important ramifications for education in general and school counseling even today.

As the Progressive Movement continued to gain strength in the early 1900s, both groups of progressive reformers worked together to change the nature and structure of education by introducing the concept of industrial education (vocational education).

The dual value orientations of progressivism – efficiency and social control on the one hand and rejuvenated democracy and social service on the other – were both represented in the efforts to introduce vocationalism into the schools (Wirth, 1980, p. 68).

While both groups of progressive reformers were interested in introducing vocational education into the educational system to reform it, they had sharply different ideas about the purposes, structure and organization of vocational education in the schools. Those who favored efficiency and social control progressivism favored a dual system of vocational education similar to that in Germany while those who favored a social service democratic progressivism favored an integrated system of vocational and academic education. Mead (1914), speaking at the National Vocational Guidance Association's organizational meeting in Grand Rapids in 1913, talked in favor of an integrated system.

"A democratic education must hold together the boys and girls of the whole community; it must give them the common education that all should receive, so diversifying its work that the needs of each group may be met within the institution whose care and generous ideals shall permeate the specialized courses, while the more academic schooling may be vivified by the vocational motive that gives needed impulse to study which may be otherwise, or even deadening" (p. 19).

The difference of opinion about the nature, structure and organization of vocational education in schools had a profound effect on how individuals viewed vocational guidance.

"The question of whether guidance should be envisaged primarily as an efficient aid to industry or whether it should be viewed as a force for reform of both industry and education reflected the differences in value orientation within the larger industrial education movement" (Wirth, 1980, p. 115).

Interest in Vocational Guidance Increases

Interest in vocational guidance from 1906 to 1913 led to a number of conferences being held and many presentations being given about the importance of and the need for vocational guidance in schools. For example, Charles W. Eliot (1910) gave a presentation at the National Education Association Convention in Boston in 1910 titled "The Value During Education of the Life-Career Motive".

"Multitudes of American children, taking no interest in their school work, or seeing no connection between their studies and the means of later earning a good livelihood, drop out of school far too early of their own accord or at least offer no effective resistance to the desire of unwise parents that they stop study and go to work" (p. 1).

Eliot felt education should prepare students for their life's work with the life-career motive being central in the educational process. Bloomfield (1911) echoed this point by stating: "Until society faces the question of the life careers of its youth, the present vocational anarchy will continue to beset the young work-seekers" (p. 4).

In November 1910 the first National Conference on Vocational Guidance was held in Boston two days prior to a meeting of the NSPIE.

Presentations focused on topics such as the waste of human resources and a lack of efficiency in education because of a lack of the vocational motive in education (Stephens, 1970). A second conference on vocational guidance was held in October 1912, in New York City. Topics discussed included the need for placement bureaus and the need for "a reconstructed educational system to fit youth for the world of work" (Stephens, 1970, p. 78). At this conference a committee was appointed to consider creating a national organization for vocational guidance.

Based on this committee's work, the National Vocational Guidance Association (NVGA) was established in October 1913 in Grand Rapids, Mich. Although the NVGA organizational meeting was held in conjunction with an NSPIE meeting, the meeting's purpose was to establish a separate organization that would promote vocational guidance. In the words of NVGA's constitution:

"The objectives of this association shall be to promote intercourse between those who are interested in vocational guidance; to give a stronger and more general impulse and more systematic direction to the study and practice of vocational guidance; to establish a center or centers for the distribution of information concerning the study and practice of vocational guidance; and to cooperate with the public schools and other agencies in the furtherance of these objects" (United States Bureau of Education Bulletin, 1914, p. 7).

From 1910 on, it was apparent that schools around the country were beginning to implement vocational guidance activities. Some authors identified Boston as being the first to implement vocational guidance in its schools. Reed (1947) however, disputed that claim. She said, "The decade from 1900 to 1910 witnessed several local beginnings, but no evidence has yet been uncovered to validate the claim of any specific city being first" (p. 46).

A review of the literature during this time period revealed that numerous cities around the country were involved in initiating vocational guidance activities in their schools. To illustrate the nature and structure of this work, following are the vocational guidance plans and activities used in Grand Rapids, Mich., and Boston.

VOCATIONAL GUIDANCE IN GRAND RAPIDS

When Jessie B. Davis (1956) moved from Detroit, Mich., to Grand Rapids, Mich., to assume become principal of Central High School in 1907 he initiated a plan "to organize an entire school for systematic guidance" (p. 176). He used grade-level principals as counselors to about 300 students each. Interestingly, he did not see vocational guidance as a new profession. According to Krug (1964) he saw it as the work of school principals.

In his book "Vocational and Moral Guidance" (1914), Davis described the purposes of his plan.

"This brief description of the plan includes all of the steps which together form what may be called vocational and moral guidance. No one part of the scheme should stand alone under that name. Summing it up it means that we should first guide the pupil through education to prepare himself morally, intellectually and physically for that vocation for which he seems to be best fitted by nature, ability and opportunity. Secondly, it requires that when the time comes for him to begin the actual struggle in the fields of labor, we should still be ready to guide him – at whatever age he may be when this event arrives – into the occupation which may appear to be best suited to his needs and in which he will probably give the greatest satisfaction to his employer. This complete plan defines the use of the title 'Vocational and Moral Guidance'" (pp. 25-26).

To carry his plan he recommended establishing a Department of Vocational Guidance. The department would have an advisory board appointed by the Board of Education as well as a director. Other personnel to be included were a supervisor of instruction in vocational guidance, a chief vocational counselor responsible for overseeing teachers doing vocational counseling and various clerical personnel to handle tasks such as work permits, truancy and attendance.

As part of Davis' plan to provide systematic guidance to all students, he convinced his English teachers to set aside the English period on Fridays to use oral and written composition as a vehicle to deliver vocational guidance. The details of his plan are described in his book "Vocational and Moral Guidance" (Davis, 1914) and are outlined briefly here. Note that vocational guidance through the English curriculum began in seventh grade and continued through 12th grade. Note too, the progression of topics covered at each grade level. School counselors today will understand and appreciate the nature and structure of Davis' system.

- Grade 7: Vocational Ambition
- Grade 8: The Value of Education
- Grade 9: Character Self Analysis
  Character Analysis through Biography
- Grade 10: The World's Work – a Call to Service
  Choosing a Vocation
- Grade 11: Preparation for My Vocation
- Grade 12: Social Ethics
  Civic Ethics

In addition to what we call the guidance curriculum today, Davis also stressed that individual vocational counseling was an important part of his plan. He introduced the use of a card system to record facts and observations on each student. One side of the card was a vocational record while the other side was a social record. He also advocated that placement was a vital part of his plan, to help all students make the transition from school to work or college.

(FACE)

VOCATIONAL RECORD
GRAND RAPIDS, MICH.

Name .... School .... Grade Left ....

School Average	Personal Data	Vocational Data
Arithmetic	Honesty	Especially adapted for { Academic .... Commercial ...... Industrial ....
Grammar	Industry	
Spelling	Initiative	Pupil's ambition ....
	Leadership	Physical defects ....
History	Habits	Attitude toward school ....
Pre-Voc. Study	Health	Attitude toward work ....

Special qualities or ability shown ....

....

....

Note: This card is to be filed out for all pupils between the ages of 14 and 16 and for all those in the seventh and eighth grades. Whenever a pupil is promoted to the high school the card should be transferred to that school. If the pupil leaves school to go to work, the card should be sent to the office of the vocational director. Use the letters a, b and c to indicate whether the pupil is above, normal or below the average in his class.

(REVERSE)

SOCIAL RECORD

Parent or guardian ....Parent's vocation.................................

    "   "   "   Address ....   "   Place of business ....

Home environment ....

Neighborhood influence...

Ability to keep child in school..

Attitude of parent toward school ....

Parent's ambition for child ....

Real reason for child's leaving school...

Previous employment of child .... Av. Wage ....

Special information ....

Date of record...

From: Davis, J. B. (1914). *Vocational and moral guidance*. Boston: Ginn and Company, page 30.

VOCATIONAL GUIDANCE IN BOSTON

The work of Frank Parsons and the Vocation Bureau had a direct impact on the Boston public schools. In 1909 the Boston School Committee asked personnel in the Vocation Bureau to outline a program of vocational guidance for Boston public schools. On June 7, 1909, the Boston School Committee approved the bureau's suggestion and "instructed the Superintendent of Schools to appoint a committee of six to work with the director" (Bloomfield, 1915, p. 34). Upon completion of its work, the committee issued a report identifying three primary aims for vocational guidance in the Boston schools:

"Three aims have stood out above all others: first, to secure thoughtful consideration, on the part of parents, pupils and teachers, of the importance of a life-career motive; second, to assist in every way possible in placing pupils in some remunerative work on leaving school; and third, to keep in touch with and help them thereafter, suggesting means of improvement and watching the advancement of those who need such aid" (Bloomfield, 1915, p. 36).

These aims were implemented in 1910 with the appointment of teachers as vocational counselors. Then in 1915 a Department of Vocational Guidance was established. The work of teachers as vocational counselors continued, often with no relief from their teaching duties and with no additional pay (Brewer, 1922; Ginn, 1924). The vocational counseling duties these teachers were asked to perform were in addition to their regular teaching duties and included:

- To be the representative of the Department of Vocational Guidance in the district
- To attend all meetings of counselors called by the Director of Vocational Guidance
- To be responsible for all material sent out to the school by the Vocational Guidance Department
- To gather and keep on file occupational information
- To arrange with the local branch librarians about shelves of books bearing upon educational and vocational guidance
- To arrange for some lessons in occupations in connection with classes in oral English and vocational civics, or wherever principal and counselor deem it wise
- To recommend that teachers show the relationship of their work to occupational problems
- To interview pupils in grades six and above who are failing, attempt to find the reason and suggest a remedy
- To make use of the cumulative record card when advising children
- To consult records of intelligence tests when advising children
- To make a careful study with grades seven and eight of the bulletin *A Guide to the Choice of Secondary School*
- To urge children to remain in school and to recommend conferences with parents of children who are failing or leaving school
- To interview and check cards of all children leaving school, making clear to them the requirements for obtaining working certificates
- To be responsible for the filling in of Blank 249 and communicate with recommendations to the Department of Vocational Guidance when children are in need of employment (Ginn, 1924, pp. 5-7)

In addition to teachers serving as vocational counselors in the schools, the central office Department of Vocational Guidance employed 1- full time vocational instructors (men) and vocational assistants (women) besides the director and two clerks. Their duties included registration, vocational and educational counseling, placement, follow-up, personal interviews, keeping records, teaching of occupations and conferences (Ginn, 1924).

Progress and Challenges in Implementing Vocational Guidance in the Schools

Interest was high, and progress was being made in developing and implementing vocational guidance in the schools from 1910 to 1920. Teachers and administrators were being appointed to positions of vocational counselor. Some training was being provided, and central office departments of vocational guidance were being created in some school districts.

At the same time progress was being made in institutionalizing vocational guidance in the schools substantial challenges to this process were also present. Brewer (1942), in his history of vocational guidance, described a number of these challenges. One challenge he noted was high interest followed by a loss of that interest due to personnel changes. Another challenge was from conservatives "who began their barrage of criticism when the traditional curriculum was in any way endangered" (p. 87).

In addition to these challenges, other challenges included a lack of a practical plan to develop and implement vocational guidance, a lack of adequate preparation of teachers to carry out vocational guidance work and the lack of resources and equipment. Two quotes from Brewer's history illustrate these challenges and their consequences.

"Vocational guidance is not a job for amateurs, to be assigned to a person because he or she has a warm heart. It should not be regarded as an adjunct to the teaching of English or mathematics. It is not a side issue of the work of dean of men or women. It is not a pastime to be indulged in during odd moments by a school principal, vice principal, placement officer, registrar or attendance officer. Vocational guidance is a distinct profession, just as independent as the work of the physician, the lawyer, the nurse or any other highly specialized worker" (Brewer, 1942, p. 88, quoting Harry D. Kitson).

"Another common reason for abandoned plans was because the vocational counselor had nothing but an office and his mental equipment behind him. Vocational training, on the other hand, had back of it an investment of thousands of dollars in machines and equipment and could not so easily be 'folded up.' It was simple enough in times of financial stress, or for other reasons, to assign a vocational counselor back to a 'more important' teaching or administrative position" (Brewer, 1942, p. 88).

Even with the challenges Brewer identified, progress was being made in developing and implementing vocational guidance in the schools. Clearly Grand Rapids and Boston were making strides, but what about progress in other cities across the country? Brewer (1942) and Reed (1947) described efforts in many cities including Boston, New York, Cincinnati, Lincoln, Minneapolis, Oakland, Chicago and Seattle. Most of these efforts involved establishing a department of vocational guidance, although titles of these departments varied by city. In some cities the department was vocational guidance while in other cities it was called attendance and guidance; educational research, information and guidance; or research and guidance. Brewer (1942) commented on the use of different titles by stating:

"It must be noted, moreover, that anxious superintendents were often misled into hitching vocational guidance to other innovations in education, perhaps on the score of financial expediency. These combinations often were (and still are) curious, the chief fallacy involved being confusion between a part and the whole. 'Child welfare,' for example, is a totalitarian term: it indicates the aim of the whole work of the school system. Secondary education covers a vast area: vocational guidance is merely one activity therein. Counseling, testing and placement are merely steps or factors of vocational guidance, not the whole; consequently the term 'vocational guidance and placement' logically resembles the expression 'New England and Vermont' (p. 99).

In 1918, Ryan's report on the status of vocational guidance in the public schools was published in the U.S. *Bureau of Education Bulletin, Number 24.* In his report, he provides an overview of vocational guidance work in the schools from 1910 to 1918. His report describes the field of vocational guidance's growth and development including studies of school leaving and employment and occupational information and its use. He presented a general guidance plan based on work by W.A. Wheatley. It is presented here in full because it is a good description of vocational guidance activities taking place in schools between 1910 and 1918 and to capture the language being used to describe vocational guidance activities during that time period.

- In all the grades discuss the salient vocational facts found in each of the grade subjects, especially in literature, geography and community civics.
- In geography, what cities or regions are noted for important productions and industries? What is the home city or region noted for? Discuss the more common occupations connected with these productions and industries.
- In civics make as concrete as possible the occupations of the various public officers and workmen.
- In all grade subjects it would be well to dramatize a number of the life careers found.
- In all the grades, but more especially in the sixth, seventh and eighth grades, base much of the English composition on the vocational interests, experiences, preferences and expectations of the children.
- In grades six, seven and eight send letters to parents on educational and vocational guidance, together with high-school courses of study and explanations of what each course is intended to prepare for. Arrange conferences with teachers and parents of these pupils for mutual enlightenment, encouragement and cooperation.
- Besides the vocational enlightenment given sixth-, seventh- and eighth-grade pupils by their teachers, have the teachers of the vocational information course in the high school and the high school principal talk with these pupils about their future.
- Have pupils on entering high school express on their enrollment blanks their choice of a high school course and, if possible, of a life vocation.
- Take great pains in helping first-year high school pupils select the right course of study and the right electives in that course.
- Provide in the high school library a large amount of helpful vocational literature for teachers and for pupils.
- Throughout the high school course have the English teachers base considerable composition work on the vocational interests, experiences, preferences and expectations of the pupils.
- Organize a survey of the city's vocational opportunities and limitations, getting whatever assistance possible from the (men's) local chamber of commerce and (the women's) social-service league or their equivalents.

- Offer first- and second-year high school pupils an elective course in vocations for which credit toward graduation is given. Make this course as vital as possible by means of visits to nearby farms, factories, stores, etc.; talks on their vocations before the class by successful men and women; and by investigations of local and nearby vocational opportunities and limitations.
- Devote an occasional assembly period to a talk on some interesting vocational by an enthusiastic man or woman engaged in this life work.
- Encourage pupils to work Saturdays and vacations in trying out occupations they think they might prefer for life vocations. Also, make use of agricultural clubs; have the boys who like woodworking assist the janitor or carpenter in minor alterations about the building; have the girls who are interested in nursing assist the school nurse, and those who are thinking of becoming teachers help the grade teachers in some of their work.
- Organize a placement and follow-up bureau for pupils who wish to work afternoons, Saturdays and vacations; for those who must leave before completing the course; and for those whose formal education is completed at graduation.
- Arrange conferences with members of the third- and fourth-year pupils to discuss what they expect to do after leaving high school. (Ryan, 1915, p. 82).

Major Trends and Issues

By the close of the second decade of the 20th century what can be said about the status of vocational guidance in the schools? First, interest in vocational guidance was high, and progress was being made in implementing it in schools. Ryan (1918), in his report on vocational guidance, noted that by April 1914, some 100 public high schools, representing some 40 cities had organized plans for vocational guidance. Ryan went on to report that by 1918 "932 four-year high schools reported vocation bureaus, employment departments or similar devices for placing students" (p. 36).

Second, at the same time progress was being made in institutionalizing vocational guidance in the schools, Ryan (1918) also noted that the vocational guidance plans of typical school districts between 1910 and 1918 showed little uniformity. Some districts had fairly complete organizational plans while others only stressed research or emphasized placement. He pointed out that Boston was the only school district that had vocational counselors (teachers) in every school.

The literature from this time period reveals the following:

- Industrial education (career and technical education today) and vocational guidance were part of an effort to reform elementary and secondary education.
- Some leaders, particularly from industrial education, saw vocational guidance as a way to sort individuals according to their various capacities preparing them to obtain a job. This was the social efficiency philosophy. Other leaders, outside of industrial education, viewed vocational guidance as a way to change conditions of industry as well as to help students make educational and occupational choices. This was the democratic, humanitarian philosophy. The differences between these two philosophies created differences of opinion about the purposes of vocational guidance (now school counseling) and how it should be organized and implemented throughout the ensuing decades to today.
- Teachers were assigned the position of vocational counselors with no organizational structure to work in other than a list of duties and often with little training and no release from their teaching duties.
- Placement and follow-up were seen as important parts of vocational guidance.

References

Bloomfield, M. (1911). *The vocational guidance of youth.* Boston, MA: Houghton Mifflin Company.

Bloomfield, M. (1915). *Youth, school, and vocation.* Boston, MA: Houghton Mifflin Company.

Brewer, J. M. (1922). *The vocational-guidance movement: Its problems and possibilities.* New York: The Macmillan Company.

Brewer, J. M. (1942). *History of vocational guidance: Origins and early development.* New York, NY: Harper & Brothers.

Davis, H. V. (1969). *Frank Parsons: Prophet, innovator, counselor.* Carbondale, IL: Southern Illinois University Press.

Davis, J. B. (1914). *Vocational and moral guidance.* Boston, MA: Ginn and Company.

Davis, J. B. (1956). *The saga of a school master.* Boston, MA: Boston University Press.

Eliot, C. W. (1910). The value during education of the life-career motive. In M. Bloomfield (Ed.), *Readings in vocational guidance* (pp. 1-12). Boston, MA: Ginn and Company.

Ginn, S. J. (1924). Vocational guidance in Boston public schools. *The Vocational Guidance Magazine, 3*, 3-7.

Hale, M., Jr. (1980). *Human science and social order.* Philadelphia, PA: Temple University Press.

Krug, E. A. (1964). *The shaping of the American high school.* New York: Harper & Row.

Mead, G. H. (1914). The larger educational bearings of vocational guidance. *United States Bureau of Education Bulletin Number 14.* Washington, DC: Government Printing Office.

Parsons, F. (1909). *Choosing a vocation.* Boston, MA: Houghton Mifflin.

Reed, A. Y. (1947). *Guidance and personnel services in education.* Ithaca, NY: Cornell University Press.

Richards, L. S. (1881). *Vocophy: The new profession.* Washington, DC: Bratt Brothers, Steam Job Printers.

Rudy, W. S. (1965). *Schools in an age of mass culture.* Englewood Cliffs, NJ: Prentice-Hall.

Ryan, W. C. (1918). Vocational guidance and the public schools. *Washington, DC Bureau of Education Bulletin, Number 24.* Washington, DC: Government Printing Office.

Savickas, M. L., & Baker, D. B. (2005). The history of vocational psychology: Antecedents, origin, and early development. In W. B. Walsh, & M. L. Savickas (Eds.), *Handbook of Vocational Psychology* (3rd cd.), pp. 15-50). Mahwah, NJ: Lawrence Erlbaum Associates.

Stephens, W. R. (1970). *Social reform and the origins of vocational guidance.* Washington, DC: National Vocational Guidance Association.

United States Bureau of Education Bulletin Number 14 (1914). Vocational Guidance. Washington, DC: Government Printing Office.

Wiebe, R. H. (1967). *The search for order.* New York, NY: Hill and Wang.

Wirth, A. G. (1980). *Education in the technological society: The vocational-liberal studies controversy in the early twentieth century.* Boston, MA: University Press of America.

CHAPTER 2

The Expansion of Vocational Guidance in the 1920s: New Purposes, Challenges and Terminology

While the 1920s witnessed the expansion of vocational guidance in the schools, those years also saw the purposes, language, practices and organization of vocational guidance change due to the impact of various social and educational movements unfolding inside and outside of education. These movements included the mental hygiene (mental health) movement, progressive education, the child study/development movement and the psychometric (measurement theory) movement. Johnson (1972) noted the impact of these movements on vocational guidance by stating that: "Vocational guidance was taking on the new vocabulary present in the culture at large and in the educational subculture; the language of mental health, progressive education, child development and measurement theory" (pp. 160-161).

The impact of these movements on the purpose, language, practices and organization was substantial. As Johnson indicated, vocational guidance was taking on a new vocabulary, consisting of words such as clinical, educational, measurement and social. As a result less attention was being focused on the industrial and national/political aspects of people, whereas considerable more attention was being given to the personal, educational and statistically measurable aspects of individuals. More specifically, at least within the school setting, there apparently was a "displacement of the traditional vocational, socioeconomic and political concerns from the culture at large to the student of the educational subculture whose vocational socialization problems were reinterpreted as educational and psychological problems of personal adjustment" (A. H. Johnson, 1972, p. 221).

As a result of this displacement of concerns, vocational guidance practices began to emphasize a more personal, diagnostic and clinical orientation to students, with an increasing emphasis on psychological measurement. "Content to explore with yet greater precision the psychological dimensions of the student, and guaranteed a demand for testing services in the public school system, the guidance movement defined its professional role to meet the expectations of its institutional colleagues. Thus there developed a mutual role expectation that requires analysis and synthesis (gathering and organizing personal data), diagnosis (comparing personal data to test norms, and occupational or professional profiles), prognosis (indicating available career choices) and counseling (or treating, to effect desired adjustment then or in the future). This formed the basis for the clinical model. Testing had created the demand for a unique technical skill around which the clinical model could develop and around which vocational guidance had established a professional claim" (A. H. Johnson, 1972, p. 138).

Further evidence of this can be seen in the 1921 and 1924 statements of the Principles of Vocational Guidance of the National Vocational Guidance Association (Allen, 1927). These principles emphasized testing, the use of an extensive cumulative record system, information, the study of occupations, counseling and case studies. Between 1925 and 1930, as the personal adjustment purpose of vocational guidance emerged, counseling became of primary concern. "Vocational guidance became problem oriented, centering on adjustable psychological, personal problems – not social, moral, religious, ethical or political problems" (A. H. Johnson. 1972, p. 201).

To help you understand and appreciate the substantial changes that were occurring in vocational guidance in the 1920s, this chapter opens by briefly describing the origins and impact of the mental hygiene, child study/development and psychometric movements on vocational guidance. The chapter continues with an examination of the clinical model of vocational guidance as an outgrowth of these three movements as well as the growing interest in educational guidance. Then attention turns to the varied and sometimes confusing terminology being used to define and describe vocational guidance, in some cases abandoning the use of the term vocational guidance altogether. Next typical activities and practices being used in the 1920s are presented as well as descriptions of the variety of personnel who were practicing in the schools during that time period. Discussion of various administrative issues in organizing and administering vocational guidance follows, including concern about the traditional position approach to assigning personnel to guidance responsibilities. Chapter 2 closes with a summary of the substantial changes in terminology, practices and administration of vocational guidance that occurred in the 1920s.

The Mental Hygiene Movement

Mental hygiene is an old term, having first been used by William Sweetzer in 1843 (Mandell, 2009). From that time until 1908 various individuals were involved in writing about the importance of mental hygiene, focusing particularly on mental illness. In 1908 Clifford Beers published a book under the sponsorship of William James and Adolph Meyer titled "A Mind That Found Itself." In it Beers called for the formation of a voluntary health agency. This led to the founding of the National Committee for Mental Hygiene in 1909 (Simpson & Thomas, 2009).

The focus of the work of mental hygienists in the 1920s was on intervention, prevention and good mental health. Schools were seen as an important setting for prevention work, work that focused on children's everyday problems. Child guidance clinics were established in the 1920s as an expression of the mental hygiene movement. The focus of these clinics was the problem child.

"Child guidance defined the problem child as a child of normal intelligence, exhibiting a range of behavior and psychological problems, which were lumped together in a category called *maladjustment*. Indications of such maladjustments ranged from thumb sucking, nail biting, enuresis and night terrors in younger children, to personality traits such as sensitiveness, seclusiveness, apathy, excessive imagination and fanciful lying. Also included was a category of undesirable behavior in older children such as disobedience, teasing, bullying, temper tantrums, seeking bad companions, keeping late hours and engaging in sexual activities" (Encyclopedia of Children and Childhood in History and Society, 2009).

According to Rudy (1965), the mental hygiene-child guidance movement brought attention to the fact "that not all unhappiness among school children was due to unfortunate course elections or vocational choices" (p. 19). Proponents of this movement saw schools as promising for preventive work because it could reach all students. "Thus, the child guidance perspective [movement] helped to emphasize the psychological and social influences of behavior and mental illness" (Plante, 2005, p. 44).

The Psychometric Movement and Vocational Guidance

According to Savickas and Baker (2005), early writers such as Lysander Richards used phrenology, physiognomy and palmistry in their vocational guidance work. "This pseudoscience recognized individual differences by assessing their meaning ... by measuring crania, facial features and body shapes" (p. 20). Although these pseudoscience techniques were still being talked about in the early 1900s, they were largely discredited as more scientific approaches to the measurement of individual differences were being developed and used.

Young (1923), in his history of mental testing, described the contributions of individuals from Germany, France, England and the United States to the measurement of individual differences. Wundt and Munsterberg (later in the United States) from Germany, Binet in France, and Galton and Pearson in England all played substantial roles, but it was to Binet, Galton and Cattell that the honor belongs "of having begun the mental testing movement" (p. 6). Savickas and Baker (2005) credit Cattell with coining the term "mental test."

The psychometric movement exploded with activity in the second decade of the 20th century. Tests of various kinds designed to measure individuals' various characteristics were being developed. Work on tests of intelligence; manual, mechanical and spatial abilities; clerical abilities; and interests begun in the second decade, continued into the 1920s and beyond (Brewer, 1942).

With the entry of the United States into World War I in 1917, soldiers needed to be classified. A committee, headed by Robert Yerkes, developed the Army Alpha intelligence test and the Army Beta intelligence test (nonverbal). These tests were administered in groups to over two million individuals (Plante, 2005).

Even as more and more tests were being developed and used in the schools during the teens and the 1920s, concern was being expressed about their purposes. Brewer (1942) noted that some test developers were interested in selection, not vocational guidance. Ayres (1913) divided tests into two types. The first type focused on selecting people for positions while the second type focused on selecting positions for people. He saw choosing people for positions as the best use of tests in vocational guidance.

"We must remember that we are using a false analogy when we refer to fitting square pegs into round holes in talking about vocational misfits, for people and positions are both plastic, not rigid, and much mutual change of form often takes place without injury to either person or position" (p. 237).

Brewer (1942) was also concerned about the use of tests in vocational guidance. He was concerned about the needed attention to the whole individual.

"Nor can the testing program in vocational guidance consist of a mere series of vocational selection tests. The counselor must consider the whole individual, who must be measured and sampled in all the varied aspects of his individuality. Abilities as they apply to his vocational success must be considered in relation to each other and in relation to a total pattern. These abilities cannot be isolated and measured without some assurance that the total individual has been measured. The sum of the parts is not always the whole" (p. 201).

The Clinical Model Emerges

As the mental hygiene, child study/development and the psychometric (measurement) movements continued to evolve, the impact on education in general and vocational guidance specifically was substantial and long-lasting. Johnson (1972) noted that the words counseling (the interview) and diagnosis were being used increasingly when describing vocational guidance.

"Thus, guidance had become 'problem'-oriented. However, these were adjustable, psychological, personal problems, not social, moral, religious, ethical or political problems" (p. 156).

To understand the changing language of vocational guidance due to the emergence of the clinical model, consider the words of Truitt (1925). "From the psychiatric standpoint, a prime essential in vocational guidance is a study of the individual's social background, personality make-up and intellectual capacity if he is to be guided to a vocation which will square not only with his abilities but with his fundamental emotional needs" (p. 91).

One outcome of the clinical model on vocational guidance was a shift in emphasis away from groups to the individual. Vitcles (1928) made this point as follows:

"In the practice of vocational guidance there appears to be a need for a shift of emphasis away from this consideration of the group as a unit of guidance to the more complete study of the individual. This complete study of the individual for purposes of guidance is what I have in mind by the clinical approach in guidance" (p. 3).

Educational Guidance Becomes Popular

The first use of the term "educational guidance" appeared in a dissertation in 1914 by Truman L. Kelly. By using this term, Kelley had in mind helping students select high school subjects. He saw it as a basis for vocational guidance (Myers, 1935).

The addition of an educational purpose for guidance was a natural outgrowth of a change that was taking place in education itself. With the advent of the Cardinal Principles of Secondary Education (National Education Association, 1981), education, at least philosophically, began to shift from preparation for college alone to education for total life.

"This was a life to be characterized by an integration of health with command of fundamental processes, worthy home membership, vocational competence, civic responsibility, worthy use of leisure time and ethical character ... Given these Seven Cardinal Principles, an education now appeared equally vocationally relevant – from this one could construe that all of education is guidance into later vocational living" (A. H. Johnson, 1972), pp. 27-28).

This change occurred partly because the leadership of vocational guidance, particularly on the part of people such as John Brewer (1922), increasingly was more educationally oriented. It also occurred, according to Stephens (1970), because the National Education Association (NEA) Commission on the Reorganization of Secondary Education (CRSE) "had so broadened the definition of vocation as to soften it, if not to virtually eliminate it as a cardinal principle of secondary education" (p. 113). This move by CRSE, together with the more educationally oriented leadership of guidance, served to separate what had been twin reform movements of education – vocational education and vocational guidance, as Stephens called them – leaving vocational guidance to struggle with its own identity. This point is made in a similar way by A. H. Johnson (1972):

"The 1918 report of the NEA's Commission on the Reorganization of Secondary Education construed almost all of the education as training for efficient vocational and avocational life. No element in the curriculum appeared salient after the CRSE report. This was no less true of vocational education. Thus, as a 'cardinal principle' vocational education was virtually eliminated. The once-correlated responsibility of vocational guidance lost its historical anchorage to vocational education and was set adrift in the public school system to be redefined by the logic of the education subculture" (p. 204).

Varied and Confusing Terminology

By the 1920s varied and sometimes confusing terminology was being used to define and label guidance. Although vocational guidance continued to be the predominate term, words other than vocational were often being used to modify the word guidance. Also, varied definitions of the term vocational guidance were appearing as well.

Payne (1925) noted the problem of terminology. "Whenever any advance is made in any field of human endeavor, difficulty develops in regard to terminology. No field of endeavor can be classed as a science until its terminology is standardized. Education is now in the process of changing from an art and a philosophy to a science. In all the divisions of education there is more or less difficulty with terminology. This is particularly true in the field of vocational guidance" (p. 34).

Out of the early 1900s came the words moral and educational to replace the word vocational. Then in the 1920s words such as occupational, social, avocational, health, life, civic and recreational were being used in addition to the word vocational.

In "Vocational Guidance and Counseling (1926), Edgerton used a number of terms:

- vocational counselors
- counselors
- vocational counseling
- guidance
- united guidance programs
- educational guidance
- organized vocational guidance and systematic counsel
- organized guidance
- comprehensive guidance programs
- school counseling programs

The variety of words used to label, define and describe personnel and guidance work caused confusion among administrators, teachers and the public. deSchweinitz (1925) said, "The greater awareness on the part of superintendents, teachers or the general public of 'guidance' had not clarified the ambiguity ... it had only proliferated that ambiguity" (p. 218). As a result it is not surprising that there was confusion among practitioners as they attempted to implement guidance activities in the schools. Interestingly, the problem of terminology continues to exist today.

Typical Vocational Guidance Activities and Practices

Although different words were used to label, define and describe guidance in the schools, the term vocational guidance remained as the most frequently used term in the 1920s.

This section of Chapter 2 presents typical activities and practices found in the literature during the 1920s.

Land (1926) reported the results of a study of activities and practices in 635 secondary schools in 143 cities across the country conducted by Edgerton (1926). The results of the survey indicated the following frequency of activities and practices:

- survey local occupational opportunities – 244 schools
- test abilities and interests of pupils – 212 schools
- assist individual pupils in choosing vocational possibilities – 351 schools

- assist pupils in selecting educational possibilities – 537 schools
- vocational placement for part-time or full-time employment – 440 schools
- employment supervision and follow-up – 195 schools

Land (1926) also reported the results of a study by McDougal of guidance activities in 130 high schools. McDougal found similar results to Edgerton's study but added some activities as follows:

- prevocational courses of vocational guidance in grades seven and eight
- discover vocational aptitudes through English
- teachers acted in the capacity of vocational counselor
- courses in vocational civics or occupations
- class visits to industry
- employment or placement bureaus
- use of mental tests to determine vocational aptitude

Based on these studies, Land (1926) suggested the following as a reasonable and comprehensive program of vocational guidance.

- An industrial and occupational survey of the community.
- The testing and studying of pupils' possibilities.
- Guidance in choosing a vocation.
- Educational guidance for preparation for vocation selected.
- Provision for educational opportunities.
- Guidance on entering work "placement" (p. 146).

Haney (1925) described vocational guidance in Philadelphia high schools. He identified the following activities including counseling, placement, classes in occupations the use of psychological tests and medical exams, publicity and information about occupations. Teeter (1928) outlined a process for students to study occupations. He described teaching material, purposes and an outline of a course in occupational civics. Lane (1927) described a course as a part of a social science curriculum to teach about occupations in the eighth grade.

The National Vocational Guidance Association (1929) in a draft document pointed to the following methods for vocational guidance:
1. Individual counseling
   - Interviews with individuals at regular intervals
   - frequent interviews with parents
   - use of cumulative records

- keep careful records
- use social case worker (visiting teacher)
2. Group counseling – Giving occupational information
3. Placement and follow-up
4. Testing – Administration and supervision of the testing program should be a trained and experienced psychologist
5. Occupational studies – surveys of local businesses and industries
6. Research (pp. 221-223)

Vocational guidance was also taking place in elementary schools. Allen (1930) described the functions of guidance and the organizational structure necessary for efficient work in elementary schools. The goal he stated was "to ensure the effective coordination of all guidance functions so that each child may receive the individual attention to which he is entitled without the necessity of becoming a 'problem pupil'" (p. 219). He felt that the "individual adjustment of each child to his school task" (p. 219) was critical for guidance. He also felt that there "must be personal responsibility for individual adjustment and guidance" (p. 220).

Allen identified the following list of guidance functions for elementary schools:

1. Personnel records and research – a graphic guidance card containing:
   - Records of physical and health examinations
   - Personal information, family, outside activities
   - Records of educational achievement – teachers' marks, educational tests
   - Records of psychological tests and school adjustment
   - Records of special assets and liabilities
   - Ratings on personality and social traits
2. Counseling. – the room teacher must usually be relied upon for the personal contacts with her pupils. If she is permitted to retain her pupils for from one to three years the task will have sufficient continuity to prove a challenge to her human interest and professional spirit. This is done in some school systems.
   - Personal and social adjustment
   - Attendance, health
   - Discipline/school citizenship
   - Parents, physician, nurse, home visitor
   - Special teachers – music and drawing/auditorium/nature/study/science

(The home room teacher puts the picture together if she has time to study the child – one to three years.)

3. Orientation or group guidance – the following elements may be found in most good elementary schools. They should be organized in a unit and given a definite place in the program.
   - Personal and social relations (case conference)
   - Manners and conduct.
   - Self-government/school citizenship
   - Thrift, safety, health
   - Desirable personal and social traits
   - Inspirational material, stories, poems, plays
   - Moving pictures, music appreciation
   - Radio talks, dramatization (p. 221)

A Variety of Personnel

One of the issues being faced in the 1920s was the addition of a variety of new personnel in the schools. When new personnel were added, questions often arose as to their duties. When school counselors (only a few full-time, others were teachers who were assigned guidance duties part-time) were added to the Minneapolis high schools, concern was expressed about overlapping duties with other personnel, such as visiting teachers (social workers). McCradie and Ferguson (1929) conducted a job analysis of school counselors and visiting teachers. The following is a list of duties for each position that gives you a picture of the duties of school counselors and visiting teachers.

DUTIES OF THE COUNSELOR

1. To interview
   - New pupils for purposes of making adjustments, and to give them educational and vocational information
   - Withdrawing pupils for purposes of explaining opportunities at vocational, Dunwoody and evening Schools
   - Pupils who wish program planning, including all 9A pupils
   - Pupils who desire employment
   - Pupils referred to her as dull or superior pupils, therefore requiring special programs
   - All seniors to
     - Check credits for university entrance
     - Interpret for each student the significance of his rating in the college aptitude tests
     - Help in securing placement

2. To do other educational and vocational counseling
   - Collect and record data necessary for counseling the individual child
   - Explain the high school program of studies and educational opportunities of city to groups entering from other schools, parents and teachers
   - Collect occupational information and make it available and useful to pupils, parents and teachers
   - Arrange vocational conferences for groups of seniors definitely interested in special occupations
   - Arrange for individual conferences between students and businessmen
   - Handle placement by
     - Preparing card file of seniors for Placement Bureau
     - Arranging for part-time work
     - Assisting girls to find homes in which to work for room and board
   - To keep records of cases handled
3. To collect information about occupations and educational opportunities by
   - Directing an investigation of an occupation as part of a program of occupational research planned by the central office
   - Assisting in other occupational studies by visiting places of business and interviewing businessmen
   - Collecting and filing information about educational institutions
4. To counsel failing students by
   - Acting as chairman of Scholarship Committee of the senior high school
   - Interviewing students, teachers and parents regarding causes of failure and plans for eliminating failures
   - Organizing plans for recognition and encouragement of honor pupils (p. 107)

DUTIES OF THE VISITING TEACHER

1. To interview
   - Principal, assistant principal, vocational counselors, nurse, parents and teachers in regard to referred problem pupils
   - Pupils
     - Referred as problems
     - Referred for PTA Scholarship Aid
     - Asking for employment certificates or home permits

2. To visit homes on matters pertaining to
   - Attendance
   - Treatment of problem pupils
   - Part-time work
   - Scholarship failure
   - Eligibility for PTA Scholarship Aid
   - Writing of social histories for pupils studied in the Child Guidance Clinic
   - Financial conditions when books or clothing are to be supplied, or when employment certificates or home permits are requested
   - Withdrawals
     - Monthly
     - Summer (these are usually about 300 to be located by close of September)
3. To write histories of pupils
   - Studied in Child Guidance Clinic
   - Referred to the Juvenile Court
   - Applying for PTA Scholarship Aid
   - Applying for employment certificates or home permits
4. To carry the treatment of
   - Pupils studied in the Child Guidance Clinic (this treatment is indicated by and is under the direction of the Child Guidance Clinic)
   - Court cases in cooperation with the probation officer
   - Pupils referred as problems by the school
   - To keep detailed records of all major and minor services to problem pupils
   - To supervise attendance in the school
   - Miscellaneous
   - To attend court hearing, Child Guidance Clinic and bi-weekly family welfare conferences
   - To cooperate with and make connections in the school for social agencies and outside school agencies
   - To certify and sign permanent record cards of withdrawing pupils
   - To make monthly report

From "A counselor and a visiting teacher describe their jobs by A. McCradie and B. Ferguson, 1929. The Vocational Guidance Magazine, 8, pp. 106-107. Copyright 1929 by the American Counseling Association. Reprinted with permission.

Administrative Issues: Leadership

As vocational guidance was taking hold in the schools, concerns were being expressed about its administration. Hanna (1925) talked about the need for the proper scheduling of vocational guidance functions. He was concerned about this because he stated that unscheduled and sometimes added functions were very unpopular with teachers who were already busy teaching as well as carrying many guidance responsibilities. He also stated that keeping the many kinds of guidance functions in schools responsible to central authority was difficult. In addition he pointed out the difficulty of monitoring regular and systematic contact between pupils' special advisors and the advisors' pupil charges. Finally, he stressed the need for constant advertising of guidance activities among teachers to include objective results that could be graphed and charted to present at general teacher meetings.

Holbrook (1927) pointed to the importance of vocational guidance. "Vocational guidance has become the head of a guidance family, including educational guidance with much of tests and measurements, and social guidance, including services of deans of girls and visiting teachers" (p. 178). He also expressed the need for central leadership and the problem of promoting school counselors to become administrators. "One of the outstanding needs is for central leadership and coordination of guidance in the larger school districts. The tendency at present in some cities seems to be to assign guidance leadership to the director of some existing departments, often with conflicting duties elsewhere" (p. 178).

"There is a tendency to promote school counselors out of guidance and into general school administration, rather than to set up an adequate salary reward and professional counseling status" (pp. 178-179).

Rynearson (1925) spoke about the importance of vocational guidance in the schools. He pointed out the school is the one institution organized to provide systematic and continuous guidance. To that end he stated that the vocational guidance program should touch every point in a pupil's life, not just at a few times. He also stressed the economic value of the work of counselors.

"Who can estimate the value of a counselor's work in dollars if he helps only one child in school? Don't say we cannot afford one more salary" (p. 119).

Early Concerns About the Position of Vocational Counselor

By the 1920s, as the vocational guidance movement was spreading across the United States, concerns were being expressed about the way vocational guidance was organized, was being perceived by others and was being practiced. In a review of the Boston School system, Brewer (1922) stated that the work was "commendable and promising" (p. 36). At the same time he expressed concern about a lack of effective centralization and supervision. What was done and how well it was done were left up to individual principals and counselors. Myers (1923), in "A Critical Review of Present Developments in Vocational Guidance with Special Reference to Future Prospects," also expressed concern:

"The first development to which I wish to call attention is a growing recognition of vocational guidance as an integral part of organized education, not as something different and apart from education that is being wished upon the schools by a group of enthusiasts because there is no other agency to handle it (p. 139)… Second, vocational guidance is becoming recognized as a specialized educational function requiring special natural qualifications and special training (p. 139) … A third development that claims attention is an increasing appreciation that a centralized, unified program of vocational guidance for the entire school system of a city is essential to the most effective work. We are rapidly passing out of the stage when each high school and junior high school can be left to organize and conduct vocational guidance as it sees fit" (pp. 139-140).

In expressing these concerns, Myers was calling attention to problems associated with the position model for vocational guidance in which teachers were designated as vocational counselors with no structure to work in and little or no released time from their teaching duties. Apparently, the position model for vocational guidance caused it to be seen as an ancillary activity that could be conducted by anybody. In contrast, he stressed the need to view vocational guidance as an "integral part of education" that required "trained personnel" working in a "unified program" of guidance. Myers's words were prophetic. These are the same words we use today to describe the importance, personnel requirements and structure of comprehensive guidance and counseling programs in our schools.

Myers (1923) made another astute observation about some unanticipated outcomes the prevailing way of organizing vocational guidance (the position model) was causing in the schools:

"Another tendency dangerous to the cause of vocational guidance is the tendency to load the vocational counselor with so many duties foreign to the office that little real counseling can be done. The principal and often the counselor ... [have] a very indefinite idea of the proper duties of this new officer. The counselor's time is more free from definite assignments with groups or classes of pupils than is that of the ordinary teacher. It well-chosen he [or she] has administrative ability. It is perfectly natural, therefore, for the principal to assign one administrative duty after another to the counselor until he [or she] becomes practically assistant principal, with little time for the real work of a counselor. In order to prevent this tendency from crippling seriously the vocational guidance program it is important that the counselor shall be well-trained, that the principal shall understand more clearly what counseling involves and that there shall be efficient supervision from a central office. (p. 140)

Myers's words were again prophetic. They pointed directly at the heart of the problem with the position model, that is, the ease at which "other duties as assigned" can become part of the work of school counselors, a problem that continues to plague school counselors even today.

Major Trends and Issues

The decade of the 1920s was an exciting and challenging time for vocational guidance in the schools. New terminology, new practices and new ideas were emerging in response to the changes that were occurring in and out of education. Following are some of those key changes and challenges.

- While the term vocational guidance continued to be used throughout the 1920s, other words such as educational and social guidance appeared with increasing frequency in the literature. Also the term the clinical model of vocational guidance appeared, focusing attention on individual counseling.
- As new terminology and ideas emerged there was a shift away from economic problems to personal psychological dynamics and adjustment. "Here, by 1926, one found and tested and refined conceptualization of a vocational and educational program incorporating the

technology of intelligence and personality testing, and, in addition, including the findings of mental hygiene, depth psychology, the interviewing techniques of the social case workers and the case study method of the clinical psychologist to focus on the individual person" (Johnson, 1972, p. 153).

- The words educational guidance were being used together with vocational guidance and sometimes separately.
- Vocational guidance activities in the schools began to solidify around the major headings of occupational/industrial surveys, individual counseling, courses in occupations or vocational guidance units in English or civics, assessment, placement and follow-up.
- Administrative concerns were also present including how best to organize and implement vocational guidance and the assignment and supervision of vocational guidance duties.
- Concern was expressed about the position approach to vocational guidance, the assignment of duties to a counselor (teacher) without a structure in which to organize the assigned duties. As we will see this was a continuing problem into the 1930s and 1940s and beyond.

References

Allen, H. C. (1930). The functions of guidance in the elementary schools (Grades 1-6) and the organization necessary for efficient service. *The Vocational Guidance Magazine, 8,* 219-223.

Ayers, L. P. (1913). Psychological tests in vocational guidance. *Journal of Educational Psychology, 4,* 232-237.

Beers, C. (1908). *A mind that found itself.* New York: Longmans, Green & Company.

Brewer, J. M. (1922). *The vocational-guidance movement.* New York: Macmillan.

Brewer, J. M. (1942). *History of vocational guidance.* New York: Harper & Brothers.

deSchweinitz, D. (1925). A message from the president of the National Guidance Association. *The Vocational Guidance Magazine, 3,* 218-219.

Edgerton, A. H. (1926). *Vocational guidance and counseling.* New York: The Macmillan Company.

Edgerton, A. H. (1926). *Vocational guidance and counseling.* New York: The Macmillan Company.

Encyclopedia of Children and Childhood in History and Society. *Child Guidance.* Retrieved, January 9, 2009, from http://www.faqs.org/childhood/bo-ch/child-guidance.html.

Haney, J. L. (1925). Vocational guidance in the Philadelphia high schools. *The Vocational Guidance Magazine, 4*, 49-50.

Hanna, J. V. (1925). Some administrative problems involved in the guidance of high school pupils. *The Vocational Guidance Magazine, 4*, 10-14.

Holbrook, H. L. (1927). In school administration. *The Vocational Guidance Magazine, 5*, 178-179.

Johnson, A. H. (1972). *Changing conceptions of vocational guidance and concomitant value-orientations, 1920-1930.* Unpublished doctoral dissertation. Indiana State University, Terre Haute, Indiana.

Land, S. L. (1926). The organization and administration of vocational guidance. *The Vocational Guidance Magazine, 4*, 145-152.

Lane, M. R. (1927). Providing vocational information. *The Vocational Guidance Magazine, 6*, 1-8.

Mandell, W. (n.d.). *The realization of an idea.* Retrieved, January 5, 2009, from http://www.jhsph.edu/dept/mh/about/origins.html.

McCradie, A., & Ferguson, B. (1929). A counselor and a visiting teacher describe their jobs. *The Vocational Guidance Magazine, 8*, 106-107.

Myers, G. E. (1923). A critical review of present developments in vocational guidance with special reference to future prospects. *The Vocational Guidance Magazine, 2*, 139-142.

Myers, G. E. (1935). *Relations between vocational and educational guidance.* Ann Arbor, MI: University of Michigan.

National Vocational Guidance Association (1929). A statement of principle and practices submitted for adoption by the National Vocational Guidance Association. *The Vocational Guidance Magazine, 7*, 219-226.

Payne, A. F. (1925). *Organization of vocational guidance.* New York: McGraw-Hill.

Plante, T. G. (2005). *Contemporary clinical psychology* (2nd Ed.). Hoboken, NJ: John Wiley & Sons.

Rudy, W. (1965). *Schools in an age of mass culture.* Englewood Cliffs, NJ: Prentice-Hall.

Rynearson, E. (1925). The high school principal's responsibility for vocational guidance of the adolescent. *The Vocational Guidance Magazine, 3*, 115-119.

Savickas, M. L., & Baker, D. B. (2005). The history of vocational psychology: Antecedents, origin and early development. In W. B. Walsh & M. L. Savickas (Eds.), *Handbook of vocational psychology* (3rd ed.) (pp. 15-50). Mahwah, NJ: Erlbaum.

Simpson, B. W., & Thomas, M. *Meeting on the same errand: Origins of mental hygiene*. Retrieved, January 6, 2009, from http://www.jhsph.edu/dept/mh/originsofmentalhygiene,pdf.

Stephens, W. R. (1970). *Social reform and the origins of vocational guidance*. Washington DC: National Vocational Guidance Association.

Truitt, R. P. (1925). *The psychiatric element in vocational guidance*. The Vocational Guidance Magazine, 4, 87-92.

Viteles, M. S. (1928). The clinical approach in vocational guidance. *The Vocational Guidance Magazine, 7,* 1-9.

Young, K. (1923). *The history of mental testing*. The Pedagogical Seminary, 31, 1-48.

CHAPTER 3

The 1930s: A Decade of Turbulence, Retrenchment and the Formation of a New Organizational Structure

In the 1930s interest in guidance in the schools continued unabated. Numerous articles were published, and many books were written. Some reported on the results of surveys of actual practices while others offered ideas and opinions about what guidance in the schools should be. Differing perceptions existed about the definition and scope of guidance (the terminology issue), the types of guidance activities, the appropriate organizational framework for guidance and the different kinds of personnel involved in providing guidance as well as the duties for which these personnel were responsible.

Reavis (1933) suggested there were four compelling conditions in society and education nurturing this continued interest in guidance in the 1930s. "Guidance services on the part of the secondary school are rendered necessary by at least four conditions, namely: (1) the character of the demands for modern secondary education, (2) the changes in the social and economic order to which the secondary-school pupil must adjust himself, (3) the needs of the adolescent for counsel and guidance and (4) the necessity of avoiding waste in the process of education" (p. 1).

It is interesting to note his descriptions of the four conditions. He emphasized the complexity of education, something that had been talked about in the 1920s. He also focused on pupils adjusting themselves to the social and economic order of the day. The adjustment theme was discussed in the 1920s but became a dominant theme for guidance in the 1930s. Finally note his concern about avoiding waste, again a theme from the early 1900s.

Before discussion of guidance in the 1930s begins, it is important to understand how turbulent and trying the 1930s were. This was the decade of the Great Depression, in which the economy and society in general and education specifically went through some extremely difficult times. Some guidance programs begun in the teens and 1920s were either curtailed substantially or closed entirely. There often was a reduction in the number of individuals serving in guidance roles in the schools.

At the same time, however, while some programs were being curtailed or closed and personnel were being laid off, the 1930s also witnessed a time of innovation and new ideas about the purposes, scope and organization of guidance. It was a time of beginning professional consensus about the needs of children and adolescents for guidance. It was a time for a new organizational framework for guidance in the schools. It was a time for increased discussion of the need for standards for the selection and train-ing of guidance personnel. Finally it was a time of a beginning federal presence in guidance in the schools in the form of legislation and the cre-ation of a national office in the federal government as well as state offices for guidance.

Chapter 3 opens with discussion of the continuing issue of terminology for guidance in the schools. Next, the chapter describes the array of per-sonnel responsible for guidance followed by discussion of their many duties. Then the chapter turns to the issue of the selection and training of guidance personnel. Following this, the chapter describes a new organiza-tional structure, called pupil personnel services, under which guidance would be placed. The chapter closes with an examination of the impact the beginning federal presence in the 1930s had on guidance in the schools and ends with a brief review of the major trends and issues of the 1930s.

The Continued Struggle with Terminology

Differences of opinion concerning the terminology for guidance continued to exist in the 1930s. Modifiers such as vocational, educational, recre-ational, health, civic-social-moral and personal continued to be used in front of the word guidance by various authors. Substantial debate centered particularly on the uses of the words vocational and educational. Brewer (1932), a proponent of educational guidance in the teens and 1920s, went even further in the 1930s to suggest in his book that education was guidance. Myers (1935a) took issue with this by expressing concern that educational guidance as well as other forms of guidance was being exalted at the expense of vocational guidance.

"Indeed, this tendency to emphasize other forms of guidance has made such progress that one wonders at times if vocational guidance is not in danger of being thrown out of this house – a house which he has builded with great labor and care during the past twenty-five years" (p. 20).

Koos and Kafauver (1937) also expressed concern about terminology. There were concerned about too narrow and too broad definitions of guidance. "Besides taking issue . . . with the narrow concept which would restrict guidance to vocation, [they] disagree with the broader concepts which make 'guidance' synonymous with 'education'. Guidance is only a part of the educative process, not the whole of it" (p. 609).

Although many types of guidance were still being talked about in the 1930s, there were glimpses of possible consensus around language to describe guidance. For example Reavis and Woellner (1930) used just three terms to describe guidance: educational, personal and vocational. Notice how close these terms are to the domains of guidance we use today: academic, personal/social and career.

At the same time some writers noted the increasing use of the word guidance without any modifiers. For example, Fitch (1936) pointed out that most books published before 1930 used the word vocational as in vocational guidance, but after 1930, the word guidance more often appeared alone. In the same article Fitch used the expression "the vocational aspects of guidance" (p. 761). This is interesting because in the 1960s and 1970s, this phrase was popular as a way to label vocational guidance.

Smith (1931) wanted to make sure vocational guidance was understood as a process not an event. He stated, "Vocational guidance, therefore, is not an event which may happen to an individual, but is a process extending over an indefinite period of time. In a letter recently received from a lady in a nearby state appears this request: 'This June my son graduates from the ———- high school and is then ready for that thing called vocational guidance. Will you send him some?' Guidance cannot be given like a dose of medicine any more than can education be taken as a solidified essence or concentrated form in a few weeks" (p. 188).

Confusion also existed with the term vocational counseling. Campbell (1932) stated that some workers in the field thought the term vocational counseling was too narrow. She pointed out that there had even been several attempts to remove the word vocational from the name of the National Vocational Guidance Association. She went on to say that she used the term vocational very broadly "applying (it) to educational, personal and social problems" (p. 42).

In addition, Campbell (1932) pointed out that the issue of terminology wasn't just centered on what to call guidance. The problem extended to the use of the term counselor as well. "The term counselor is loosely used. Investigations in this field show that some counselors are in reality doing work that is often thought of as that of the visiting teacher, or the psychologist, and still others are engaged in educational guidance almost to the exclusion of vocational guidance" (p. 40).

The Personnel Responsible for Guidance

During the 1930s, a number of school personnel were responsible for guidance in the schools. They included administrators, teachers and a few full-time counselors. They also included individuals with the titles of dean of girls and dean of boys. In addition social workers, sometimes called visiting teachers, and attendance personnel were also involved.

Reavis and Woellner (1930) reported on a study of the office practices of principals in secondary schools in which a survey was sent to 967 principals; 522 responded. Included in the survey were questions about guidance including "(1) the extent to which educational, personal and vocational guidance are given, and (2) what school officers are called upon to assume the responsibility for such guidance" (p. 190). They found that guidance programs were reported in a large majority of the schools and that principals assumed most responsibility for providing guidance, followed by assistant principals, counselors, and deans of boys and deans of girls.

Allen (1931) described the guidance functions of a variety of school staff, indicating that all faculty members and administrators have guidance responsibilities. The principal was responsible for the organization of the guidance program as well as the supervision of individuals with guidance responsibilities. Classroom teachers stressed the occupational information of their subjects while homeroom teachers (classroom teachers) provide friendly and personal interest in each pupil and orientation to school activities as well as keep records and attendance. Next class advisors had special training and provided individual counseling and orientation instruction dealing with educational, vocational and social problems. Of these personnel, the class advisor in Allen's terms is closest to school counselors today, although it must be remembered that class advisors were teachers who taught regular courses along with their work as class advisors. In a report issued in 1933, Reavis described guidance functionaries in secondary schools. He found that the principal was most often responsible for guidance in small schools, but homeroom advisors and deans of boys and girls were most often responsible in large schools. He also indicated that specialists in counseling (counselors) were found most often in large schools.

PRINCIPALS AS GUIDANCE FUNCTIONARIES

In small schools (fewer than 200 students) principals were chiefly responsible for guidance activities (Reavis, 1933). In schools with more than 1,000 students, principals provided leadership in a general way but relied on others for carrying out most of the guidance activities. Reavis (1933) pointed out that when administrators were responsible for guidance their guidance work was often less of a priority.

"In the schools which develop their guidance programs around general administrative officers, guidance activities are often subordinated to other administrative duties. Furthermore, in dealing both with individuals and with groups the administrative officer is sometimes inhibited in the performance of a guidance activity by the urgency of prior performance of some nonguidance administrative activity. In practice administration may interfere with guidance, and guidance may interfere with administration. This relation often renders guidance difficult by officers whose primary responsibility is administration" (p. 9-10).

DEANS OF GIRLS AND BOYS AS GUIDANCE FUNCTIONARIES

In the 1930s large secondary schools often employed deans of girls and boys in guidance work. They often taught part-time. Their duties were a mixture of administration and guidance. The following nine duties were common:

- Discipline
- Oversight of social conduct
- Supervision of extracurriculum activities
- Control of attendance
- Guidance concerning quality of work
- Curriculum guidance
- Vocational guidance
- Placement service
- Follow-up work

(Reavis, 1933, p. 10)

HOMEROOM ADVISORS AS GUIDANCE FUNCTIONARIES

Regular teachers often served as homeroom advisors. According to Reavis (1933) the chief purpose of homeroom was guidance, not instruction. He referred to a study of 336 schools indicating homeroom advisors often gave more attention to non-guidance administrative duties than to guidance. Among the duties homeroom advisors performed included "discipline, oversight of social conduct, direction of special homeroom activities, guidance concerning quality of work, curriculum guidance and vocational guidance" (p. 12).

TRAINED COUNSELORS AS GUIDANCE FUNCTIONARIES

Beginning in the 1930s specialists in guidance called counselors were beginning to be employed in schools.

"Whether the emphasis is placed on the vocational, educational or personal aspects of guidance, certain schools have conceived of the activities of counseling and guidance as involving knowledge and technical skill beyond that possessed by the teacher and general administrative officer. Such schools regard guidance as an act of skill, which requires for its successful execution training of a technical character. Accordingly, in these schools guidance becomes the responsibility of the specialist, who may be developed from the staff through special training or be added to the staff for the specific purpose" (Reavis, 1933, p. 13).

If counselors were to be employed Reavis (1933) stated they should become members of the school staff with clearly defined duties. He also stated that having counselors in schools did not relieve teachers and administrators of their guidance responsibilities. In addition he added that counselors should not be overloaded with pupils or have their energy diverted with administrative work.

THE VISITING TEACHER AS A GUIDANCE FUNCTIONARY

Based on his study Reavis (1933) found that visiting teachers were typically found in large schools. Visiting teachers were trained social workers or sometimes psychiatric social workers. Often they were responsible for both attendance and home adjustments. Because of their specialized training, not many schools employed these personnel.

Later in the decade, Allen (1937) wrote about the variety of personnel involved in guidance activities. He described various titles given to teachers who performed guidance functions, and he emphasized an interesting point when he stated these assignments did not add additional personnel to schools.

"The counselor is essentially a teacher who deals with the common problems of youth by means of class instruction and with individual problems by means of personal interviews. Often the special title of 'counselor' or 'dean' or 'adviser' tends to set apart the work of the guidance worker from that of the rest of the faculty. This fact is unfortunate and has retarded the development of guidance programs because it implies an increased personnel rather than merely a different plan of assignment for the various instructional tasks" (p. 16).

In the same article Allen (1937) pointed out that sometimes teachers thought class counselors had an easy program because they spent time in individual interviews without realizing that interviews required preparation and involved outside work. He stated that it was important to differentiate guidance responsibilities among homeroom teachers, subject teachers and class counselors so it was clear as to who did what. This, he said, was the responsibility of the principal and superintendent.

Concern was expressed about the variety of titles given to guidance personnel. Fitch (1935) noted that principals, vice principals, deans of girls, deans of boys, various advisors and counselors including pupil counselor, student counselor, teacher counselors and visiting counselors were titles used in the 1930s. There was little standardization of titles as Fitch noted.

Duties of Individuals Responsible for Guidance

One of the tasks of the profession in the 1930s was to establish the preferred list of duties to be carried out by individuals who had guidance responsibilities in schools. The task was to decide which duties would constitute a complete program or, as Procter (1930) stated, the "standard set up" for guidance. To accomplish this task it was first necessary to find out what counselors were actually doing. Myers (1931) asked some counselors to record their activities hour by hour for a week. He also consulted various papers and reports on counseling available in the literature. From these sources he prepared a list of 37 actual duties for which counselors were responsible. There was no indication that any one counselor was responsible for all 37 items, rather it was a total list.

Among the 37 items were traditional duties such as teaching classes in occupational information, conducting individual interviews with pupils, conferring with parents, and gathering and preparing vocational information. Also among the 37 items were other duties including handling discipline cases, handling absence and tardiness cases, having charge of the all-school assembly program, presiding over study halls, lending money from the school loan fund and performing corridor duty.

After reviewing the list, Myers stated, "Here is, indeed, a formidable list of things which counselors do. It is obvious that many of these are essential to an effective guidance program and may properly be expected of a counselor. It is equally obvious that some of them are routine administrative or clerical matters which have nothing whatever to do with counseling. Evidently, under the guise of setting up a counseling program, some junior and senior high school principals have unloaded a large number of their office duties upon the counselor" (p. 344).

Myers went on to point out that counselors should have some duties other than ones essential to counseling. At the same time he stressed the need for counselors to have time for counseling. "Superintendents and principals who are genuinely interested in guidance will do all that they can under the conditions which exist to allow the counselor time for real counseling duties" (p. 347).

Later Fitch (1936) pointed out that school principals typically determined the duties individuals assigned guidance responsibilities would carry out. According to Fitch this has led to an undesirable expansion of duties assigned. He explained the problem as follows:

> "Where the principal has an intelligent and sympathetic interest in the practice of vocational guidance this is less likely to occur, but there is always danger that the counselor may come to be regarded as a handyman on whom may be unloaded any sort of task no one

else has time to do. Thus we often find counselors performing the function of visiting teachers, director of the lunch room, substitute teacher, counselor of problem pupils, etc. They may be called upon to act in all sorts of roles from that of chairman of the committee on social activities to that of assistant principal" (pp. 761-762).

Koos and Kefauver (1937) also expressed concern about the assignment of guidance duties. They pointed out that some duties that some schools listed as guidance were not guidance duties at all.

"[Guidance] is significantly related to, but does not include such matters as discipline, methods of teaching, curriculum-making, vocational training and directing the extra-curriculum" (p. 609).

As guidance was becoming institutionalized in schools and was in the process of being defined and implemented in the 1930s, the expectations of other educational personnel concerning guidance and counseling also were being shaped. This seemed to be particularly true for school administrators. Johnson (1972) underlined this when he pointed out that administrative obligations were a substantial part of the new professional responsibilities. In fact, many suggested vocational guidance responsibilities delineated by the profession became administrative obligations when incorporated into the school setting. "Professional responsibilities became in fact administrative obligations for which guidance would be held accountable not to professionally determined values but values of the education subculture interpreted through its administrative structure" (Johnson, 1972, p. 191).

Reavis (1933) also reported on typical duties guidance personnel performed in schools based on a survey of high schools. The following list represents an accumulation of duties across a number of schools. No one school had personnel performing all of these duties, but the list provides an idea of the variety of guidance duties being carried out in the early 1930s.

- Instructing pupils regarding occupations
- Carrying on occupational research
- Rendering placement services
- Making follow-up investigations
- Effecting adjustments between employees and employers
- Visiting homes of pupils
- Compiling case histories of pupils

- Administering tests to pupils
- Preparing guidance bulletins
- Giving information to pupils in groups
- Counseling individual pupils
- Holding case conferences with groups
- Sponsoring pupil activities
- Conferring with teachers and sponsors regarding individual pupils
- Serving on committees of teachers to develop materials for try-out courses
- Conducting guidance clinics
- Making reports of activities to administrative offices

In an article on guidance in a large city Weglein (1935) described a number of duties that should be carried out by guidance personnel in a guidance program. Individual guidance consisting of the use of cumulative records beginning in elementary school and individual interviews with all pupils beginning in elementary school continuing on through junior and senior high school were two important duties. The goal of these duties was adjustment to school. As Weglein noted, "Adjustment is the keynote of guidance" (p. 13). Group guidance including classes on educational information and occupations was also popular according to Weglein. He also indicated that placement and follow-up work, the keeping of records on students, publicity and information and research on vocational opportunities and follow-up studies were important duties for guidance personnel.

Lee (1934) highlighted the following duties in describing what he called functions of guidance: counseling individual students; teaching exploratory classes, occupational information classes, personality development classes; conducting placement and follow-up; testing and keeping records; and researching occupational trends and requirements, personality traits and characteristics and the actual effectiveness of the guidance program. Other authors also described the functions or duties of guidance personnel. Rutledge and Yockey (1932) talked about the importance of interviews with students individually or in groups, cooperating with agencies within school and outside of school, research, and routine and clerical studies to include making pupils programs and filling out personal data cards. They did state that "a counselor should not be asked to perform administrative and clerical functions" (p. 129). And Myers (1931) classified what he thought the preferred duties should be as follows:

- Interviewing or conferring with individual pupils
- Meeting with pupils in groups

- Conferring with teachers and other members of the school staff
- Conferring with special officers of the school system
- Conferring with parents
- Conferring with representatives of industry, business and the professions
- Working with social agencies of the community (pp. 345-347)

Based on a survey of 336 high schools of various sizes across 44 states, Koos and Kefauver (1937) identified common guidance duties as follows:

1. Informing the student concerning educational and vocational opportunities by means of:
   - Information through publications
   - Information through organization of offering: curricula
   - Information through content and experience within the offering: courses on occupations, exploratory courses
   - Information through other agencies
2. Securing information concerning the student through:
   - Information from students: educational and vocational plans
   - Records concerning school activities
   - Information derived from measurement
3. Guiding the individual student through individual counseling

The Selection and Training of Individuals Who Carried out Guidance Duties

Concern about the selection and training of the personnel who performed guidance duties in the schools has a long history dating back to Lysander Richard in the 1880s. In his book "Vocophy" (1881) he envisioned a profession for counselors (he labeled them vocophers) similar to that of law and medicine. His plan for preparing "vocophers" was as follows:

"A professorship of Vocophy might be added to some College, Institute or University, where especial attention could be given to its study. The other method, which is the most preferable, is the establishment of an institution, well-equipped with teachers and professors who are experts in the studies to be flowed and can impart their knowledge to the students in a practical manner. The time occupied in preparation for this profession should be no less than in the profession of law, and even after its practice begins, he who would expect to reap the greatest success will continue his studies until becomes master of his profession" (pp. 41-42).

Frank Parsons also saw the need for training individuals to serve as counselors. According to Brewer (1942) he inaugurated a course of study for prospective counselors. He died before the course began, but Ralph Albertson taught the course for 16 meetings on Saturday evenings.

In 1910, the Vocation Bureau organized a course for Boston school teachers who had been named counselors. These courses continued until 1913. Then the Boston School Committee took over teaching the course. Brewer (1942) reported that the first university course on vocational guidance was held at Harvard University in summer 1911. The Harvard catalog described the course as follows: "Vocational Guidance – The duties and equipment of teachers as vocational counselors; the theory and practice of vocational guidance. Lectures, readings, conferences. Ten lectures beginning Friday, July 7, and continuing on Mondays, Wednesdays and Fridays at 4 P.M. for three weeks" (p. 184).

By the 1920s most major universities were offering course work to train individuals who had guidance responsibilities in schools. Brewer (1942) reported that in 1925, 35 colleges were offering summer courses in vocational guidance. By 1928 that number had increased to 70 colleges and universities.

As more and more colleges and universities offered courses in the 1920s some authorities raised questions about how training should be delivered and what the content should be. Payne (1925), for example, raised the following questions.

"What is the best method of training vocational advisers? Directors of vocational and educational guidance? Visiting teachers? Placement officers? What required courses should they take? What elective courses should be offered them? What institutions offer such training in the form of systematic curricula; what should be the prerequisites for entrance to such courses? What training have present holders of such positions received" (p. 399)?

In the 1930s more and more articles and book chapters appeared in the literature on the topic of the selection and training of individuals responsible for guidance in the schools. While teachers, administrators and social workers all had some time for guidance responsibilities, the 1930s was the time when the number of individuals spending half or more time in guidance work began to increase. Brewster and Greenleaf (1939), specialists with the Occupational Information and Guidance Service of the U.S.

Office of Education, reported on a study of public high schools (23,032 high schools with a total enrollment of 7,163,919 pupils). One part of their study provided data about the number of counselors in these schools. For this study, counselors or guidance officers were defined as "any member of the high school staff who spends half or more than half time in counseling and guidance" (p. 83). They found that there were 1,484 women and 802 men serving as guidance officers or counselors. Given these figures the ratio of counselors to students was one counselor for every 3,100 pupils. They pointed out that these ratios ignored the fact that less-than half-time personnel may work in these schools.

As more and more individuals were being employed half or more time in the schools with guidance and counseling responsibilities, discussion in the literature began to focus on standards for counselors. Fuller (1935) reported on discussions held at a conference that focused in part on these questions.

Who should set the standards, and by what methods should they be made effective? What personal qualifications should the counselor possess, and what preparation should he have in terms of training and practical experience (p. 219)?

In addition to discussions concerning the personal qualifications of counselors and their preparation, discussions in the literature focused on counselors' backgrounds. Fuller (1935) recommended counselors be recruited from the teaching staff. He stated that teaching experience was a "*sine qua non* of the counselor's experience" (p. 220). Fitch (1936) suggested that another view of training for counselors emphasized economics over pedagogy and that their "experience should include other occupations than teaching" (p. 763).

Whatever differences existed concerning the best background for counselors, there was some agreement about the training of counselors. Fuller (1925) suggested the following courses should be considered.

"The training of the counselor, it was asserted, should relate chiefly to courses which would help in understanding the individual; these would include not only the psychology of individual differences, mental tests and measurements and such, but mental hygiene as well" (p. 220).

As the 1930s came to a close, it was clear that there was a need for high standards for counselor selection and education. Williamson (1939) noted this point when he stated counselors must be well-trained. "A simple course in guidance may be sufficient for teachers but not for counselors" (p. 12).

Another interesting point was made about the need for guidance training for other personnel in schools. As the 1930s closed Altstetter (1938) noted that teachers and administrators needed training too.

"Not until guidance training becomes a recognized part of a teacher's and administrator's preparation can good guidance be expected in the schools. Hasten the time" (p. 520).

A New Organizational Structure for Guidance: Pupil Personnel Services

The organization of guidance in the schools continued to be of concern in the 1930s. Fitch (1935) stated that where guidance was being carried out in schools, there were two types of organization; centralized and decentralized. In the centralized system a central office is established with a director in charge of guidance for the entire school system. The decentralized approach featured each building in the district carrying out its work independently. These variations in the organization of guidance led Fitch (1935) to state:

"A careful examination of practice in different cities reveals the fact that guidance has become standardized neither in organization, method, nor purpose. In one city it may be that organized guidance is rejected altogether; in another, it may be the keynote of the school system. Where it is accepted and a program is in operation we find one city devoting itself to educational guidance, another to vocational activities, while a third includes both. Furthermore, even in the cities where the vocational aspects of guidance are in the ascendancy, the particular emphasis tends to differ. In one system the specialty is placement, in another follow-up, while another may expend its energies on occupational research and counseling and ignore placement altogether" (pp. 17-18).

While discussion continued in the 1930s about various organizational patterns for guidance, other specialists were being added to the staffs of schools, a trend that began in the 1920s. They included attendance workers, visiting teachers (social workers), school nurses and school physicians.

In addition, guidance responsibilities were being incorporated into the work of administrators, deans of boys and girls and teachers. Also, by this time some full-time counselors were being employed in the schools.

As a result of adding more staff members who were working in various guidance capacities (educational, vocational and personal-social), it became apparent that a new organizational system was needed to coordinate their work. The traditional system of lists of duties (the position approach) was no longer adequate. Overlapping lists of duties often occurred among these staff members resulting in role confusion among themselves, other professionals in the schools and the public.

The question was, what organizational system was available to coordinate the work of these specialists? Borrowing a term from industry, the word personnel was chosen along with the word pupil to designate services in elementary and secondary schools. Putting these two words together gave birth to pupil personnel services (Heck 1935a, 1935b; Myers, 1935; Shear, 1965). At the college level the term was student personnel services. According to Shear (1965) these terms were used in the literature beginning in the 1930s. "Items labeled 'pupil personnel' and 'student personnel' appeared in any appreciable numbers in bibliographies and reference lists" (p. 134).

As we will see pupil personnel services became the dominant organizational framework for all of the specialists in schools including counselors and other individuals responsible for guidance and other special services in the 1940s, 1950s, 1960s and beyond. It remains so today in many schools. In fact, in the 1950s and 1960s some writers suggested that the term school guidance be dropped "in favor of the concept of pupil personnel services or pupil services" (Koeppe & Bancroft, 1966, p. 228).

Given the introduction of the pupil personnel services organizational framework, what happened to guidance in the schools? Sturtevant (1938) stressed that in any "discussion of the organization of pupil personnel work ... the purposes of the guidance program can be met only insofar as that program is an integral part of education" (p. 14). Myers (1935) pointed out that when guidance is compared with the activities in the other pupil personnel services "... no activity ... suffers as much as a lack of a coordinated program as does guidance and especially the counseling aspect of it" (p. 807).

Given Myers's point about the lack of a coordinated program for guidance (remember that the prevailing organization for guidance and counseling at that time was a position with a list of duties), what would be the best way to provide a more coordinated program for guidance and counseling? The concept that emerged was *guidance services*. Five services were typically identified, including individual inventory, information, counseling, placement and follow-up (Smith, 1951). According to Roeber, Walz and Smith (1969):

"This conception of guidance services was developed during a period in the history of the guidance movement when it was necessary to have some definitive statement regarding the need for and nature of a more organized form of guidance. This delineation of guidance services generally served its purpose and gave the guidance movement something tangible to 'sell' to state departments of education and to local schools" (p. 55).

Within the guidance services model, counseling began to assume more importance than the other services. It was the result in part of the work of American psychologist and pediatrician Arnold Gesell and the mental hygiene movement. It was also a result of the increasing number of pupils who were experiencing personal problems.

"Up to 1930, ... not much progress had been made in differentiating this function [personal counseling] from the preexisting programs of vocational and educational guidance. After that date, more and more of a separation appeared as guidance workers in the high schools became aware of increasingly large numbers of students who were troubled by personal problems involving hostility to authority, sex relationships, unfortunate home situations and financial stringencies" (Rudy, 1965, p. 25).

Bell (1939), in a book on personal counseling, stated that the goal of counseling was student adjustment through personal contact between counselor and student. Adjustment in his thinking included all phases of an individual's life: school, health, occupational, motor and mechanical, social, home, emotional and religious. Koos and Kefauver (1937) also noted the theme of adjustment when they stated that guidance programs had two phases, (1) the distributive and (2) the adjustive. The goal of the first phase was to distribute students to educational and vocational opportunities. The goal of the second phase was to help students make adjustments to educational and vocational situations. Finally, Campbell (1932) made the same point by stating that guidance needed to focus on "problems of adjustment to health, religion, recreation, to family and friends, to school and to work" (p. 4).

As this was occurring, the original term for guidance, vocational guidance, was being defined more narrowly as: "the process of assisting the individual to choose an occupation, prepare for it, enter upon and progress in it. As preparation for an occupation involves decisions in the choice of studies, choice of curriculums and the choice of schools and colleges, it becomes evident that vocational guidance cannot be separated from educational guidance" (Campbell, 1932, p. 4).

Interesting to note is that vocational guidance was seen as a process that helped individuals examine all occupations, not just those for which vocational education provided training.

"As vocational guidance and vocational education are linked together in many minds, a statement about this relationship may clarify the situation. Vocational education is the giving of training to persons who desire to work in a specific occupation. Vocational guidance offers information and assistance which leads to the choice of an occupation and the training which precedes it. It does not give such training. The term *vocational* refers to any occupation, be it medicine, law, carpentry or nursing. Preparation for many occupations and professions must be planned in the secondary school and in college by taking numerous courses, which are not usually known as vocational. Vocational guidance concerns itself, therefore, with pupils in the academic courses in high school or students of the liberal arts in college, as well as with the pupils in the trade and commercial courses, which have become known as vocational education" (Campbell, 1932, p. 4).

This distinction is important because, from the 1960s to the present, this was and is a point of contention in defining the focus and scope of guidance and counseling in career and technical education legislation. Some individuals contend that vocational guidance is guidance and counseling for career and technical education students only and that if money were made available it should be spent only for the guidance and counseling of students in these programs.

The Beginning Federal Presence

Although the educational and personal adjustment themes for guidance continued to play a dominant role in guidance practice in the schools during the 1930s, the vocational emphasis also continued to show strength. In February 1933 the National Occupational Conference, funded by a Carnegie grant, opened its doors. The activities of the National Occupational Conference included studies and research related to the problems of occupational adjustment, book publication and the development of a service that provided information and consultation about vocational guidance activities. The National Occupational Conference for a time also provided joint support for Occupations, the official journal of the National Vocational Guidance Association.

In 1938, a national advisory committee on education, originally appointed in 1936 by President Franklin D. Roosevelt, issued a report that pointed to the need for an occupational information service at the national level as well as for guidance and placement services as a part of a sound program of vocational education. As a result of these recommendations, and with funds from Vocational Education and from the Commissioner of Education (Studebaker, 1938), the Occupational Information and Guidance Service was established in 1938 in the Vocational Division of the U.S. Office of Education. Richard Allen served for a few months as the chief of the unit before Harry Jager assumed the post (Wellman, 1978). Although the service was located in the Vocational Division, it was not designed to be exclusively vocational in nature. This point was made clear in a document, "Principles Underlying the Organization and Administration of the Occupational Information and Guidance Service," issued by the U. S. Office of Education in 1940.

"The functions to be performed by the Occupational Informational and Guidance Service are to be as broad and complete as it is practicable for the Office to provide for at any given time within the limits of funds, cooperative assistance from various organizations, both within the government and outside, and other assets. The activities in which the service will be interested will include such phases of guidance as vocational guidance, personal guidance, educational guidance and placement. While, with respect to personnel, no service in the Office can now be said to be complete, the various divisions or services go as far as possible in their respective fields in meeting needs or requests for services. Thus, for example, in the field of education for exceptional children, a service which would require 15 or 20 professional workers in the office if it were even to approximate completeness in numbers and types of persons needed, we have only one specialist. Yet this specialist is responsible for representing the Office in handling all problems and service in this particular field" (Smith, 1951, p. 66)

Of particular importance was the statement, "The activities in which the service will be interested will include such phases of guidance as vocational guidance, personal guidance, educational guidance and placement." Not only did the statement clearly outline the broad mission of the service and, as a result, of guidance in the schools, but it also described a currently popular way of describing guidance as having three phases; vocational, personal and educational." Once the Occupational Information and Guidance Service was established at the federal level, it also became possible to establish guidance offices in state departments of education. Such funds could be used only for state offices, however. No funds could be used to support guidance and counseling at the local level.

"Reimbursement was provided for state supervision under the George Dean Act [An Act to Provide for the Further Development of Vocational Education in the several states and territories; Public Law No. 673, 1936] and the number of states with a state guidance supervisor increased from two to 28 between 1938 and 1942. The Occupational Information and Guidance Service was instrumental in initiating conferences of state supervisors to consider issues in the field. This group subsequently became the National Association of Guidance Supervisors, then National Association of Guidance Supervisors and Counselor Trainers and finally the current Association for Counselor Education and Supervision" (Wellman, 1978, p. 2).

Major Trends and Issues

During the turbulent 1930s various conceptions about guidance, its activities and the personnel involved that had emerged in the teens and 1920s continued to be debated. The debate about guidance terminology continued as well, although some consensus appeared. Now, instead of many forms of guidance, only three forms – educational, vocational and personal-social – began appearing more often in the literature. And, increasingly a number of authors were using the word guidance alone without any modifiers.

The 1930s also witnessed increasing discussion about the various personnel responsible for guidance and the duties they performed. Concern began to be expressed about their selection and training. There was growing recognition of the need for well-trained individuals and the need for standards for counselor preparation. There also was concern about some of the duties counselors were performing, particularly those that were administrative and clerical.

One of the duties some counselors were asked to perform was discipline. This was not surprising since many administrators and later deans had dual roles of counselor and administrator in a school. This pattern goes back to the time of Jessie B. Davis, first in the Detroit Public Schools and then in Grand Rapids, Mich., where administrators served as counselors. It was natural for them to serve as the disciplinarian of the school as well as the school's counselor. Once individuals other than administrators or deans became counselors however, the issue of discipline as a duty became of real concern. Today we call this having dual relationships, which are to be avoided according to the ethical standards of the American School Counselor Association (2004).

A major milestone in the 1930s was the creation of a new organizational structure for all of the individuals who had guidance responsibilities. It was called pupil personnel services. And, within that structure, the concept of guidance services emerged. The field of guidance had moved from a position with a list of duties to a position with a list of duties organized by guidance services all under the overall structure of pupil personnel services. The five most typical services mentioned were assessment, information, counseling, placement and follow-up, although some writers added other services to the list.

It is important to remember that most of the work of guidance in the schools under this new organizational structure of guidance services continued to be carried out by teachers teaching part-time and providing guidance services part-time as well as administrators fulfilling some guidance roles in addition to their administrative responsibilities. This pattern of staffing would not change until the 1950s and 1960s when more full-time counselors began to be employed in the schools.

Also, as we will see in the next chapter, the emergence of a federal presence for guidance in the 1930s was to have substantial impact on the nature, structure and growth of guidance in the schools. The establishment of the Occupational Information and Guidance Service in 1938 at the federal level provided leadership and resources for the then new state leaders of guidance to meet and carry on leadership activities at the state level. The federal presence also raised awareness at the national level of the need for guidance services in schools.

Finally, due to the dire economic times in the 1930s, guidance programs and personnel were often cut or reduced in scope and numbers. The cost of guidance in the schools was discussed in a number of issues of

Occupations, the journal of the profession. In response to the cost issue, the NEA Committee (1937) made the following pronouncement:

"Costs may be always a consideration; if they are reasonable they ought never to be a barrier. The best way to prevent waste of money in education is to use the services of guidance to make education function for each pupil. Cost of effective guidance is not an expense but is an investment; it is not an extravagance, but is an economy – if evaluated in terms of successful and competent personalities developed and failures avoided" (p. 876).

References

Allen, R. D. (1931). Delegating the guidance functions within a secondary school. *Occupations, 10*, 14-19.

Allen. R. D. (1937). How a principal can direct guidance. *Occupations, 16*, 15-20.

Altstetter, M. L. (1938). Guidance service in two hundred secondary schools. *Occupations, 16*, 513-520.

American School Counselor Association (2004). *Ethical standards for school counselors*. Alexandria, VA: Author.

Bell, M. M. (1939). *Theory and practice of personal counseling*. Stanford, CA: Stanford University Press.

Brewer, J. M. (1932). *Education as guidance*. New York: The MacMillan Company.

Brewer, J. M. (1942). *History of vocational guidance*. New York: Harper & Brothers Publishers.

Brewster, R. E., & Greenleaf, W. J. (1939). A roll-call of counselors. *Occupations, 18*, 83-89.

Campbell, M. E. (1932). Study of the individual; counseling; scholarships; curriculum work in educational and vocational guidance. In F. J. Kelly, *Section III, Education and Training, Committee D on Vocational Guidance and Child Labor, Anne S. Davis, Chairman, White House Conference on Child Health and Protection* (pp. 19-161). New York: The Century Co.

Fitch, J. A. (1935). *Vocational guidance in action*. New York: Columbia University Press.

Fitch, J. A. (1936). Professional standards in guidance. *Occupations, 14*, 760-763.

Fuller, R. G. (1935). Trail-markers of guidance. *Occupations, 14*, 218-222.

Heck, A. O. (1935a). Pupil-personnel services in pupil schools. *Educational Research Bulletin, 14,* 57-61.

Heck, A. O. (1935b). Administrative organization. *Educational Research Bulletin, 14,* 214-216.

Johnson, A. H. (1972). Changing conceptions of vocational guidance and concomitant value-orientations 1920-30. *Dissertation Abstracts International, 33,* 3292A. (University of Microfilms No. 72-31, 933).

Koeppe, R. P., & Bancroft, J. F. (1966). Elementary and secondary school programs. *Review of Educational Research, 24* (2), 219-232.

Koos, L. V., & Kefauver, G. N. (1937). *Guidance in secondary schools.* New York: The Macmillan Company.

Lee, E. A. (1934). Functions of guidance. *Occupations, 12,* 36-37.

Myers, G. E. (1935a). *Relations between vocational and educational guidance.* Ann Arbor, MI: The Vocational Education Department, University of Michigan.

Myers, G. E. (1935b). Coordinated guidance. *Occupations, 13,* 804-807.

Myers. G. E. (1931). What should be the duties of the counselor? *Occupations, 9,* 343-347.

N. E. A. Committee (1937). The function of guidance in secondary education. *Occupations, 15,* 874-876.

Payne, A. F. (1925). *Organization of vocational guidance.* New York: McGraw-Hill Book Company, Inc.

Proctor, W. M. (1930). Evaluating guidance activities in high schools. *Occupations, 9,* 58-66.

Reavis, W. C. (1933). *Programs of guidance* (Bulletin, 1932, Number 17, Monograph Number 14). Washington, DC: U.S. Government Printing Office.

Reavis, W. C., & Woellner, R. C. (1930). *Office practices in secondary schools.* Chicago, IL: Laidlaw Brothers.

Richards, L. S. (1881). *Vocophy: The new profession.* Marlboro: Bratt Brothers, Steam Job Printers.

Roeber, E. C., Walz, G. R., & Smith, G. E. (1969). *A Strategy for guidance.* New York: Macmillan.

Rudy, W. S. (1965). *Schools in an age of mass culture.* Englewood Cliffs, NJ: Prentice-Hall.

Rutledge, R. E., & Yockey, F. M. (1932). The functions of the counselor. *Occupations, 11,* 128-129.

Shear, B. E. (1965). Pupil personnel services: History and growth. *Theory into practice, 4,* 133-139.

Smith, F. C. (1931). Vocational guidance as a national movement. *Education, 52,* 185-188.

Smith, G. E. (1951). *Principles and practices of the guidance program.* New York: The MacMillan Company.

Studebaker, J. W. (1938). The new occupational information and guidance service. *Occupations, 16,* 101-105.

Sturtevant, S. M. (1938). Organizing a guidance program. *Teachers College Record, 40,* 5-15.

Weglein, D. E. (1935). Guidance in a large city. *Occupations, 14,* 10-20.

Wellman, F. E. (1978). *U. S. Office of Education Administrative Unit: past, present, and future.* Unpublished manuscript, University of Missouri, Columbia, Missouri.

Williamson, E. G. (1939). Training and selection of school counselors. *Occupations, 18,* 7-12.

CHAPTER 4

The 1940s and 1950s: Expanding and Extending Guidance in the Schools

The decades of the 1940s and 1950s witnessed times of turmoil and times of progress. World War II in the 1940s, the Korean War in the 1950s and the Cold War beginning in the 1940s all presented substantial challenges to our economy and our society. It was the beginning of the atomic age. At the same time the civil rights movement began in earnest in the 1950s. What about guidance in the schools during these two decades? Discussion in the literature concerning the purposes, organization and operation of guidance in the schools as well as the personnel involved intensified in the 1940s and 1950s. The two decades also saw the continued discussion and debate of guidance terminology, the personnel involved in providing guidance and their selection and training, as well as the organizational structures for guidance. Even during the World War II years of 1941 to 1945, but particularly afterward, from 1945 through the 1950s, increasing numbers of articles and books were being written on these topics.

The 1940s and 1950s witnessed the passage of two major pieces of federal legislation that would have a substantial, long-lasting impact on school counselor training and section and the continuing evolution of guidance in the schools. The 1950s also saw the formation of the American School Counselor Association (ASCA) as a division of the American Personnel and Guidance Association (APGA). In addition, the beginnings of elementary guidance appeared as did increasing interest in the need for adequate physical facilities for school counseling.

Chapter 4 begins by addressing the continuing guidance terminology issue followed by a presentation of data concerning the numbers of personnel involved in providing guidance in the schools. Then the chapter focuses on the selection and training of school counselors with particular attention being given to two pieces of federal legislation: the George-Barden Act of 1946 (P.L. 586) and the National Defense Education Act of 1958 (P.L. 85-864). Chapter 4 continues with a description of the formation of ASCA and a review of the various roles of school counselors and the organizational structures in which they worked. Next, the chapter describes the emergence of counseling as a major service in guidance highlighting the directive/nondirective debate of the 1940s and 1950s. This is followed by a review of the literature concerning physical facilities for guidance and the emergence of guidance in the elementary school. The chapter closes with a summary of the major issues and trends of the 1940s and 1950s.

The Terminology Issue Continued

As guidance in the schools continued to expand and evolve, concern about what to call it increased. Barry and Wolf (1957) expressed their concerns about this issue as follows: "Terminology tangles have complicated the guidance-personnel worker's attempts to explain his work to the public. Philosophical developments within the field have been impeded by misunderstandings about and difficulties with the language used to describe them" (p. 58).

Wrenn (1940) suggested the very word guidance had "lost its usefulness through excessive use" (p. 409). He felt a term such as "student-personnel work could profitably be substituted for guidance" (p. 409). His suggestion was in keeping with the pupil personnel services model that had evolved in the 1930s. Interestingly, 11 years later Wrenn (1951) wrote that while he had fought for the use of the title student personnel work, he had come to the conclusion that guidance would be used in the public schools for some time into the future.

Other writers such as Hale (1952) had difficulty differentiating the terms vocational guidance and vocational counseling. He felt some writers unfortunately were using the terms interchangeably. Arbuckle (1951) worried that some individuals were clinging to the notion that guidance was "strictly vocational in nature" (p. 595) and perhaps it was too prescriptive in practice. He suggested a broader meaning for the word guidance focusing on "a process which accentuates the work of the individual to work up to his capacity, and achieve what he can ..." (p. 598).

Davis (1950) felt that some individuals confused the terms pupil personnel services and guidance. He stated that guidance was one of the services of pupil personnel services, hence the term pupil personnel services was broader than the term guidance. He also felt the term guidance had limitations in that to some it meant vocational guidance, to others educational guidance and still to others personal, health or leisure-time guidance. Myers (1941) too felt there was confusion surrounding the term personnel work. He said, "Recent educational literature offers few terms concerning which there is greater confusion than that pertaining to personnel work" (p. 40). He went on to say that when the word guidance is used it includes educational, vocational, recreational and community service. Note that he did not use the modifier personal or social as other writers had done in the 1930s.

While confusion existed in the literature concerning how to label guidance, confusion also existed in the titles of the personnel involved in guidance work. Polmantier (1950) found that 1,565 school guidance workers (grades 1-12) listed in the "National Vocational Guidance Association Yearbook, 1948-1949" fell into 53 title categories. A table from his article is reproduced here to illustrate the wide range of titles being used during this time. Polmantier closed his article by suggesting that these results could indicate a lack of maturity in the development of school guidance, a lack of stability or movement toward clarification of terms since a large number of titles fall into 18 common titles.

Numbers of School Counselors

As indicated previously, confusion about what to label guidance continued in the 1940s and 1950s as did confusion concerning the appropriate titles of guidance personnel in the schools. This leads to the question, how many individuals carried the title of counselor or guidance officer during the 1940s? An answer to this question was provided by Greenleaf (1943) and Froehlich (1948). Greenleaf reported on a survey conducted in 1942 of guidance in 25,000 high schools across the country. Among the questions asked were who directed guidance in the school and what percent-

Table 1

NUMBER AND DISTRIBUTION OF SCHOOL GUIDANCE WORKERS BY TITLES COMMON TO MORE THAN ONE PERSON

Title	Number of Members	Title	Number of Members
Counselor, High School	446	Coordinator, Advisory Services, Public Schools	3
Counselor, Public Schools	265	Adviser, Junior High School	3
Director of Guidance, Public Schools	107	Assistant Supervisor, Advisory Services, Public Schools	3
Director of Guidance, High School	106	Coordinator of Guidance, Public Schools	3
Counselor, Junior High School	90	Director of Placement, Public Schools	2
Teacher, High School	86	Principal, Elementary School	2
Principal, High School	58	Director of Pupil Personnel Services, Public Schools	2
Teacher, Public Schools	51	Teacher-Adviser, High School	2
Assistant Principal, High School	50	Counselor, Trade School	2
Dean of Girls, High School	33	Assistant in Division of Instruction, Public Schools	2
Counselor-Teacher, High School	32	Administrative Assistant, High School	2
Superintendent of Public Schools	31	Assistant Director of Guidance, Public Schools	2
Counselor-Teacher, Public Schools	26	Director of Guidance and Placement, Public Schools	2
Teacher, Junior High School	18	Guidance Coordinator, High School	2
Principal, Junior High School	17	Librarian, High School	2
Supervisor of Guidance, Public Schools	10	Supervisor of Counselors, Public Schools	2
Adviser, High School	10	Supervisor of School-Work Program, Public Schools	2
Psychologist, Public Schools	10	Supervisor of Special Education, Public Schools	2
Dean of Girls, Public Schools	9	Supervisor of Vocational Guidance, Public Schools	2
Director of Guidance, Junior High School	7	Teacher-Coordinator, Public Schools	2
Director of Vocational Education, Public Schools	7	Vocational Adviser, High School	2
Counselor-Teacher, Junior High School	7	Vocational Assistant, Public Schools	2
Dean, High School	7	Total	1,565
Coordinator of Diversified Occupations, High School	5		
Assistant Superintendent of Public Schools	5		
Dean of Boys, High School	5		
Coordinator, High School	5		
Coordinator, Public Schools	4		
Counselor-Coordinator, High School	4		
Assistant Principal, Junior High School	3		
Counselor-Coordinator, Vocational Education and Extension, Board of Public Schools	3		

From "Titles of school guidance workers" by P. C. Polmantier, 1950, *Occupations, 28*, p. 350. Copyright 1950 by the American Counseling Association. Reprinted with permission.

age of school time was devoted to it. In reporting his findings, he compared the results of the 1942 survey with data from a 1937-1938 survey as follows:

"In 1937-1938 a total of 2,286 counselors and guidance officers in 1,297 schools served 2,062,341 pupils; approximately an average of one counselor to 900 pupils. In 1942 a total of 1,662 counselors and guidance officers, on at least a half-time basis, in 1,233 schools served 1,659,744 pupils; approximately an average of one counselor to 1,000 pupils. In addition, there were 113 schools whose principals said they served as counselors, and 5,453 high schools that reported part-time counselors who spent less than half time in counseling" (p. 603).

By the school year 1945-1946, the number of persons designated as counselors had increased. Froehlich (1948) reported on a survey of 24,314 secondary schools in 1945-1946 and found there were 8,299 persons called counselors and guidance officers; 3,618 were men and 4,681 were women. Although this was a substantial increase from the 1942 school year, he noted that "of the 24,314 secondary schools only 3,990 or 16.4 percent of the schools have counselors" (p. 522). So while there was an increase of counselors only a small number of the secondary schools actually employed counselors.

In viewing these numbers it is important to remember that during this time many of these individuals were part-time. The teacher-counselor or administrator-counselor was still common. Although there had been an increase in the number of full-time counselors from the 1930s into the 1940s and 1950s, part-time counselors were very common.

The Selection and Training of School Counselors

Although the 1930s certainly saw interest in school counselor selection and training, interest increased substantially in the 1940s and 1950s. The decade of the 1940s opened with the issuance of a report of the Section on Preparation for Guidance Service of the National Vocational Guidance Association (National Vocational Guidance Association, April & May, 1941). The committee that prepared the report described the functions of successful school counselors and their characteristics and competencies essential to their work.

The use of the term school counselor in this report may be misleading to some today who think of that term specifically identifying a full-time certified school counselor. That is not the case in this report. Note the following:

"The term 'school counselor' is used throughout these suggestions to indicate the personnel worker whose chief responsibility is to stimulate, initiate, develop and coordinate the guidance work of the entire school. He will in many schools also perform some one or more forms of specialized guidance service; what this is will be determined by the type of other personnel available. He just acts as guidance leader and as a resource person in the school and should have superior qualifications and training for the task. The particular name given to this type of personnel worker is not important. In actual practice such duties are now performed by personnel workers who are variously known as deans, advisers, educational and vocational counselors, coordinators, head guidance workers or counselors.

The school counselor is an educational worker and should have basic training as such. This does not mean that the counselor must be a teacher in some subject field, but it does mean that at least the basic training should already have been achieved and that the advanced training for the more specialized task is to be built upon an adequate undergraduate foundation" (National Vocational Guidance Association, April 1941, p. 534).

In the second section of this report appearing in the May 1941 issue of *Occupations* the details of requirements and training were presented. The report recommended that school counselors have a teaching certificate and have completed graduate work. The graduate work should include human growth and development, tests and measurements, clinical techniques, general methods of evaluation, counseling techniques, the educational program of the school and an internship. The report also described the preparation that teachers and administrators needed for their guidance responsibilities.

Harry A. Jager (1945), chief of the occupational information and guidance service, U.S. Office of Education, reported on a conference on Training on the Undergraduate and Graduate Levels in the Principles and Practices of Guidance Work in Secondary Schools. The participants outlined what they thought all candidates for teaching in secondary schools should know. In addition they recommended a minimum of 30 semester hours of graduate work for counselors. Of the 30 hours they recommended the following core coursework:

- A basic overview or introductory course: Three hours. Credit for this might be secured from the undergraduate course already described.
- Understanding the individual: Six hours
- Occupational information and training opportunities: Six hours
- Counseling procedures: Six hours
- Organizational relationships of the guidance program: Three hours (Jager, 1945, p. 154).

Important Federal Legislation

VOCATIONAL EDUCATION ACT OF 1946 (P.L. 586)

In 1946, an event occurred that was to have substantial impact on school counselor training as well as the growth and development of guidance and counseling in the schools. The event was the passage of the Vocational Education Act of 1946 (P.L. 586), commonly referred to as the George-Barden Act after the two legislators who sponsored the legislation. As a result of the act, funds could be used to support guidance and counseling activities in a variety of settings and situations. More specifically, the U.S. commissioner of education ruled that federal funds could be used for the following four purposes:

- The maintenance of a state program of supervision
- Reimbursement of salaries of counselor-trainers
- Research in the field of guidance
- Reimbursement of salaries of local guidance supervisors and counselors (Smith, 1951, pp. 67-68)

For the first time, because of this ruling, guidance and counseling received material, leadership and financial support. Consequently, guidance and counseling grew rapidly at state and local levels. Jager (1947) provided an overview of the George-Barden Act, describing how federal policy derived from the act evolved, focusing on federal-state relationships and the act's potential influence on vocational guidance as he called it. He went on to describe the act's impact on the profession including clearer definitions of counselor duties. He felt that this would:

"Protect professional personnel in the guidance field from that dispersion of their efforts which is now one of the curses of our work. A counselor whose administrative superior steals him from his counseling work and the activities basic to it, to set him in charge of study halls or lunch room duty or teaching some allegedly related class, will meet the fact that these are not professional counselor duties" (pp. 486-487).

Jager (1947) was also concerned about barriers he felt were present that would block the path toward full implementation of guidance programs in schools. One barrier he identified was the guidance terminology issue. He said "guidance," "counseling" and "the guidance program" needed common definitions that would be accepted by professionals. A second barrier was the lack of agreement about counselor duties, and a third barrier was the lack of agreement about the training of school counselors.

Concern about the training of school counselors had been discussed over the past decades as noted in previous chapters. The National Vocational Guidance Association had taken a leadership role by establishing standards for counselor preparation. Now, with the passage of the George-Barden Act, it was possible to use state funds to reimburse counselor training (or counselor education as we call it today). This made the recurring question of what a counselor training program should entail of extreme importance.

In spring 1948, the Occupational Information and Guidance Service staff called a meeting of state guidance supervisors and counselor trainers in cooperation with the Division of Higher Education of the U.S. Office of Education to discuss counselor preparation. Eight major subtopics were identified, and subcommittees were established to study each subtopic. Reports were presented for consideration at the National Conference of State Supervisors of Guidance Services and Counselor Trainers in Washington, D.C., Sept. 13-18, 1948. These reports were then revised with others participating in the work. Six of the seven were published between 1949 and 1950 by the Federal Security Agency, Office of Education.

- "Duties, Standards and Qualifications for Counselors," February 1949, co-chairpersons, Eleanor Zeis and Dolph Camp
- "The Basic Course" (never published)
- "Counselor Competencies in Occupational Information," March 1949, chairperson, Edward C. Roeber
- "Counselor Competencies in the Analysis of the Individual," July 1949, chairperson, Ralph C. Bedell
- "Counselor Competencies in Counseling Techniques," July 1949, chairperson, Stanley R. Ostrom

- "Administrative Relationships of the Guidance Program," July 1949, chairperson, Glenn Smith
- "In-Service Preparation for Guidance Duties, Parts One and Two," May 1950, chairperson, John G. Odgers

An additional report had been issued on supervised practice at the eighth National Conference but was referred back to committee. After revision it was considered at the ninth National Conference in Ames, Iowa, Sept. 11-15, 1950, and, with subsequent revision, was released as the eighth report in the series:

- "Supervised Practice in Counselor Preparation," April 1952, chairperson, Roy Bryan

All of the published reports were edited by Clifford P. Froehlich, specialist for the training of guidance personnel, under the general direction of Harry A. Jager, chief, guidance and personnel services branch.

Later, in fall 1948, the National Vocational Guidance Association issued a manual on counselor preparation. The manual listed seven broad areas of preparation:

- Philosophy and principles
- Growth and development of the individual
- Collecting, evaluating and using occupational, educational and related information
- Administrative and community relationships
- Techniques used in counseling
- Supervised experience

(Froehlich, 1949, pp. 542-543)

NVGA prepared the manual to help institutions plan training programs around the seven broad areas and to help students plan their training programs.

In the 1940s and early 1950s concern was being expressed about school counselor certification. Kremen (1951) made this statement about the need for certification.

"It is becoming increasingly apparent that we as counselors must either adopt certification regulations which represent our best thinking up to this time and take our chances on coping with the many issues which certification procedures inevitably raise or take the risk of having the counseling field filled with persons having inadequate, insufficient or inappropriate training because of a lack of certification regulations" (p. 584). Kremen analyzed the existing certification requirements of 23 states, which all required a teaching certificate and two years teaching experience as well as some work experience. The certificates in these states were valid for life. He also found a wide range of semester hours required, from 12 to 48 with a median of 20.5 semester hours. Finally he found the states required these areas of study:

- Philosophy and Principles of Guidance
- Understanding the Individual
- Occupational and Educational Information
- Organization and Administration of Guidance Programs

In addition to focusing on the initial training of school counselors, some writers emphasized the need for in-service education of teachers, administrators and counselors. Copenhart (1951) stated it this way:

"Since a guidance program cannot function without the active support and cooperation of all school personnel, the in-service education program must provide for all these persons. It must provide for teachers, for counselors and for the visiting teacher (in some schools), for the psychologist and for other special staff personnel who may be working in the school system" (p. 198).

Other writers during this time stressed the need for supervised internship in a school setting. Landy (1953) wrote, "One of the most serious lacks in counselor training has been the absence or near absence of any provision for a thorough-going, carefully supervised internship program in a school setting. Counselor training has too often depended largely on formal courses, sometimes carefully organized in a comprehensive, planned sequence, sometimes not. Occasionally students are assigned to schools where counseling programs are supposed to exist and where, too often, much of the student's training is inadequately supervised or where it consists largely of clerical work" (p. 310).

THE NATIONAL DEFENSE EDUCATION ACT OF 1958

In 1958 another event occurred that had a substantial impact on guidance and counseling in our schools, the roles of school counselors, and the selection and training of school counselors throughout the 1960s and beyond. The event was the passage of the National Defense Education Act (NDEA) of 1958 (P.L. 85-864). In passing the act, Congress said, "The Congress hereby finds and declares that the security of the nation requires the fullest development of the mental resources and technical skills of its young men and women. The present emergency demands that additional and more adequate educational opportunities be made available. The defense of this nation depends upon the mastery of modern techniques developed from complex scientific principles. It depends as well upon the discovery and development of new principles, new techniques and new knowledge.

"We must increase our efforts to identify and educate more of the talent of our nation. This requires programs that will give assurance that no student of ability will be denied an opportunity for higher education because of financial need; will correct as rapidly as possible the existing imbalances in our educational programs which have led to an insufficient proportion of our population educated in science, mathematics and modern foreign languages and trained in technology."

To respond to this national emergency Congress deemed it necessary to expand testing programs in schools and increase the number of guidance programs and school counselors so students could be advised about course selection and encouraged to be ready for college and enroll in college. Title V, Guidance, Counseling and Testing; Identification and Encouragement of Able Students of the NDEA had two major parts. Part A provided funds in the form of grants to states to establish statewide testing programs; Part B provided funds for training institutes to prepare individuals to be counselors in secondary schools. (See Appendix A for the full Text of Title V)

The Formation of the American School Counselor Association

In late 1947 and early 1948 the trustees of the National Vocational Guidance Association discussed the possible creation of a school counselor association. The question was should school counselors remain NVGA members, or should they have a separate organization? According to Odell (1971), Edward Roeber of the University of Michigan and Glenn Smith, chief of guidance and counseling for Michigan, were instrumental in getting a separate organization, now called the American School

Counselor Association (ASCA), started. ASCA was organized in 1952 and officially became a division of the American Personnel and Guidance Association (APGA) in 1953. ASCA's first journal, *The School Counselor*, started as a newsletter in 1953 and became a regular journal in 1955. This was followed by the publication of the journal *Elementary School Guidance and Counseling* in 1967. In 1997, ASCA combined these two journals into one titled *Professional School Counseling*. The first issue of the new journal was published in October 1997. Later, ASCA published *ASCA School Counselor.*

Counselor Roles and Guidance Program Organization

The 1940s and '50s saw the publication of many articles and books describing the variety of guidance activities being provided in schools. These articles and books also presented discussion concerning school counselors' roles as well as the needed organizational structure for guidance in the schools. During this time period it is important to remember that while more and more full-time counselors were being hired, much of the work was still being conducted by teacher-counselors, administrators and deans. Also, the terminology issue was still of concern: Should it be called vocational guidance, educational guidance, personal/social guidance, just plain guidance or the newer term, personnel work? All of these terms were used in the 1940s and 1950s by various authors leading to continued confusion among professionals and the public.

One of the major ways to deliver guidance activities to students was group guidance. Sachs (1945) reported that group guidance activities were usually classified as the homeroom plan or the guidance-teacher plan. Contrasts between these two types follow:

GUIDANCE-TEACHER PLAN
- A few teachers, selected because of special interests and training, serve as guidance workers.
- The guidance teacher usually has a load of 100 or more pupils depending on the amount of non-teaching time allowed.
- The group guidance period is usually a full class period.
- The degree of organization of content varies with the school district. Definite areas of instruction are often assigned to each grade level. Sometimes the content is highly organized.

- Individual guidance is a definite part of the guidance teacher's responsibility, a free period or two daily often being assigned for this work.

HOMEROOM PLAN

- All, or almost all, teachers serve as guidance workers.
- Each homeroom teacher usually works with 25 to 40 pupils.
- The homeroom period is usually a short daily period of 15 to 25 minutes.
- The content is usually highly flexible. Often very little cooperative planning is done by teachers.
- Individual guidance is incidentally given by the homeroom teacher. The counselor or school director of guidance usually has full responsibility for individual guidance work. (p. 2)

In the 1944-1945 school year, counselors in the Minneapolis Public School System conducted a survey of guidance at the secondary level. The focus was on the work counselors were doing at the junior and senior high school levels (Wright, 1946). What follows is a summary of the duties common to counselors in senior high schools.

- Teaches one or two classes and may have a homeroom
- Handles special assignments
- Supervises orientation of new pupils and assignment of incoming students to sections and remedial classes
- Advises pupils regarding choice of electives during their period in high school
- Advises pupils regarding transfers to vocational school
- Advises pupils regarding vocational planning and further training
- Supervises the testing program in the building
- Checks credits for high school graduation and for university entrance
- Advises boys entering and those in military service
- Interviews and counsels pupils who are failing in school
- Handles employment, including routines for excusing pupils for Christmas work
- Arranges group conferences
- Writes letters of reference
- Confers with pupils planning to withdraw from school
- Confers with teachers in regard to individual pupils who present particular problems
- Does clerical work involved in the routines and services mentioned above. Some of this clerical work requires counseling skills but much

is routine, such as alphabetizing tests, checking cards, preparing pass slips, typing letters, writing interview notes, pulling cards from files and returning cards to files (pp. 217-219).

During the 1940s and 1950s a number of studies were conducted to determine the time spent by counselors on various guidance activities. Arnold (1949) reported on a study conducted in Ohio in 1947 asking counselors to identify the amount of time they spent on various activities. He concluded from the data that "more time and effort are being given to attendance, tardiness, discipline and school failure than are being given to counseling about vocational and educational plans and about personal, social and school problems" (p. 392). He raised the following questions based on his data.

"Are counselors themselves clear as to what they really want to do? Do they not enjoy being jacks-of-all-trades rather than masters of counseling? Could a lack of mastery of effective counseling techniques be one aspect of the confused situations?" (p. 393).

A short article from the *California Guidance Newsletter* that appeared in the January 1951 issue of Occupations reported on a study asking 35 counselors in five schools in California to show the amount of time spent on clerical work. They were given a list of 10 typical clerical duties for this purpose. The study found that counselors in these schools were spending "as much as 80 percent of their time on clerical duties" (*California Guidance Newsletter*, 1951, p. 194). Other writers picked up on the issue of other duties including Feldman (1951). She stated that the "trend seems to be to make guidance a catch-all for all services that should be in the school system and for which there seems to be no other place" (p. 265). Hitchcock (1953) reported on a survey of 1,282 counselors from 1,255 schools in the United States. He found that counselors believed they should not be involved in the following:

- Duties of a clerical nature
- Scoring tests and recording tests results
- Securing and filing occupational and educational information
- Checking absentees
- Checking the halls and washrooms
- Substituting for absent teachers (p. 72)

Roeber (1955) also was concerned about counselor role and the forces at work in schools buffeting the school counselor. He stated:

"On the one hand, we see the counselor's functions inextricably bound to a fixed confining pattern of activities which neglect some fundamental pupil needs. On the other extreme, where the counselor's position is still at the Neanderthal stage of development, we see the counselor in such a fluid pattern of activities that no one understands or recognizes his functions. Somewhere between the extremes are found the majority of counselors who are buffeted continually by the pressure of immediate crises in the lives of pupils and the pressures of co-workers who have their own conceptions of the counselor's role. Unless the counselor is alert, he may early become the victim of forces which can pervert his functions and thereby decrease his effectiveness as a counselor (p. 7).

Keppers (1955) conducted a survey of state supervisors, counselor trainers and persons in charge of guidance programs representing all states except Oklahoma, Wyoming and Delaware. On the basis of his survey he drew the following conclusions:

- The principal should give administrative support to the program.
- The coordinator of guidance services should provide leadership in coordinating the program as well as perform specific services.
- The counselor should work with boys and girls on an individual basis and act as a consultant to the teacher.
- The teacher contributes through classroom activities and by referring pupils for counseling.
- Counseling is considered the most important service of the guidance program.
- An adequate cumulative folder is an important adjunct to the program.
- Counseling services should be limited in a beginning program.
- Qualified personnel cooperating with other staff members are essential for the program's success.
- The guidance program and the curriculum should supplement one another.
- If counselors are to teach, the class work should be definitely related to guidance.
- Beginning should be with a few services available for all rather than all services for a few.
- Time for counseling should be flexible so as to meet the needs of the pupils and changes in the program.
- Group-guidance activities should not be an end in themselves but should supplement counseling (p. 276).

Keppers closed his article by stating that organization is not a panacea for effective programs, but without sound organization, the services of guidance will be ineffective.

An interesting question was asked in 1955. What should be the pupil load for the school counselor? Hoyt (1955) answered this question with the statement, "nobody knows" (p. 86). He went on to analyze the job of school counselors listing percent of counselor time as follows:

Function	Per Cent of Counselor's time
Counseling	50
Appraisal	10
Working with Teachers	10
Group Activities	5
Environmental Information	10
Administrative and Clerical Work	5
Working with Parents and Community	5
Local Research	5

(p. 86)

Based on his analysis he concluded that "a full-time counselor is needed for every 400 students in the school in order for the counselor to perform at a minimal level of effectiveness" (p. 88).

In the 1950s articles continued to appear about the role of counselors in high schools. Ellis (1950), writing on this topic, described the early years of the guidance movement as focusing on group guidance and every teacher being a guidance teacher. Homerooms were featured as a way to provide group guidance activities. "While counseling was talked about, the contribution of the trained counselor in the total school program was not fully recognized" (p. 206).

Ellis went on to describe what he thought the role of high school counselors should be. He described the role in terms of the guidance services concept that had emerged in the 1930s as follows:

"The school counselor is gradually emerging as a trained person who has an important role to play in the modern school. He provides individual counseling, supervises the individual inventory, and provides informational, placement and follow-up services. He works cooperatively with teachers, administrators and community agencies in the systematic collection and use of information concerning student needs in order that more intelligent decisions can be made in the process of curriculum planning" (p. 209).

Wrenn (1957), also writing on school counselors' status and role, found a wide variety of opinions in the literature on these topics. Based on his analysis of this literature he drew the following conclusions. All of his conclusions are reported here because they capture the essence of the status and role of schools counselors during that time.

- The school counselor is an educator with special professional training at the M.A. level and beyond.
- The school counselor is a generalist in a number of school functions and may be a specialist in at least one type of service. The nature of this specialization may vary with each counselor's unique personal qualifications and with the specific emphasis of his professional education.
- The school counselor's clients include teachers, parents and administrators as well as students.
- The school counselor's skills should include not only those necessary for the individual counseling relationship but those essential to working effectively with groups.
- The school counselor is concerned primarily with the normal growth needs of students, more with personality development than with problem crises.

The school counselor, because of the expectations of student, teacher, administrator and parent, must have a fairly high level of psychological sophistication in his professional education and in-service development. Current developments suggest that this calls not only for a sound knowledge of personality dynamics in individuals and in groups, appraisal techniques, knowledge of the psychological effect upon the individual of educational, vocational and other environmental demands but also for supervised experience in working with both individuals and groups (p. 178-179).

In an interesting article dealing with the need to develop a genuine profession of school counseling Pierson and Grant (1959) lamented the fact that school counselors lacked professional identity. They recommended that the term counselor be the focus rather than the term guidance worker. They said, "Personnel and guidance workers should build their profession around the concept 'counselor' rather than around the concept 'guidance worker'" (p. 207).

A growing debate in the 1940s and 1950s focused on the educational background needed to become a school counselor. It is not surprising that in the 1900s, 1920s, 1930s and even the 1940s and 1950s, common wisdom portrayed school counselors as educators rather than clinicians even though there was some emphasis on clinical work in the schools. When translated to state certification this meant that a teaching certificate, two years of teaching experience and one or more years of work experience outside of education was required. Lloyd-Jones (1947) supported these requirements stating that "an important part of the responsibility of the guidance worker is to work with teachers" (p. 88). On the other hand, Wertz (1958) wondered if many young people trained as guidance workers were barred from work in the schools because they did not possess a teaching certification or have teaching experience. He conducted a survey of state leaders on this topic. He found out that most state leaders supported teacher certification and teaching experience because they felt guidance workers could not perform adequately without teacher certification and teaching experience.

The Growing Importance of Counseling in the Guidance Services

In the 1930s the guidance services model emerged as a part of pupil personnel services. While various authors identified somewhat different lists of guidance services, counseling was always on the list. Some confusion apparently did exist with the terms guidance and counseling, however. Fenton (1943) pointed out that sometimes the words guidance and counseling were being used interchangeably. In his mind the word guidance was the broader term because it included other things besides counseling. Even though counseling was only one of the services of the guidance services model in the 1930s, by the 1940s and 1950s counseling was increasingly being "recognized as the heart of the guidance program" (Tennyson, 1958, p. 131) and "the service of the guidance program around which all others develop and function" (Smith, 1951, p. 75). This same idea was used by Jager (1950) and was further supported by Dugan (1941), who stated "the counseling service is very definitely the 'heart and core' of the personnel program ..." (p. 577). Dugan made this statement based on his analysis of his interview contacts with 374 high school pupils over a period of one school year.

As the counseling service assumed a more dominant position in the guidance services model, questions arose as to what form counseling should take. Remember that early forms of counseling owed their beginnings to the work of Parsons (1909) and the legacy of the mental hygiene and child-study movements. Based on Parson's work one form of counseling became known as trait and factor counseling, which, in turn, was labeled later as "directive or counselor-centered" (Aubrey, 1977, p. 291).

Then in 1942 and 1951, Rogers published two books that would change how counseling was viewed and practiced. And, in turn, guidance in the schools would be greatly influenced as well. Aubrey (1977) used the expression "steamroller impact" to describe the full effects these books would have on guidance in the schools.

"The influence of Carl Rogers on the counseling profession can hardly be underestimated. In particular, the literature pertaining to the practice of counseling and guidance would change dramatically. Before Rogers, this literature was practical in nature and dealt with such topics as testing, cumulative records, orientation procedures, vocations, placement functions and so on. In addition, this early literature would deal extensively with the goals and purpose of guidance. With Rogers, a sudden change occurred, and there was a new emphasis on the techniques and methods of counseling, research, refinement of counseling technique, selection and training of future counselors and the goals and objectives of counseling" (p. 292).

Rogers' client-centered approach to counseling came to be known as non-directive counseling in contrast to the existing trait-factor or directive counseling model. Combs (1947) pointed out that while "the dichotomy 'directive' versus 'non-directive' ... seem to imply two techniques which are poles apart ... it is necessary to remember all counseling has the same end in view no matter what it may be called. That end is the optimum adjustment of the individual" (p. 261). Combs went on to suggest that the choice of which technique to use isn't based on either/or but both/and. He offered two criteria to use in the choice of a technique for counseling.

"Directive techniques seem most useful where the client's primary need is for information, education or an opportunity for clarification of thinking through discussion. Non-directive techniques have most to offer where the primary need of the client is for social or emotional adjustment, clarification of feelings and attitudes or where a shift in personality integration or self concept is necessary" (p. 266).

Traxler (1950) supported the both/and approach by stating there was a trend toward a middle position between directive and nondirective guidance. Both are useful.

Physical Facilities for School Guidance

As the move from part-time teacher-counselor or administrator-counselor to full time counselors was occurring, questions were raised about the needed physical space for these full-time personnel. Harris (1940) described the use of a classroom across from the main office at Taft Union High School in Taft, Calif., to house school counselors. Fladseth (1946) noted that counselors are often considered as a part of administration so offices should be near that of the principal within easy access to the central office system. In stressing the importance of physical facilities, he pointed out that: "the character and philosophy of the school's administration and its guidance program are continually reflected by its physical facilities" (p. 171).

In a review of the literature on physical facilities for guidance, Bedard (1951) concluded that the need for adequate facilities is still great and that physical facilities have not kept pace with guidance program development. Shear (1950) echoed the same point with specific illustrations from a report of supervisors of the Bureau of Guidance of the New York State Education Department, Albany based on their visits to schools in 1948-1949 to inspect space allocations for guidance. In the report Shear stated that words such as "vaults, ends of corridors, storerooms and balconies as makeshift counseling offices" (p. 25). He went on to use these words: "inadequate lighting, no ventilation, inaccessibility, no equipment, interruption, too small" (p. 25).

What should space for guidance look like? Shear suggested the following guidelines.

Central Location. The suite should be located so as to be easily accessible to pupils, teaching staff, administrators, new pupils and other persons coming into the building (out-of-school youth, parents, employers). Its location should also foster use at times when the school may be otherwise closed. As stated by Dr. Don L. Essex, "Facilities used by the community should be so located and grouped that they are readily accessible from the main entrance."

Relative Location. The unit should be adjacent to the administrative offices. When not included in the suite, a classroom for group testing and instruction should be available near the personnel unit. Nearness to the school library is a possible advantage.

Space Provided. The amount and type of space available will depend on such factors as the size of school and whether it is a new or remodeled school building. Inclusions, in a rough order of desirability, should be: a health suite, one or more private offices for counseling and interviewing, a waiting room, an available classroom for group testing and group instruction in guidance topics, an office for individual psychological examination and for psychological counseling and therapy, storage and vault space. Each counselor on duty should have a private counseling office available. The equivalent of one full-time counselor for each 400 pupils is recommended. The waiting room might well be large enough to house the central records file and clerical offices. Some schools may wish to provide space for test scoring and a one-way vision room in connection with the psychologist's room.

Equipment. Each counselor's office should contain a desk and desk chair, two other chairs, at least one four-drawer vertical letter file, bookcase and a telephone. The waiting room should be furnished with comfortable chairs, table, display and bulletin boards; the records alcove of this room should have desk(s) and chairs, vertical files with four or five lock drawers, telephone and typewriter(s). The room for psychological examination and therapy should have a table, chairs and storage cupboard. If a classroom is provided for group testing and guidance instruction, it should be equipped with movable student desks and chairs, blackboards and plenty of bulletin board space, a large table, a bookcase and four-drawer vertical file. Rugs, draperies and suitable pictures would be desirable extras for the suite (p. 26).

While discussion was continuing about office space for counselors, concern was also being expressed about the location of the space for counselors in the school building. Most writers placed office space in and/or near administrative space. Parke (1957) surveyed principals, counselors and counselor-trainers and found the following:

"Generally, principals seem to hold to a philosophy of guidance that is more 'authoritative, directive' than the philosophy held by counselors and counselor-trainers, as determined by the questionnaire. That is, principals appear to think of the counselor as an administrative assistant or assistant principal. Thus, they prefer to have the counselor located within the main administrative office, where he can more conveniently assist in performing these administrative duties.

Counselors, on the other hand, prefer to separate themselves, insofar as possible, from administrative duties. Thus, counselors tended to choose the plans which had separate facilities for guidance, removed in distance from the administrative office. This, they felt, helped to create a more permissive atmosphere around the counseling function and helped to encourage self-referrals" (p. 254).

Roeber, Smith & Erickson (1955) stressed the need for counselors to have a voice in planning the physical space for guidance. They stated: "Developments in the past 10 years and the need for guidance services in the years ahead have made it imperative that the counselor have some voice in planning adequate guidance facilities, that he is articulate in making known his needs and that he is aware of and understands suitable standards for his facilities" (p. 252).

The Emergence of Elementary School Counseling

Although elementary school counseling as we know it today emerged in the 1960s, its historical roots go back into the 1920s. One of the major figures who provided a foundation and a perspective for elementary guidance was William Burham. According to Faust (1968) Burham (1926) "established him[self] as the father of what was to become modern elementary school counseling with the publication of his book 'Great Teachers and Mental Health'" (p. 11). Previous mental hygiene efforts of Beers (1908) and others who followed, focused more on clinical concerns, not on the educative process of children. Burnham, on the other hand, emphasized viewing all children "within a framework of the normal educative process" (p. 12). This, Faust stated, led to the creation of the developmental approach to school counseling that emerged in the 1960s.

The 1930s and 1940s witnessed an increasing number of articles and books focusing on school counseling at the elementary level. Much of the literature was conceptual in nature expressing the need for guidance at the elementary level with particular emphasis on the role of the teacher (Strang, 1938). Some articles, such as the one by Noonan (1931), pointed out that although there was growth in guidance in secondary schools, elementary schools were slow "in adopting a guidance organization of its own" (p. 205).

The purpose of elementary guidance also received attention in the 1930s. Driscoll (1938) made the point that guidance should focus on education not therapy.

"In summary, we may say that guidance in the elementary school is a process of education by which the growth and development of the individual child is given major emphasis. Educators and psychologists must cooperate closely if sound methods for stimulating emotional growth are to be found. In addition, a guidance program must provide remedial help for children who are handicapped in any one aspect of growth. Children who are too seriously disturbed to respond to a limited period of remedial help should be referred to a clinic or private psychiatrist. However, education and not therapy should be the major emphasis of the guidance program" (p. 33).

In the 1940s Berger (1947) noted that while guidance at the secondary level was seen by some as a distinct part of education, guidance at the elementary level was an essential part of good teaching. Berger went on to add that "an elementary school guidance program places the teacher in the central position as counselor" (p. 47). He did suggest that specialists would supplement the work of teachers but that teachers would be the major delivers of services.

"The specialist may act as the dispenser of therapy. The teacher retains responsibility for maintaining within the school the wholesome atmosphere that is not only prophylactic but ameliorative in nature" (p. 48).

By the 1950s more attention was being paid to guidance in elementary schools. Strang (1950) described three essentials for effective guidance to take place in elementary schools. These essentials were administrative leadership, qualified guidance-minded teachers and specialists who work with teachers and with individual students. She also pointed out that the goals of guidance in elementary schools are obtained through individual and group work.

Similar to Strang, Wilson (1950) stated that if a guidance program is planned and carried out by administrators, guidance specialists and classroom teachers, it would result in a "carefully conceived, practically administered and dynamically functioning program which will be characterized by a mental hygiene point of view, broad design and adequate coverage of the needs of every child" (p. 173). Martinson (1951) reported on a study of individuals responsible for elementary guidance in schools in California. She reported that these individuals had responsibilities for many duties other than guidance work. She stated, "One may well wonder at the opportunity left for the counselor to perform guidance functions in view of other assignments" (p. 169). Just as secondary guidance personnel had to deal with other assignments, so did guidance personnel in elementary schools.

One of the ongoing issues in elementary guidance was what should be done about vocational guidance. After all, in some people's minds vocational guidance should be provided in secondary education guidance programs only. Kobliner (1955) reviewed literature dealing with vocational guidance in elementary schools. He described the work of seven authors who had emphasized the need for vocational guidance at the elementary level. He concluded his article by stating they all felt vocational guidance in elementary schools laid "the foundation for future vocational choice and counseling and that it instills in children good social attitudes toward all kinds and levels of occupations" (p. 276).

Two of the authors he mentioned were McCracken and Lamb, who in 1923 published a book, "Occupational Information in the Elementary School." In their book they provided a rational for occupational information in elementary schools, pointing out that many students left education at grade five or six and therefore needed information about the work world. They went on to describe lessons, beginning in kindergarten through grade six, that teachers could teach presenting various aspects of the work world.

Major Trends and Issues

The 1940s and 1950s saw the expansion and extension of guidance in the schools. The professional literature during years 1941-1945 often focused on the contributions of guidance to the war effort. However, after 1945, attention once again returned to the need for guidance in the schools and on ways to improve the guidance services being provided.

Concern about guidance terminology, or as some author labeled it, the guidance terminology tangle, continued. What do we call guidance in the schools? Is it guidance? Vocational guidance? Personnel work? Educational guidance? What titles should we use for the personnel involved? Should we use counselor? Vocational counselor? Personnel worker?

These two questions continued to be debated during the 1940s and the 1950s with many opinions but no clear answers forthcoming.

The selection and training of counselors also continue to be widely discussed in the literature. Having a teaching certificate and some teaching experience was deemed necessary as was some work experience outside of education. Consensus was beginning to form around the necessary coursework (knowledge and skills) needed to become a counselor, although universal agreement was still far off. Work experience was part of most state certification requirements because, in the minds of some, counselors needed real-world experience to help them provide vocational guidance to students. Teaching certificates and teaching experience were required because, in the minds of most, counselors needed to understand education, its culture and the work of teachers. Interestingly a few authors did question the need for teaching as necessary background for counselors, particularly in the light of what they identified as a shortage of counselors.

The selection and training of school counselors and school guidance received substantial attention and support in the 1940s and 1950s with the passage of the Vocational Education Act of 1946 (P.L. 586), commonly known as the George-Barden Act, and the National Defense Education Act (NDEA) of 1958 (P.L. 85-864). The George-Barden Act provided funding for state supervisors, counselor-trainers, research and salaries for local guidance supervisors and counselors. NDEA provided monies for training counselors in summer and yearlong institutes. It also provided funding to establish statewide testing programs in schools. Building on the test and measurement movement, federal funds were now available to states to establish testing programs in public secondary schools. In the language of Title V of the NDEA, guidance, counseling and testing were firmly connected and were part of a national effort to meet the security needs of the United States through the full development of the mental resources and technical skills of its young men and women.

The formation of the American School Counselor Association in 1952 was a milestone event for school counselors. Now school counselors had their own professional association with their own journals. They had a voice in national affairs.

Continued discussion occurred in the 1940s and 1950s concerning the role of school counselors and the organizational framework in which they worked. While the guidance services model received some attention, most discussion focused on counselors' roles and the tasks they performed in schools. As reported, a number of studies investigated the tasks school counselors performed while other articles focused on what was called "other duties as assigned." Although an organizational framework called the guidance services model had emerged in the 1930s, the most common framework still being used to organize the work of school counselors in the 1940s and 1950s was a position (the school counselor full or part-time) with a list of duties, all of which unfortunately, were still not actually guidance tasks.

The emergence of counseling (the counseling services) as predominant in the work of counselors was another major development in the 1940s and 1950s. This trend had begun to emerge in the 1930s, but it became even more apparent in the 1940s and 1950s. Two broad categories of counseling emerged, namely, directive and nondirective. The debate between the two camps that evolved from these two categories continued into the 1960s.

Physical facilities for counselors received attention too in the 1940s and 1950s. As more and more counselors were being employed concern was expressed about the nature and location of their office space. Some writers recommended placement in or near administrative offices while others, particularly school counselors, felt their office space should be located away from administrative space. This debate had a lot to do with the perceived roles of counselors. Are counselors a part of administration or part of the instructional staff? Where counselors were located in buildings during this time had a lot to do with how counselors were perceived.

A final trend in the 1940s and 1950s was the increasing attention being given to elementary guidance. It was clear in the minds of most authors that elementary schools needed a different model for guidance than that used by secondary schools. The term developmental was being used increasingly to describe the overall perspective needed for guidance in the elementary school. As we will see, the elementary school guidance movement blossomed in the 1960s.

References

Arbuckle, D. (1951). Guidance is shacked. *Occupations, 29,* 595-598.

Arnold, D. L. (1949). Time spent by counselors and deans on various activities. *Occupations, 27,* 391-393.

Aubrey, R. F. (1977). Historical development of guidance and counseling and implications for the future. *The Personnel and Guidance Journal, 55,* 288-295.

Barry, R., & Wolf, B. (1957). *Modern issues in guidance-personnel work.* New York: Bureau of Publications, Teachers College, Columbia University.

Bedard, J. A. (1951). Physical provisions for guidance services. *Occupations, 29,* 354-357.

Beers, C. (1908). *A mind that found itself.* Garden City, NJ: Doubleday.

Berger, D. (1947). Guidance in the elementary school. *Teachers College Record, 49,* 44-50.

Burham, W. (1926). *Great teachers and mental health.* New York: D. Appleton and Company.

California Guidance Newsletter (1951). Counselors revealed as clerical workers. *Occupations, 29,* 294.

Combs, A. W. (1947). Non-directive techniques and vocational counseling. *Occupations, 25,* 261-267.

Copehart, B. E. (1951). Try training them. *Occupations, 30,* 198-201.

Davis, F. G. (1950). Pupil personnel services in the public schools. *Education, 70,* 512-514.

Driscoll, G. P. (1938). Guidance at the elementary level. *Teachers College Record, 40,* 25-33.

Dugan, W. E. (1941). Counseling quantitatively analyzed. *Occupations, 19,* 573-577.

Ellis, G. G. (1950). The emerging role of the high school counselor. *High School Journal, 33,* 206-209.

Faust, V. (1968). History of Elementary School Counseling. Boston, MA: Houghton Mifflin Company.

Feldman, E. E. (1951). Jobs in guidance ... City director. *Occupations, 29,* 264-266.

Fenton, N. (1943). *Mental hygiene in school practice.* Stanford, CA: Stanford University Press.

Fladseth, F. R. (1946). Streamlining the counselor's office. *Occupations, 25,* 169-171.

Froehlich, C. P. (1948). Counselors and guidance officers in public schools. *Occupations, 26,* 522-527.

Froehlich, C. P. (1949). Content of the manual on counselor preparation. *Occupations, 27,* 541-545.

Greenleaf, W. J. (1943). Guidance in public high schools—1942. *Occupations, 21,* 599-604.

Hale, P. P. (1952). Defining vocational counseling & vocational guidance. *The Personnel and Guidance Journal, 31,* 171-172.

Harris, G. E. (1940). A special room for counseling. *Occupations, 19,* 106-110.

Hitchcock, W. L. (1953). Counselors feel they should. *Personnel and Guidance Journal, 32,* 72-74.

Hoyt, K. B. (1955). What should be the pupil load for the school counselor? *Personnel and Guidance Journal, 34,* 86-88.

Jager, H. A. (1945). Training in guidance work for teacher and counselor: A conference report. *Occupations, 24,* 151-155.

Jager, H. A. (1950). The guidance movement is larger than you think. *Occupations, 29,* 98-102.

Jager, H. A., (1947). The George-Barden Act as an influence in the further development of guidance work. *Occupations, 25,* 483-489.

Keppers, G. L. (1955). Guidance services in order of importance. *The Clearing House, 29,* 274-276.

Kobliner, H. (1955). Literature dealing with vocational guidance in the elementary school. *Personnel and Guidance Journal, 33,* 274-276.

Kremen, B. G. (1951). Counselor certification in the United States. *Occupations, 29,* 584-586.

Landy, E. (1953). Counselor training through practice. *The Personnel and Guidance Journal, 31,* 310-314.

Lloyd-Jones, E. (1947). Some current issues in guidance. *Teachers College Record, 49,* 77-88.

Martinson, R. A. (1951). Duties of elementary school counselors. *Occupations, 30,* 167-170.

McCracken, T. C., & Lamb, H. E. (1923). *Occupational information in the elementary school.* Boston, MA: Houghton Mifflin.

Myers, G. E. (1941). *Principles and techniques of vocational guidance.* New York: McGraw-Hill Book Company.

National Defense Education Act of 1958, Pub. L. No. 85-864, 72, Part 1, Stat 1580 (1958).

National Vocational Guidance Association (1941, April). The preparation and certification of the school counselor. *Occupations, 19,* 533-538.

National Vocational Guidance Association (1941, May). The preparation and certification of the school counselor: The certification of counselors. *Occupations, 19,* 589-594.

Noonan, D. J. (1931). The place of guidance in the elementary schools. *Education, 52,* 205-210.

Odell, L. (1971). *American School Counselor Association: The historical growth and development of a professional organization.* Unpublished doctoral dissertation. George Washington University.

Parker, K. H. (1957). Location of guidance facilities within the school plant. *Personnel and Guidance Journal, 36,* 251-254.

Parsons, F. (1909). *Choosing a vocation.* Boston, MA: Houghton Mifflin.

Pierson, G. A. (1954). AESOP and the school counselor. *Personnel and Guidance Journal, 32,* 326-329.

Pierson, G. A. (1965). *An evaluation—Counselor education in regular session institutes.* Washington DC: U. S. Department of Health, Education, and Welfare, Office of Education.

Pierson, G. A., & Grant, C. W. (1959). The road ahead for school counselors. *The Personnel and Guidance Journal, 38,* 207-210.

Polmantier, P. C. (1950). Titles of school guidance workers. *Occupations, 28,* 349-352.

Roeber, E. C. (1944). High school students need vocational information. *Occupations, 23,* 97-101.

Roeber, E. C. (1955). What is your batting average? *The School Counselor, 3,* 6-9.

Roeber, E. C., Smith, G. E., & Erickson, C. E. (1955). *Organization and administration of guidance services* (2nd ed.). New York: McGraw-Hill Book Company.

Rogers, C. R. (1942). *Counseling and psychotherapy.* Boston, MA: Houghton Mifflin.

Rogers, C. R. (1951). *Client-centered therapy.* Boston, MA: Houghton Mifflin.

Sachs, G. M. (1945). *Evaluation of group guidance work in secondary schools.* Los Angeles, CA: The University of Southern California Press.

Shear, B. (1950). Physical facilities for pupil personnel services. *American School Board Journal, 120,* 25-27.

Smith, G. E. (1951). *Principles and practices of the guidance program: A basic text.* New York: The MacMillan Company.

Strang, R. M. (1938). The teacher's contribution to guidance of children. *Teachers College Record, 40,* 14-16.

Strang, R. M. (1950). Guidance in the elementary school. *Education, 70,* 492-494.

Tennyson, W. W. (1958). Time: The counselor's dilemma! *The Personnel and Guidance Journal, 37,* 129-135.

Traxler, A. E. (1950). Emerging trends in guidance. *School Review 58,* 14-23.

Tyler, L. E. (1960). *The national defense counseling and guidance training institutes program: A report of the first 50 institutes.* Washington DC: U.S. Department of Health, Education, and Welfare, Office of Education.

Vocational Education Act of 1946, Pub. L. No. 79-586, 60, Part 1, Stat. 775-778 (1946).

Weitz, H. (1958). The role of the guidance worker in the schools. *Personnel and Guidance Journal, 37,* 266-272.

Wilson, F. M. (1950). Guidance in elementary schools. *Occupations, 29,* 168-173.

Wrenn, C. G. (1940). The evaluation of student personnel work: A critique of the "guidance movement". *School and Society, 52,* 409-414.

Wrenn, C. G. (1951). Training of vocational guidance workers. *Occupations, 29,* 414-419.

Wrenn, C. G. (1957). Status and role of the school counselor. *The Personnel and Guidance Journal, 36,* 175-183.

Wright, B. H. (1946). Minneapolis school counselors analyze their jobs. *Occupations, 24,* 214-219.

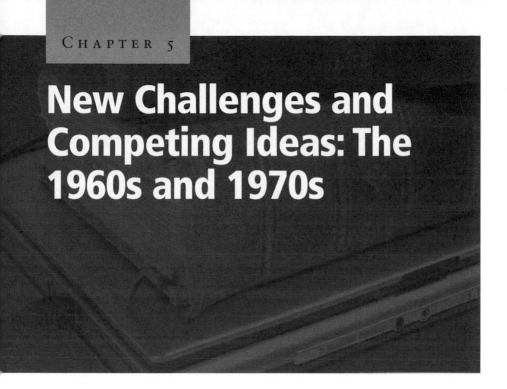

CHAPTER 5

New Challenges and Competing Ideas: The 1960s and 1970s

The 1960s and 1970s saw the continuation of the civil rights movement, concerns about gender equity and an increasing focus on multiculturalism and diversity. The rate of change in values, beliefs and ways of living seemed to accelerate. The Vietnam war, although war was never declared, was a flash point for social protest and social unrest.

What happened to guidance and counseling in the schools during these two decades of rapid social change? Interestingly, the 1960s and 1970s witnessed the rapid growth of guidance and counseling in the schools. This growth was stimulated in part by Title V, Guidance, Counseling and Testing of the National Defense Education Act (NDEA) of 1958. It was also stimulated by the passage of the Vocational Education Act of 1963 (P.L. 88-210), the Vocational Education Amendments of 1968 (P.L. 90-576), and the Education Amendments of 1976 (P.L. 94-482).

The rapid growth of guidance and counseling in the schools during these two decades saw the writing of many articles and books on a wide array of topics including the role of school counselors, elementary guidance and counseling, guidance terminology, the selection and training of school counselors, and leadership and supervision. Competing philosophical orientations, organizational frameworks and strategies for guidance and counseling in the schools also filled the pages of these articles and books.

Interestingly, most of these topics were carried over from the 1940s and 1950s to be discussed and debated again.

The chapter begins by presenting discussion about the competing philosophical orientations and organizational frameworks for guidance and counseling. The dominant pupil personnel services model of the time with its subset of guidance services is highlighted, but other ideas that were evolving about philosophical orientations and organizational frameworks are highlighted as well. Then the chapter describes the continuing debate about the appropriate roles for school counselors followed by a review of the continuing emergence of guidance and counseling in elementary schools. Next, the selection and training of school counselors as affected by NDEA is discussed. Following this is discussion of the calls for change in the way guidance is practiced in the schools. Then the chapter focuses on the emergence of the concept of comprehensive guidance programs as a way to organize guidance in the schools. The chapter closes with a description of the renewed interest in guidance through the curriculum, stimulated in part by the passage of the Vocational Education Act of 1963 and the amendments of 1968 and 1976, discussion of concerns about leadership and supervision and a summary of the major issues that surfaced during the 1960s and 1970s.

The Continued Search for Identity: Educator or Psychologist?

Up until the 1950s many school counselors were teachers or administrators serving as school counselors part-time. Thus it was not surprising that the general wisdom was that anybody serving as a school counselor should have an educational background; they should be teachers first. As more and more school counselors became full-time in the 1950s, but particularly in the 1960s and 1970s, the question of whether teaching experience was necessary, was being asked more frequently. This question raised the question, if school counselors aren't teachers first, who are they?

The 1960s and 1970s saw intense debate in the literature concerning the school counselor identity issue. As we will see some writers identified school counselors as educators so they felt teaching experience was necessary to become a school counselor. Other writers identified school counselors more with psychology and psychologists so they questioned the necessity of teaching experience as a prerequisite to becoming a school counselor in the schools.

Stefflre (1964) was concerned about the name of our occupation because he felt that the name was our identification. What name did he suggest? He wanted to end up using the term psychologist. "From guidance worker, to guidance counselor, to school counselor, to psychological counselor, to psychologist is one possible path toward 'professionalization'" (p. 655). Odell (1973) also raised questions about labels for school counselors. She stated that some groups would like to use labels such as "advisor," "human relations specialist," "psychologist" or "applied behavioral scientist" to replace the label school counselor. She felt these groups thought these titles more clearly described the work of school counselors.

An interesting exchange occurred between Brammer (1968) and Felix (1968) on this same topic. Brammer stated the field should drop the guidance model and adopt a counseling psychologist model for school counseling. "Where will school counselors play ball? I have suggested the counseling psychology ball park, not as an ideal solution, but as the possibility most compatible with evolving school counseling functions" (p. 8).

Felix (1968) disagreed sharply with Brammer in a rejoiner to Brammer's article. Felix strongly defended the guidance model for school counseling. He ended his rejoiner with the following statement using the same ball park analogy that Brammer used. "We have let some psychologists come into our park, even though the place is not really suited to the game at which they excel. They have put down the floor they brought with them. Now they want us to change the way we train and practice and even change the name of our team. Next thing you know, they will want to rename the park" (p. 11).

Aubrey (1969) sided with Felix (1968) by stating that "many psychotherapeutic models are at odds or even totally incongruent with educational objectives" (p. 273). He went on to state his position as follows: "What the schools need are theoretical models congruent with educational purposes and/or realistic designs which will enable guidance personnel to modify or change existing educational structures and practices. Those psychotherapeutic methods and techniques which fail to take into account the counselor's training and background, the conditions under which he works, the involuntary nature of many counselees in a school setting, the limitations of time and scheduling, the institutional expectations and the structure of the school setting should be approached with extreme caution" (p. 277).

Another interesting exchange on this topic occurred between Hoyt (1961) and Stewart (1961). Hoyt felt teaching experience was absolutely necessary. He stated his position as follows: "Those who today are arguing that the school counselor needs neither a teaching certificate nor teaching experience are as wrong as were those who were arguing 10 years ago that they could specify exactly how many years' teaching experience are needed before one could be expected to counsel students" (p. 129).

Stewart, in his response to Hoyt's position, took the opposite position. He felt only a few individuals would argue that teaching experience was necessary. "That actual teaching experience is the only way to demonstrate a commitment to education would have to be seriously questioned" (p. 134).

Pupil Personnel Services Become Dominant

Concurrent with the influence of NDEA and Vocational Education legislation on the development of guidance and counseling in the schools was the influence of the pupil personnel services movement in the 1960s. What began in the 1930s, and was nurtured in the 1940s and 1950s, finally matured in the 1960s. According to the Council of Chief State School Officers (1960), pupil personnel services included "guidance, health, psychological services, school social work and attendance" (p. 3).

Of particular importance to the development of the pupil personnel services concept was the creation in 1962 of the Interprofessional Research Commission on Pupil Personnel Services (IRCOPPS). IRCOPPS was created by the U.S. Office of Education and financed by the National Institute of Mental Health. It was composed of 18 professional member associations. The commission's aims were threefold:

- To provide through research a body of knowledge that will increase the effectiveness of all professions and services collaborating to provide the total learning experience
- To demonstrate efficient programs of pupil personnel services for various sizes and types of communities
- To carry on and stimulate research on preventive mental hygiene related to the schools (Eckerson & Smith, 1966, p. 4)

In the IRCOPPS conception of pupil personnel services, guidance and counseling were viewed "as a lifetime service, from preschool to retirement, with the goal of increasing each individual's capacity for self-direction" (Eckerson & Smith, 1966, p. 24).

Pupil personnel services in the elementary school was a topic of discussion in the 1960s. Of particular concern was the overlapping duties of elementary school counselors, school psychologists and school social workers (Lorimer & Haddad, 1969). Eckerson (1967) stressed the importance of elementary school guidance establishing its unique role. She stated:

"The great potential of elementary school guidance and its uniqueness may be realized if, and only if, it will take its mandate from the needs of normal children as revealed by analyses of research and collaborative thinking of pupil personnel specialists. Herein elementary school guidance has the opportunity to carve out its own identity. It cannot flourish within the shadow of secondary school guidance. On the contrary, as it develops from the needs of young children, it may force change and spur counselors in junior high school and at higher levels to face the needs of students realistically and help them make a better world than ours" (p. 354).

As you will remember some writers in the 1940s and 1950s wanted to do away with the term guidance and replace it with the term pupil personnel services. The same was true in the 1960s and 1970s. McCully (1962) urged the field to abandon the term guidance in favor of the term pupil personnel services. Tyler (1960) felt it was "desirable to replace the ambiguous work 'guidance' with the clearer term 'pupil personnel work'" (p. 77). Hoyt (1962), on the other hand, felt the word guidance should be retained to keep our connection to education.

In 1970 an article appeared that suggested a new worker be employed in elementary schools. Seidman, Peterson, Byrne, Dayton and Bock (1970) conducted a study to compare school counselors and social workers trained in traditional ways with a new worker called a child development consultant (CDC). Although this person's role wasn't clearly defined and the study's results didn't reveal any significant differences in the outcomes of the work of these two groups, it is interesting that there was even a suggestion that a new professional should take the place of school counselors and social workers.

As the 1960s and 1970s continued to unfold, the impact of the pupil personnel services movement on guidance and counseling became increasingly apparent. Many state departments of education and local school districts placed guidance and counseling and the positions of school counselors administratively under the pupil personnel services umbrella (Warner, 1969). In addition, textbooks written in the 1960s on the organization and administration of guidance and counseling adopted the pupil personnel services model as the way to organize guidance in the schools.

The Question of Counselor Role and Functions

During the 1960s and 1970s, the services model for guidance, with its position orientation within pupil personnel services, focused heavily on school counselors' role and functions. In fact, to many individuals, what school counselors did became the program. Literally hundreds of articles were written about the role and functions of school counselors. The need for such statements was heightened considerably by competition from other pupil personnel workers as they too sought to establish themselves and their role in the schools, particularly when Wrenn (1962) recommended in his book "The Counselor in a Changing World" that, "the confusing term guidance services be abandoned and that pupil personnel services be seen as the activities of the school counselor, the school psychologist, the school social worker, the school health officer and the school attendance officer. Pupil personnel services thus became broader than any so-called guidance services, and yet a central function of such services is the work of the school counselor."

In his book Wrenn also emphasized the work of the school counselor. He recommended: "The professional job description of a school counselor specify that he perform four major functions: (a) counsel with students; (b) consult with teachers, administrators and parents as they in turn deal with students; (c) study the changing facts about the student population and interpret what is found to school committees and administrators; (d) coordinate counseling resources in school and between school and community. From two-thirds to three-fourths of the counselor's time, in either elementary or high school, should be committed to the first two of these functions. Activities that do not fall into one of these four areas neither should be expected nor encouraged as part of the counselor's regular working schedule (p. 137).

Wrenn was concerned particularly about what had come to be known as "other duties assigned." What were they? He identified duties such as "class sponsorship, study hall supervision, routine discipline and the mechanics of psychological testing," (p. 119) which he stated kept school counselors from doing what they should be doing.

Of the other duties list, he was particularly concerned about discipline, particularly what he called routine discipline mechanics. He stated, "In some of these areas, discipline for example, professionals in both teaching and counseling must be involved, but it is a mistake to use either for routine discipline mechanics. It is also a mistake to have an administrative policy which requires counselors to be responsible for study hall and detention hall supervision or which requires $6,000-a-year counselors to do $3,000-a-year clerical jobs" (p. 119).

In a similar fashion, Roeber (1963) outlined proposed school counselors' functions. He suggested that school counselors engage in helping relationships, including individual counseling, group procedures and consulting. In addition, the counselor should have supporting responsibilities, including pupil-environment studies, program development and personal development. This emphasis on the school counselor during the 1960s came at a time when some individuals were calling for "the abandonment of the term guidance as it is associated with services provided by a counselor" (Roeber, 1963, p. 22).

In an article titled "A new strategy for assessing counselor role," Stevic (1966) expressed concern about the lack of understanding of the functions of the school counselor. He stressed that school counselors must assume an active role in role definition.

"Unless and until the function of the school counselor is established, understood and accepted by the counselor and his public, the growth of guidance and the movement toward professionalization will be halting at best. Any change must begin with the active involvement of the counselor in redefinition or perhaps definition of his role" (p. 96).

Arbuckle (1968) noted that the question of what school counselors do has been of concern for a long time and that disagreement concerning what they do is a major barrier to school counselor effectiveness. He stated that the disagreement in the field is between those who "see the counselor as having special functions and responsibilities, quite distinct from those of teacher and administrator, and those who see the counselor as being basically a teacher or administrator, with similar functions and responsibilities" (p. 341). Later, Arbuckle (1972) weighed in on this issue again and came to the following conclusion:

"It would be eminently reasonable for counselors to accept as their professional responsibility the functions of the psychological counselor, who works primarily with individuals or small groups of individuals. His task is therapeutic and preventive, helping individuals to attain a higher level of individual freedom, dignity and pride in self. Thus these individuals become contributing rather than destructive members of their society" (pp. 789-790).

Who is responsible for determining the role of school counselors? A number of authors in the 1960s and 1970s expressed their opinions. Shertzer and Stone (1963) for example stated that occupational identity formulation is the responsibility of school counselors. Later Stone and Shertzer (1963) pointed out, "The counselor who waits upon an externally supplied solution to the questions 'Who am I?' and 'What do I do?' does a disservice to himself and to the professions" (p. 346).

Of particular concern was the issue of role conflict between school counselors and administrators. Hart and Prince (1970) stated that the conflict was real.

"The conflict is real: school counselors are taught many role philosophies and behaviors which are in conflict with the expectations of the principals. Disagreement exists on basic issues such as confidentiality, clerical responsibilities, nonrelated counseling functions and total adjustment counseling" (p. 379).

Wrenn (1979) and Carroll (1968) were concerned particularly about the need for school counselors to define their role based on their expertise and school needs and then communicate this to administrators. Bradley (1978) recommended that counselors needed to fill the role of change agent in their schools. Other writers such as Kahnweiler (1979) recommended the consultant role for counselors. He summed up his article with the following statement:

"In summary, significant needs for the future concern the transmission of specific consultation techniques, new training approaches, results of research and program-development models. If these shortcomings can be overcome, the difference between theory and practice can be minimized. Perhaps our profession will then witness a real commitment to the counselor-as-consultant concept where it counts – in the field" (p. 378).

Knapp and Denny (1961) justified the consultant role for school counselors because they stated school counselors were staff, not line personnel, and as a result, should work in a consultant and service capacity. Pine

(1974) similarly urged the field to give their skills away, becoming consultant-trainers and psychological educators; to become change agents concerned with organizational development. Skovholt (1977) suggested that the way out of clerical and quasi-administrative tasks was for school counselors to embrace psychological education. He stated, "Let us hope counselors increasingly devote themselves to entering the curriculum and creating powerful preventive-educational programs" (p. 475).

Some writers, including Zerface and Cox (1971), were concerned about the current role of school counselors given what they called the suppressive environment of the school. They were concerned because they said school counselors did not counsel (they called them "noncounseling counselors"). They pointed out that organizational constraints causing school counselors to carry out clerical chores, attendance duties, scheduling and discipline but not counseling were a major problem. As a result of these environmental issues, they went so far as to recommend relocating school counselors to a community setting. In effect, it would become a community-based program with school counselors housed in the community but working the schools.

During the 1960s the centrality of the counseling service also continued to be featured. Stripling and Lane (1966) stressed the centrality of counseling – both individual and group. A second priority area was consultation with parents and teachers. Other traditional guidance functions such as appraisal, placement and evaluation were seen as supplementary and supportive to counseling, group procedures and consultation. Ferguson (1963) emphasized the same theme that counseling was the core service: "No longer is it viewed merely as a technique and limited to vocational and educational matters; counseling is regarded as the central service in the guidance program" (p. 40).

This emphasis on counseling during the 1960s has deep historical roots. It began to emerge in the 1920s under the services model and the intense interest in personal adjustment that followed. It was reinforced further, according to Hoyt (1974), by the NDEA Title V-B training institutes whose enrollees by law were either counselors or teachers and by the standards used by the U.S. Office of Education to judge whether or not a proposed training institute was acceptable for funding. These factors, Hoyt suggested, led the training institutes to place "a heavy emphasis on the counseling function ... The emphasis was on counseling and counselors, not on guidance and guidance programs" (p. 504).

Finally, how did others view the role of school counselors? During the 1960s and 1970s a number of articles were written assessing the role of school counselors as perceived by students, teachers, administrators and parents (Bergstein & Grant, 1961; Gibson, 1965; Hart & Prince, 1970; Wells & Ritter 1979). All of the studies indicated that differences of opinion were present concerning school counselor role among these groups. Why? All of the studies pointed to lack of school counselor role definition generally and to the fact that "... many counselors feel confused about what their role really is" (Wells & Ritter, 1979, p. 170).

In an attempt to clarify the role of school counselors, the president of the American School Counselor Association appointed a National Planning Committee for the Counselor Role and Function Study in 1962 (Fitzgerald, 1965). Many groups were involved in this study, which culminated in the approval of the report of this committee in 1964. Two documents were approved. They were "Statement of Policy for Secondary School Counselors" and "Guidelines for Implementation of the ASCA Statement of Policy for Secondary School Counselors." "This policy statement sets forth the essential elements needed to identify and clarify the role of the secondary school counselor ..." (p. 41).

Elementary Guidance and Counseling

The 1960s also witnessed the birth of elementary school guidance and counseling, after a gestation period of more than 50 years. Professional literature indicated that teachers were appointed as elementary counselors as early as 1910 in the Boston schools. Apparently, however, the secondary school emphasis was so strong during the early years that little attention was paid to the work of counselors in elementary schools. What attention there was proved to be heavily occupational in nature. Witness, for example, the publication of a book by McCracken and Lamb in 1923 titled "Occupational Information in the Elementary School."

Faust (1968), in his history of elementary school counseling, divided the emergence of elementary school counselors into three time periods. The first period, which he titled *traditional*, stretched from the beginnings of the guidance and counseling movement in 1908 through the 1940s. During this period, elementary guidance and counseling borrowed methods and techniques extensively from secondary school guidance and counseling practice. For the next 15 years, from 1950 to 1965, elementary guidance and counseling began to change. Faust called this the *neotradi-*

tionalist period. It was characterized by a de-emphasis on traditional secondary methods coupled with more emphasis on group counseling and learning climates. In the middle 1960s, according to Faust, the *developmentalist* period emerged.

The developmental emphasis was reinforced by a preliminary report of the Joint Association for Counselor Education and Supervision and the American School Counselor Association (ACES-ASCA) Committee on the Elementary School Counselor that appeared in the February 1966 issue of the Personnel and Guidance Journal. Its central focus was "on the child and teacher in the educative process" (Faust, 1968, p. 74). Effective learning climates were to be central to the work of school counselors.

The neotraditionalist period began the process of conceptually separating elementary school from secondary school counseling and the developmentalist period carried that separation even further. A unique identity was beginning to form for elementary school counselors conceptually and in practice. Many articles and books were written about this emerging identity offering a variety of opinions concerning its major features.

Dinkmeyer (1966) wrote about the need for what he called developmental counseling in elementary schools. He stressed that developmental counseling was not adjustment or crisis counseling. Rather, it focused on "helping the individual know, understand and accept himself ... The child learns not only to understand himself but to become ultimately responsible for his choices and actions" (p. 264).

As progress was being made in establishing elementary guidance in schools, some writers expressed caution. They felt there were some unresolved issues and possible barriers that needed attention. Aubrey (1967) was one of those authors. He felt that as elementary guidance continued to evolve, the training of elementary school counselors needed attention. He stated that "all too often the training, preparation and models of elementary counselors are those originally devised for secondary school pupils and seen grossly inadequate for elementary age children" (p. 355). He also was concerned about the paucity of elementary guidance theory and research as well as what he felt were possible barriers to implementing elementary guidance including the possible negative views of teachers and the control of administrators over the work of elementary school counselors.

What was the status of elementary guidance during this time period? Three studies were completed between the time period 1967 and 1970-71. The first study by Van Hoose and Vafakas (1968) reported that 3,837 school counselors were providing services in the elementary schools with 73 percent being employed full-time. By the school year 1968-1969, Van Hoose and Kurtz (1970) found that the number of elementary school counselors had increased to 6,041 with 70 percent being full-time. This increased to 7982 with 78 percent being full-time elementary school counselors (Van Hoose & Carlson, 1972).

As more and more elementary school counselors were being employed discussion in the literature continued to appear concerning the nature of their work. Most writers agreed that elementary school counselors' work should be developmental in nature and should "reflect a collaborative relationship with teachers, parents and other pupil personnel specialists" (Dinkmeyer, 1968, p. 41). The guidance services typically identified were pupil appraisal, consulting, counseling, classroom guidance, group guidance and information services and administration. Other authors talked about the three C's – counseling, consulting and coordination – as being the preferred work of elementary school counselors. Consultation in particular was identified as a most important service (Aubrey, 1978; Eckerson & Smith, 1968).

Some authors chose to use the term school guidance worker to label the person providing guidance in the elementary school rather than the term school counselor. Patouillet (1968) used the term to label counselors, psychologists and visiting teachers in keeping with the organizational concept of pupil personnel services and because of what he perceived as similar roles.

"I have grouped counselors, psychologists and visiting teachers together under the general heading of guidance worker because I see an increasing number of similarities and a decreasing number of differences among their respective roles" (p. 60).

One of the issues being discussed during the 1960s and 1970s was the nature and structure of preparation programs for elementary school guidance workers. The title guidance worker was used often at this time by a number of writers rather than school counselors because of the strong influence of the pupil personnel services organizational model. Instead of singling out school counselors, school psychologists and school social workers by title, these writers put them all together under the title guidance workers, particularly at the elementary school level.

A study by Hill and Nitzschke (1961) found there wasn't much difference between the preparation of elementary and secondary guidance workers (to use their term). Nitzschke (1965) in his study found there still was not much difference between elementary and secondary preparation programs although more emphasis was being placed on child development and child study at the elementary level.

Eckerson (1967) wrote about the need for elementary guidance to have its own identity. She stated that elementary guidance "cannot flourish within the shadow of secondary school guidance" (p. 354). She went on to point out that as elementary guidance flourishes, it may change the way school counselors in junior and senior high school carry out their work.

Aubrey (1967) was concerned about the inadequate preparation of elementary school counselors. He was also concerned about the lack of appropriate theory and research at the elementary level. Berry (1979) echoed this concern by stating, "There is no developmental theory to explain adequately the connection between human development and elementary counseling theory" (p. 513).

Several writers also expressed concern about the role of administrators in the elementary guidance program. Dinkmeyer (1973) expressed his concern about the "tyrannical and ineffectual qualities of some administrators" (p. 174). Aubrey (1967) also was concerned about the role of administrators. "As long as the notion prevails that the school principal is the duly constituted authority in determining guidance policy and practice, counselors will be forced to take a back seat to teacher and curricular considerations" (p. 358)

In a survey of California elementary school counselors, teachers and principals McCreary and Miller (1966) found a unique role for school counselors wasn't apparent, and elementary school counselor roles overlapped with other pupil personnel workers such as school psychologists and school social workers. Because of the lack of clear statements about the role of elementary school counselors, Cottingham (1966) called for the creation of a national commission to study and clarify the role of elementary school counselors in relationship to other personnel workers and then issue a position statement on this topic.

The Selection and Training of School Counselors

The decade of the 1960s opened with the full implementation of Title V – Guidance, Counseling and Testing: Identification and Encouragement of Able Students of the National Defense Education Act of 1958 (See Appendix A). Of particular interest is Part B of Title V titled Counseling and Guidance Training Institutes, funds for sponsored summer and year-long institutes to train school counselors. Between the years 1959 and 1965, 65 full-year institutes were conducted, attended by 1955 individuals (Pierson, 1965). During this same period of time 401 summer institutes were conducted in 127 colleges and universities throughout the country training a total of 13,220 students (Townsend, 1965).

During the first six years of summer and full-year institutes only secondary school counselors were trained. This changed in 1964. The amended Title V(b) of NDEA, which became effective Oct. 16, 1964, provided for the U.S. Commissioner of Education to arrange, through grants or contracts, with institutions of higher education for the operation by them of short-term or regular session institutes for advanced study, including study in the use of new materials, to improve the qualifications of individuals who are engaged, or are teachers preparing to engage, in counseling and guidance of students in elementary or in secondary schools or in institutions of higher education, including junior colleges and technical institutes. Thus, for the first time in the history of the program there were, during summer 1965, some short-term counseling and guidance institutes for elementary school personnel and also for higher education (including junior college and technical institute) personnel (Townsend, 1965, p. 2).

Over the years NDEA was in force Jennings (1982) reported that the number of school counselors more than tripled from 13,000 in 1958 to 43,500 in 1967. He went on to report that the ratio of students to counselors dropped from 960 to 450 in high schools and from 17,500 to 6,500 in elementary schools. He was of the opinion that these changes in numbers were a direct consequence of this legislation.

Unfortunately, in the late 1960s, Title V of the NDEA of 1958 became involved in the politics of the times. It was a time of program consolidation. According to Jennings (1982), "In the Education Amendments of 1970, the NDEA program was consolidated with the federal program to encourage innovation in education: Title III of the Elementary and Secondary Education Act of 1965 (P.L. 89-10). This consolidation led to a

50 percent decline in federal support for guidance and counseling – from nearly $32 million in 1967 to $16 million in 1973. In 1974, federal support for counseling received another jolt by being moved from this 1970 consolidation to yet another, more restrictive consolidation. This new consolidation provided grants to local school districts for three purposes: purchase of library books and materials, acquisition of instructional equipment and provision of counselors' salaries. A school district could use whatever proportion it chose from its consolidated grant for each of those three purposes" (p. 122).

The purpose of this section of Chapter 5 is not to report fully on the overall impact of NDEA but rather to focus briefly on the act's impact on how school guidance and counseling and the work of school counselors were further conceptualized and institutionalized as a result of its implementation. Of particular importance was the nature of the training school counselors received and the major professional issues addressed during the courses provided for institute participants.

Peirson (1965) described five topics that seemed to be central to the training of school counselors in NDEA institutes:

- Determinism and a free society
- Mental health and individual responsibility
- Basic science and supervised practice
- Teaching and counseling
- The role of the school counselor

Of these, topics four and five related most directly to how school counselors functioned in schools. The teaching and counseling topic was resolved according to Pierson (1965) by counselor educators who promoted the idea "that the services of the high school counselor are adjunct to the services of the classroom teacher" (p. 40). The role definition topic was handled by saying that the role of the counselor cannot be predetermined. School counselors were taught to develop their own role definition. "The adequately trained school counselor develops his [or her] own role, a role that tends to be unique with him [or her] and unique to the situation in which the role is developed" (p. 39).

It is interesting to note that the training individuals received stressed school counselors defining their own roles. They were to shape their roles according to the unique school settings in which they would be employed. No specific organizational structure was provided.

Further analysis of NDEA institutes also makes it clear that there was a heavy emphasis on individual and group counseling in counseling practica and group procedures courses. Placement and traditional educational and occupational information procedures (collecting, classifying and using information) as well as philosophy and principles received relatively less attention. Pierson (1965, p. 46) summarized curriculum offerings in institutes by pointing out that, "The curriculum in regular session institutes has placed great stress upon practicum; about one-third of an enrollee's time has been spent in supervised practice in counseling. At the same time, institutes have strengthened their instruction in psychology, particularly in the areas of personality, learning, growth and development and mental health.

Another aspect of the school counselor role dilemma was identified by Tyler (1960) in her review of the first 50 summer institutes conducted during summer 1959. "Before one can really define the role of the counselor, it will be necessary to clarify the roles of all workers who make up guidance staffs. It may be desirable to replace the ambiguous word *guidance* with the clearer term *pupil personnel work*." (p. 77)

Here is another reference to replacing the word guidance with pupil personnel work. Instead of being called school counselors, the term personnel worker was again suggested.

During the early 1960s many writers acknowledged the impact of Title V-B of the National Defense Education Act of 1958 (Dugan, 1960; Fossett, 1960). There were individuals, however, who were concerned about the training school counselors received in NDEA Institutes. Patterson (1960) stated he was concerned training in summer NDEA institutes alone did not make a counselor a counselor. He felt such training encouraged the creation of what he called "makeshift counselors" (p. 58).

Many articles were written in the 1960s describing and discussing the impact of Part B of Title V of NDEA. Little was written, however, about the impact of Part A of Title V (establishing and maintaining statewide programs of testing; see Appendix A for the language of Part A). And yet as Part A was put into operation, it was to have a substantial impact on school counselors' duties and responsibilities. Why? Remember that one of the services of guidance was Assessment or sometimes called Appraisal. This meant testing was seen as part of guidance in the schools, which in turn meant that school counselors were "usually delegated leadership responsibility in developing a testing program ..." (Eckerson & Smith, 1966, p. 31). School counselors could be delegated this responsibility because they had a course or two in their preparation typically labeled as "The Individual Inventory" (Polmantier & Schmidt, 1960, p. 46). This tradition has been carried over to today in that many school counselors are given the responsibility of coordinating the school's testing program.

In the 1960s, school counselor preparation standards were, once again, of concern. In May 1960, the Association for Counselor Education and Supervision (ACES) launched a five-year Planning Cooperative Study of Counselor Education Standards. The goal was to prepare guidelines to evaluate secondary school counselor preparation programs (Stripling, 1965). This work resulted in the publication of "Standards for Counselor Education in the Preparation of Secondary School Counselors" in 1964.

Calls for Change in How Guidance was Organized and Practiced

Beginning in the 1960s, but particularly in the 1970s, the call came to reorient guidance and counseling from what had become an ancillary position organized around a set of services within pupil personnel services to a comprehensive developmental program. This was not the first time calls had been made for change, however. As early as the 1920s, Myers (1923) called for the development of a centralized, unified program of vocational guidance for an entire school system. Later, Mathewson (1949) noted that the field of guidance had been searching over the years for an organizing system to free itself from other disciplines. Then in the 1950s, Willis (1957) stated that "without an organized program, effective guidance depends upon chance" (p. 489). He also said, "A guidance program goes beyond incidental guidance; it presupposes a plan" (p. 489). In addition Willis noted the need for close integration between elementary and secondary school guidance to provide for "the development of a sequential program of guidance where every pupil receives the assistance he needs" (p. 494). Mathewson (1961) said, "Research findings as well as the dictates of field experience have confirmed the validity of the need for developmental guidance" (p. 649). Similarly, Zaccaria (1966) stressed the importance of and need for developmental guidance. He pointed out that developmental guidance was a concept in transition, that it was in tune with the times, but that it was still largely untried in practice.

The calls for the reorientation of guidance in the schools came from a number of diverse sources. They included a renewed interest in vocational-career guidance and its theoretical base career development. They also included concern about the efficacy of the then-prevailing approach to guidance in the schools – the position/services model.

Vocational-career guidance: The resurgence of interest in vocational-career guidance that began in the 1960s was aided, in part, by a series of national conferences on the topic. These conferences were funded through the Vocational Education Act of 1963 (P.L. 88-210) and later amendments. It is clear from Hoyt's (1974) account of these conferences that they contributed substantially to the renewed interest in the term career guidance and its practice in the schools.

The resurgence of interest in vocational-career guidance also was aided by a number of career guidance projects begun in the 1960s. Among them was the Developmental Career Guidance Project, begun in 1964 in Detroit to provide career guidance for disadvantaged youths. It was one of the early developmental career guidance programs, one that accumulated sufficient evaluative data to support the further development of comprehensive guidance programming in schools (Leonard & Vriend, 1975).

Concern about the prevailing position service model: Paralleling the resurgence of interest in vocational-career guidance was a growing concern about the efficacy of the services model with its emphasis on the role and function – or position – of the school counselor. Particular concern was expressed about an overemphasis on the one-to-one relationship model of counseling and the tendency of counselors to focus mainly on crises and problems to justify their reason for being in a school. "The traditional one-to-one relationship in counseling, which we have cherished and perhaps over-valued will, of course, continue. But it is quite likely that the conception of the counselor as a room-bound agent of behavior change must be critically reappraised. The counselor of the future will likely serve as a social catalyst, interacting in a two-person relationship with the counselee part of the time but also serving as a facilitator of the environmental and human conditions which are known to promote the counselee's total psychological development, including vocational development" (Borow, 1966, p. 88).

During the 1960s there were also expressions of concern about the potency of the guidance services model and the need for more meaningful reconceptualizations for guidance so guidance could reach higher levels of development (Roeber et al., 1969). This same theme was echoed by Sprinthall (1971):

"It is probably not an understatement to say that the service concept has so dominated guidance and counseling that more basic and significant questions are not even acknowledged, let alone answered. Instead, the counselor assumes a service orientation that limits and defines his [or her] role to minor administrative procedures" (p. 20).

Aubrey (1979) also spoke about problems with the prevailing services model to guidance. He contrasted the service approach with a programmatic approach. "In contrast to a service approach is a programmatic position. A programmatic approach contains the essential ingredients of a service orientation, namely skills and functions, but does not view these as randomly dispensable commodities or services. Instead of focusing on problem situations or the daily needs of consumers, a programmatic position organizes functions and skills according to carefully planned short- and long-range objectives intended to deliberately and systematically influence students for guidance outcomes" (p. 159).

Comprehensive Guidance and Counseling Programs Emerge

In the early 1970s interest in career development theory, research and practice as well as in career guidance and career education, their educational manifestations, increased. Other educational movements, such as psychological education, moral education and process education, emerged as well. In addition, interest in the development of comprehensive systematic approaches to guidance and counseling program development and management continued to increase. The convergence of these movements in the early 1970s served as a stimulus to continue the task of defining guidance and counseling developmentally in measurable student outcome terms – as a program in its own right, integrated and central within the educational enterprise, rather than as services ancillary to other educational programs.

Basic Ideas, Vocabulary and Systems Thinking

By 1970 a substantial amount of preliminary work had been done in developing the basic ideas, vocabulary and constructs to define guidance and counseling in comprehensive-developmental-outcome terms. In 1961 Glanz identified and described four basic models for organizing guidance because of his concern about the lack of discernible patterns for implementing guidance in the schools. Tiedeman and Field (1962) issued a call to make guidance an integral part of the educational process, and they also stressed the need for a developmental, liberating perspective of guidance. Zaccaria (1965) stressed the need to examine developmental tasks as a basis for determining the goals of guidance. Shaw and Tuel (1966) developed a model for a guidance program designed to serve all students. At the elementary level, Dinkmeyer (1966) emphasized the need for developmental counseling by describing pertinent child development research that supported a developmental perspective.

Paralleling the preliminary work on ideas, vocabulary and constructs was the application of systems thinking to guidance and counseling. Based on nationwide survey of vocational guidance in 1968, a systems model for vocational guidance was developed at the Center for Vocational and Technical Education in Columbus, Ohio. This model focused on student behavioral objectives, alternative activities, program evaluation and implementation strategies (Campbell et al., 1971). Ryan (1969) and Hosford and Ryan (1970) also proposed the use of systems theory and systems techniques for the development and improvement of comprehensive guidance and counseling programs.

Beginning models for guidance and counseling programs: On the West Coast, McDaniel (1970) proposed a model for guidance called Youth Guidance Systems. It was organized around goals, objectives, programs, implementation plans and designs for evaluation. The primary student outcome in this model was considered to be decision making. Closely related to this model was the Comprehensive Career Guidance System (CCGS) developed by personnel at the American Institutes for Research (Jones, Hamilton, Ganschow, Helliwell, & Wolff, 1972; Jones, Nelson, Ganschow, & Hamilton, 1971). The CCGS was designed to plan, implement and evaluate guidance programs systematically. Mesa, Ariz., used this approach to design and implement a comprehensive guidance program in the 1970s (McKinnon, 1974).

Systems thinking also undergirded Ryan and Zeran's (1972) approach to the organization and administration of guidance services. They stressed the need for a systems approach to guidance to ensure the development and implementation of an accountable program. A final systematic approach to guidance was advocated in the Program of Learning in

Accordance with Needs (PLAN) System of Individualized Education (Dunn, 1972). Guidance was seen as a major component of PLAN and was treated as an integral part of the regular instructional program.

Concurrent with these efforts, a national effort was begun to assist the states in developing and implementing state models or guides for career guidance, counseling and placement. On July 1, 1971, the University of Missouri–Columbia was awarded a U.S. Office of Education grant, directed by Norman C. Gysbers, Ph.D., to assist each state, the District of Columbia and Puerto Rico in developing models or guides for implementing career guidance, counseling and placement programs in local schools. This project was the next step in a program of work begun as a result of a previous project at the university, a project that conducted a national conference on career guidance, counseling and placement in October 1969 and regional conferences across the country during spring 1970. All 50 states, the District of Columbia and Puerto Rico were involved in the 1971 project, and by the time the project ended in 1974, 44 states had developed some type of guide or model for career guidance, counseling and placement. As a part of the assistance provided to the states, project staff conducted a national conference in January 1972 and developed a manual (Gysbers & Moore, 1974) to be used by the states as they developed their own guides.

Model Development Continues

As the movement toward planning and implementing systematic developmental and accountable guidance and counseling programs in the early 1970s became more sophisticated, theoretical models began to be translated into practical, workable models to be implemented in the schools. Many of these translations were based on an expanded conception of career guidance. For example, when the guidance staff in Mesa, Ariz., felt the need to reorient their guidance program to make it more accountable in 1972, they chose a comprehensive career guidance program that included needs assessment, goals and objectives development and related guidance activities (McKinnon & Jones, 1975). To train the staff in program development and implementation methods and procedures for the new system, they wrote competency-based training packages in cooperation with the American Institutes for Research. For another example, guidance personnel at the Grossmont Union High School District in California chose the California Model for Career Development (California State Department of Education, 1971) to supply the content of their program and then proceeded to lay out a systematic, developmental career guidance program (Jacobson & Mitchell, 1975). For yet another example, the Georgia State Department of Education initiated a project funded by the U.S. Office of Education to coordinate the efforts of several Georgia school systems in planning and implementing comprehensive career guidance programs. The project goal was to develop a career guidance system based on student needs and focused on a team approach and curriculum-based strategies (Dagley, 1974).

On July 1, 1974, the American Institutes for Research began work on bringing together program planning efforts previously undertaken by the Pupil Personnel Division of the California State Department of Education and their own Youth Development Research Program in Mesa, Ariz., and elsewhere (Jones, Helliwell, & Ganschow, 1975). This resulted in the development of 12 competency-based staff development modules on developing comprehensive career guidance programs K-12. As a part of the project, the modules were field-tested in two school districts in California in summer 1975 and in a pre-service class of guidance and counseling majors at the University of Missouri–Columbia in fall 1975. A final report of this project was issued by the American Institutes for Research in January 1976 (Dayton, 1976). Jones, Dayton and Gelatt (1977) subsequently used the 12 modules as a point of departure to suggest a systematic approach in planning and evaluating human service programs.

The work that began in the early 1970s on various guidance program models was continued and expanded. *Career Development: Guidance and Education*, a special issue of the *Personnel and Guidance Journal* edited by Hansen and Gysbers (1975), contained a number of articles describing program models and examples of programs in operation. The American College Testing Program (1976) published a programmatic model for guidance in "River City High School Guidance Services: A Conceptual Model."

An Increasing Number of Publications

An increasing number of articles, monographs and books on various aspects of comprehensive guidance programming were published in the late 1970s. Brown (1977) discussed the organization and evaluation of elementary school guidance services using the three-C's approach (counseling, consulting and coordinating). Upton, Lowery, Mitchell, Varenhorst and Benvenuti (1978) described procedures for developing a career guidance curriculum and presented leadership strategies to teach the procedures to those who were to implement the curriculum. Ballast and Shoemaker (1978) described a step-by-step approach to developing a comprehensive K-12 guidance program. Campbell, Rodebaugh and Shaltry (1978) edited a handbook that presented numerous examples of career guidance programs, practices and models. Included in the handbook were descriptions by Gysbers (1978) of systematic approaches to comprehensive guidance programming, such as the Career Planning Support System (Campbell, 1977) and the Cooperative Rural Guidance System (Drier, 1976), both developed at the National Center for Research in Vocational Education, Columbus, Ohio. Peterson and Treichel (1978) wrote the Programmatic Approach to Guidance Excellence: PAGE 2, a similar systematic approach. Herr and Cramer (1979) described a further systematic planning approach for career guidance and delineated goals, objectives and activities for elementary, junior and high schools as well as for higher and adult education. Hilton (1979) provided a conceptual framework for career guidance in the secondary school. Mitchell (1978) and Mitchell and Gysbers (1978) described the need for comprehensive guidance programs and provided recommendations for how to develop and implement such programs. Halasz-Salster and Peterson (1979) presented descriptions of different guidance planning models.

An Increasing Interest in Guidance Through the Curriculum

The 1960s and 1970s also saw increasing interest in implementing guidance through the curriculum. This interest was not new either. Davis (1914) had developed a guidance curriculum to be delivered through English in Central High School in Grand Rapids, Mich., in the early years of the guidance movement. This interest continued in the 1920s and 1930s, expressed through classes in occupations and in presenting guidance units in classrooms. While interest in guidance in the curriculum waned in the 1940s and 1950s due to the increased attention being given to counseling, some articles and books were published on this topic, notably a book by Kelly (1955). In it she urged the field to recognize the centrality of the curriculum to guidance. "Guidance, instruction and curriculum need to become inseparable parts of the total educative process …" (p. vii). By the 1960s and 1970s, however, interest in guidance and the curriculum returned.

Swan (1966) wrote about the need for school counselors to be involved in the school curriculum as did Aubrey (1979). Of particular interest were the efforts to implement career development through the curriculum. In the early 1970s a number of states developed guides for implementing career development through the curriculum. One such guide was developed by the state of Wisconsin (Drier, 1971). It featured a career development model that organized knowledge and skills for K-12 students to acquire using the domains of self, work world and career planning and preparation. Another guide, the California Model for Career Development K-Adult, organized the knowledge and skills for K-12 students around the domains of education, work and leisure alternatives, career planning and decision making, and life styles and personal satisfaction. It appeared in draft form in 1971 (California State Department of Education, 1971) and then in a monograph of the California Personnel and Guidance Association (1972).

Conceptual foundations and examples of practices to implement career development in the curriculum began in the 1960s and continued into the 1970s. Of particular interest are the work of Tennyson, Soldahl and Mueller (1965) titled "The Teacher's Role in Career Development" and the Airlie House Conference in May 1966 on the topic "Implementing Career Development Theory and Research Through the Curriculum," which was sponsored by the National Vocational Guidance Association (Ashcroft, 1966). Later in the 1960s and early 1970s came the work of such theorists and practitioners as Gysbers (1969), Herr (1969), Hansen (1970), and Tennyson and Hansen (1971), all of whom spoke to the need to integrate career development concepts into the curriculum. Through these efforts and others like them, career development concepts began to be translated into individual (student) outcomes and the resulting goals and objectives arranged sequentially, K-12.

In addition to an emphasis on career, work was also underway to create a wider array of individual (student) outcomes to include the domains of educational and social. Wellman (1968) was awarded a contract at the University of Missouri to develop this taxonomy of guidance outcomes. He used the terms educational, vocational and social to label the three domains of student outcomes. The California State Department of Education (1970) used these terms in a document to help pupil personnel services personnel write operational objectives for their programs. These same terms (educational, vocational, social) were then used again by Sullivan and O'Hare (1971) in a monograph published by the California Personnel and Guidance Association. Later, in 1974, Gysbers and Moore

(1974) used the terms self-knowledge and interpersonal skills, knowledge and understanding of life roles, settings and events, life career planning knowledge and skills, and basic studies and occupational preparation to label four domains of K-12 student outcomes.

Concerns about Leadership and Supervision

Discussion about the need for leadership for school counseling began as early as the 1920s when Brewer (1922) expressed concern about the lack of effective centralization and supervision. Myers (1923) spoke about the lack of effective centralization and supervision. Later Fitch (1936) was concerned about the lack of centralized responsibility for guidance. In the 1940s Myers (1941) stressed the need for head counselors in each building who would, with the assistance of a director of vocational guidance and in consultation with the principal, plan and coordinate the vocational guidance program in the school.

During the 1960s and 1970s, guidance services in the schools were found in a wide variety of organizational patterns under a number of different types of leadership. The concerns about the organization and leadership of guidance that were present in the 1920s were still present. This was particularly true at the elementary level. The growing numbers of elementary counselors, who typically served more than one building, caused an increased need for district-based elementary counseling supervisors. Large districts were able to justify small guidance departments, comprising a guidance director, an elementary and, less frequently, a secondary counseling supervisor and a testing supervisor. In addition, in many school districts elementary school counselors were assigned the task of identifying students who would benefit from special programs. Organizationally some counselors were placed under the auspices of the newly supported (through PL94-142) Special Education administration. However, with elementary guidance, career guidance and career education movements emphasizing the developmental aspects of the guidance program, this placement produced tensions for both central office guidance supervisors and school counselors. In contrast to the guidance-as-part-of-special-education organizational pattern and in the context of expanding use of educational supervisors, some districts incorporated the central office guidance supervisor into departments of instruction.

It was also clear that, during this time, the building principals were still defining the roles and assigning the work school counselors did. Costar

(1977) pointed out, "Although every elementary and secondary school has a guidance function to perform, only a relatively small portion has a director of guidance or a coordinator other than the principal. The result in the past has often been to leave the guidance function unattended" (p. 212). In some cases in which there were directors of guidance, there were conflicts between the directors and the principals. "Building principals were reluctant to relinquish authority and autonomy to any person functioning in a staff relationship" (Aubrey, 1978, pp. 294-295), and directors seem to have been reluctant to assert themselves.

The practice of supervision within the counseling profession also was evolving during these years. Although "clinical supervision has been practiced as long as has psychotherapy" (Bernard & Goodyear, 1992, p. xv), it only became a topic of some prominence in the counseling field in the late 1960s. In 1969, the Association for Counselor Education and Supervision (ASES) through its Committee on Counselor Effectiveness recognized that "in view of the increasing pressures and demands being placed on counselors, it seems essential to implement continuing supervision if competent counseling skills are to be maintained, refined, revised and integrated with new knowledge" (Boyd, 1978, p. xiv). In his landmark book on counselor supervision, Boyd identified the purposes of supervision as "facilitation of the counselor's personal and professional development, promotion of counselor competencies and promotion of accountable counseling and guidance services and programs" (Boyd, 1978, p. 10). He also recognized that "the supervisor is an advocate for counselors" (p. 10).

Major Trends and Issues

The 1960s and 1970s were decades of rapid growth for guidance and counseling in the schools. Many articles and books were published about the nature and structure of guidance and counseling.

One of the major issues being debated concerned the nature of guidance and counseling. Was it more psychological in nature featuring counseling as a major intervention? Was it more educational in nature featuring a broader array of interventions including counseling but also including information, assessment, placement and follow-up activities? Those who favored a more psychological orientation stated that teaching certificates and teaching experience were not necessary prerequisites to become a school counselor. Those who thought guidance was more educational in nature advocated for teaching certificates and teaching experience.

Closely related to the debate about the appropriate orientation for school counselors was the debate about counselor role. Here again the lines were drawn. Is it counseling or is it a broader array of interventions? Also debated was the focus of the role of consultation. Some writers saw the role of counselors as being primarily one of consultation. Other writers recommended more direct work with students.

The 1960s saw the impact of two pieces of legislation that were to have substantial impact on the nature and structure of guidance in the schools. The National Defense Education Act of 1958 changed the selection and training of school counselors as well as increased the numbers of school counselors. The Vocational Education Act of 1963 made possible the extension and expansion of career guidance and counseling.

The issue of the title of counselors also continued to be discussed. Following the pupil personnel services model some writers wanted to re-title counselors as personnel workers. Other writers maintained that the title counselor was most appropriate. In the end those who favored counselor won the day.

Although guidance in elementary schools had been discussed over the past decades, it wasn't until the 1960s when it became a reality. Many articles were written about this focusing on various topics including a needed philosophical base and the roles and functions of the personnel involved. NDEA as amended in the 1960s stimulated training practices and procedures that set elementary guidance apart from secondary guidance.

The 1960s and 1970s also witnessed increasing concern about what had come to be known as the position in a services model of guidance. Calls for change came from a variety of sources ending up in the beginning development of a comprehensive program approach to guidance.

Finally, while the topic of leadership and supervision for school counseling had been discussed in the early decades of the 1900s, concern about the need for leadership and supervision intensified in the 1960s and 1970s. Two issues of concern were where to place school counseling organizationally and who should lead and supervise school counselors. Although no specific answers were forthcoming, it was clear there was a need to address these important issues.

References

American College Testing Program (1976). *River City High School guidance services: A conceptual model.* Iowa City, IA: Author.

American Personnel and Guidance Association (1961). Standards for the preparation of school counselors. *The Personnel and Guidance Journal, 40,* 402-407.

Arbuckle, D. S. (1968). A question of counselor function and responsibility. *The Personal and Guidance Journal, 47,* 341-345.

Arbuckle, D. S. (1972). The counselor: Who? What? *The Personal and Guidance Journal, 50,* 785-790.

Ashcroft, K. B. (1966). *A report of the invitational conference in implementing career development theory.* Washington, DC: National Vocational Guidance Association.

Association for Counselor Education and Supervision (1964). Standards for counselor education in the preparation of secondary school counselors. *The Personnel and Guidance Journal, 42,* 1061-1073.

Aubrey, R. F. (1967). The legitimacy of elementary school counseling: Some unresolved issues and conflicts. *The Personnel and Guidance Journal, 46,* 355-359.

Aubrey, R. F. (1969). Misapplication of therapy models to school counseling. *The Personal and Guidance Journal, 48,* 273-278.

Aubrey, R. F. (1978). Consultation, school interventions, and the elementary counselor. *The Personnel and Guidance Journal, 56,* 351-354.

Aubrey, R. F. (1978). Supervision of counselors in elementary and secondary schools. In J. D. Boyd (Ed.), *Counselor supervision: Approaches, preparation, practices* (pp. 293-338).

Aubrey, R. F. (1979). Relationship of guidance and counseling to the established and emerging school curriculum. *The School Counselor, 26,* 150-161.

Ballast, D. L., & Shoemaker, R. L. (1978). *Guidance program development.* Springfield, IL: Charles C. Thomas.

Bernard, J. M., & Goodyear, R. K. (1992). *Fundamentals of clinical supervision.* Boston, MA: Allyn & Bacon.

Bergstein, H. B., & Grant, C. W. (1961). How parents perceive the counselor's role. *The Personnel and Guidance Journal, 39,* 698-703.

Berry, E. (1979). Guidance and counseling in the elementary school: Its theoretical base. *The Personnel and Guidance Journal, 57,* 513-520.

Borow, H. (1964). Milestones: A chronology of notable events in the history of vocational guidance. In H. Borow (Ed.), *Man in a world of work* (pp. 45-64). Boston, MA: Houghton Mifflin Company.

Borow, H. (1966). Research in vocational development: Implications for the vocational aspects of counselor education. In C. McDaniels (Ed.), *Vocational aspects of counselor education* (pp. 70-92). Washington, DC: George Washington University.

Boyd, J. D. (Ed.) (1978). *Counselor supervision: Approaches, preparation, practices.* Muncie, IN: Accelerated Development.

Bradley, M. K. (1978). Counseling past and present: Is there a future? *The Personal and Guidance Journal, 57,* 42-45.

Brammer, L. M. (1968). The counselor is a psychologist. *The Personnel and Guidance Journal, 47,* 4-9.

Brewer, J. M. (1922). The vocational guidance movement: Its problems and possibilities. New York: MacMillan.

Brown, J. A. (1977). *Organizing and evaluating elementary school guidance services: Why, what, and how.* Monterey, CA: Brooks/Cole.

California Personnel and Guidance Association (1972). *Career development: A California model for career guidance curriculum K-Adult - monograph 5.* Fullerton, CA: Author.

California State Department of Education (1970). *Situation, population, treatment, outcome.* Sacramento, CA: Author.

California State Department of Education (1971). *Career guidance: A California model for career development K-adult.* Sacramento, CA: Author.

Campbell, R. E. (1977). *The career planning support system.* Columbus, OH: National Center for Research in Vocational Education.

Campbell, R. E., Dworkin, E. P., Jackson, D. P., Hoeltzel, K. E., Parsons, G. E., & Lacey, D. W. (1971). *The systems approach: An emerging behavioral model for career guidance.* Columbus, OH: National Center for Research in Vocational Education.

Campbell, R. E., Rodebaugh, H. D., & Shaltry, P. E. (1978). *Building comprehensive career guidance programs for secondary schools.* Columbus, OH: National Center for Research in Vocation Education.

Carroll, M. R. (1968). School counseling—Potpourri for education. *The School Counselor, 16,* 21-23.

Costar, J. W. (1977). *The relationship of counselors to school principals.* In American Personnel and Guidance Association, The status of guidance and counseling in the nations' schools: A series of issue reports (pp. 211-221). Washington, DC: Author.

Cottingham, H. F. (1966). National-level projection for elementary school guidance. *The Personnel and Guidance Journal, 44,* 499-502.

Council of Chief State School Officers (1960). *Responsibilities of state departments of education for pupil personnel services.* Washington, DC: Author.

Dagley, J. C. (1974, December). *Georgia career guidance project newsletter.* Athens, GA: University of Georgia.

Davis, J. B. (1914). *Vocational and moral guidance.* Boston, MA: Ginn.

Dayton, C. A. (1976). *A validated program development model and staff development prototype for comprehensive career guidance, counseling, placement, and follow-up* (Final Report, Grant No. OEG -0-74-1721). Palo Alto, CA: American Institutes for Research.

Dinkmeyer, D. (1966). Developmental counseling in the elementary school. *The Personal and Guidance Journal, 45,* 262 266.

Dinkmeyer, D. (1973). Elementary school counseling: Prospects and potentials. *The Personnel and Guidance Journal, 52,* 171-174.

Dinkmeyer, D. C. (Ed.) (1968). *Guidance and counseling in the elementary school.* New York: Holt, Rinehart and Winston, Inc.

Drier, H. N. (1976). *Cooperative rural guidance system.* Columbus, OH: National Center for Research in Vocational Education.

Drier, H. N. (Ed.) (1971). *Guide to the integration of career development into local curriculum: Grades K-12.* Madison, WI: Wisconsin Department of Public Instruction.

Dugan, W. E. (1960). The impact of NDEA upon counselor preparation. *The Personal and Guidance Journal, 39,* 37-40.

Dunn, J. A. (1972). *The guidance program in the plan system of individualized education.* Palo Alto, CA: American Institutes for Research.

Eckerson, L. O. & Smith, H. M. (1966). *Scope of pupil personnel services.* Washington, DC: U.S. Government Printing Office.

Eckerson, L. O. (1967). *Realities confronting elementary school counseling.* The Personnel and Guidance Journal, 46, 350-354.

Eckerson, L. O., & Smith, H. M. (1968). Elementary school guidance: The consultant. In D. C. Dinkmeyer (Ed.), *Guidance and counseling in the elementary school* (pp. 42-119). New York: Holt, Rinehart and Winston, Inc.

Eckerson, L. O., & Smith, H. M. (Eds.) (1966). *Scope of pupil personnel services* (Catalog No. FS5.223: 23045). Washington, DC: U.S. Government Printing Office.

Faust, V. (1968). *History of elementary school counseling: Overview and critique.* Boston, MA: Houghton Mifflin.

Felix, J. L. (1968). Who decided that? *The Personnel and Guidance Journal, 47,* 9-11.

Ferguson, D. G. (1963). *Pupil personnel services.* Washington, DC: Center for Applied Research in Education.

Fitch, J. A. (1936). Professional standards in guidance. *Occupations, 14,* 760-765.

Fitzgerald, P. W. (1965). The professional role of school counselors. In J. W. Loughary (Ed.), *Counseling, a growing profession* (pp. 31-41). Washington DC: American Personnel and Guidance Association.

Fossett, K. (1960). Guidance institutes—NDEA. *The Personal and Guidance Journal, 39,* 207-209.

Gibson, R. L. (1965). Teacher Opinions of high school guidance programs. *The Personnel and Guidance Journal, 44,* 416-422.

Glanz, E. C. (1961). Emerging concepts and patterns of guidance in American education. *The Personnel and Guidance Journal, 40,* 259-265.

Gysbers, N. C. (1969). *Elements of a model for promoting career development in elementary and junior high school.* Paper presented at the National Conference on Exemplary Programs and Projects, 1968 Amendments to the Vocational Education Act (ED045860), Atlanta, GA.

Gysbers, N. C., & Moore, E. J. (Eds.) (1974). *Career guidance, counseling, and placement: Elements of an illustrative program guide.* Columbia, MO: University of Missouri.

Gysbers, N. C., (1978). Comprehensive career guidance programs. In R. E. Campbell, H. D. Rodebuagh, & P. E. Shaltry (Eds.), *Building comprehensive career guidance programs for secondary schools* (pp. 3-24). Columbus, OH: National Center for Research in Vocational Education.

Halasz-Salster, I., & Peterson, M. (1979). *Planning comprehensive career guidance programs: A catalog of alternatives.* Columbus, OH: National Center for Research in Vocational Education.

Hansen, L. S. (1970). *Career guidance practices in school and community.* Washington, DC: National Vocational Guidance Association.

Hansen. L. S., & Gysbers, N. C. (Eds.) (1975). Career development: Guidance and education [Special issue]. *Personnel and Guidance Journal, 53.*

Hart, D. H., & Prince, D. J. (1970). Role conflict for school counselors: Training versus job demands. *The Personnel and Guidance Journal, 58,* 374-379.

Herr, E. L. (1969). *Unifying an entire system of education around a career development theme.* Paper presented at the National Conference on Exemplary Programs and Projects, 1968 Amendments to the Vocational Education Act (ED045860), Atlanta, GA.

Herr, E. L., & Cramer, S. H. (1979). *Career guidance through the life span.* Boston: Little, Brown.

Hill, G. E., & Mitzschke, D. F. (1961). Preparation programs in elementary school guidance. *The Personnel and Guidance Journal, 40,* 155-159.

Hilton, T. L. (1979). *Confronting the future: A conceptual framework for secondary school career guidance.* New York: College Entrance Examination Board.

Hosford, R. E., & Ryan, T. A. (1970). Systems design in the development of counseling and guidance programs. *The Personnel and Guidance Journal, 49,* 221-230.

Hoyt, K. B. (1961). What the school has a right to expect of its counselor. *The Personal and Guidance Journal, 40,* 129-133.

Hoyt, K. B. (1962). Guidance: A constellation of services. *The Personnel and Guidance Journal, 40,* 690-697.

Hoyt, K. B. (1974). Professional preparation for vocational guidance. In E. L. Herr (Ed.), *Vocational guidance and human development* (pp. 502-527). Boston, MA: Houghton Mufflin.

Hoyt, K. B. (1974). Professional preparation for vocational guidance. In E. L. Herr (Ed.), *Vocational guidance and human development* (pp. 502-527). Boston, MA: Houghton Mifflin.

Jacobson, T. J., & Mitchell, A. M. (1975). *Master plan for career guidance and counseling.* Grossmont, CA: Grossmont Union High School District.

Jennings, J. F. (1982). A federal perspective on guidance and counseling. In E. L. Herr & N. M. Pierson (Eds.), *Foundations for policy in guidance and counseling* (pp. 121-129). Washington, DC: The American Personnel and Guidance Association.

Jones, G. B., Dayton, C., & Gelatt, H. B. (1977). *New methods for delivering human services.* New York: Human Services Press.

Jones, G. B., Hamilton, J. A., Ganchow, L. H., Helliwell, C. B., & Wolff, J. M. (1972). *Planning, developing, and field testing career guidance programs: A manual and report.* Palo Alto, CA: American Institutes for Research.

Jones, G. B., Helliwell, C. B., & Ganschow, L. H. (1975). A planning model for career guidance. *Vocational Guidance Quarterly, 23,* 220-226.

Jones, G. B., Nelson, D. E., Ganschow, L. H., & Hamilton, J. A. (1971). *Development and evaluation of a comprehensive career guidance program.* Palo Alto, CA: American Institutes for Research.

Kahnweiler, W. M. (1979). The school counselor as consultant: A historical review. *The Personal and Guidance Journal, 57,* 374-380.

Kelly, J. A. (1955). *Guidance and curriculum.* Englewood Cliffs, NJ: Prentice- Hall.

Knapp, D. L., & Denny, E. W. (1961). The counselor's responsibility in role definition. *The Personal and Guidance Journal, 40,* 48-50.

Leonard, G. E., & Vriend, T. J. (1975). Update: The developmental career guidance project. *The Personnel and Guidance Journal, 53,* 668-671.

Lorimer, J., & Haddad, J. (1969). Pupil personnel services in the elementary school. *The Personnel and Guidance Journal, 47,* 975-978.

Mathewson, R. H. (1949). *Guidance policy and practice.* New York: Harper.

Mathewson, R. H. (1961). School guidance: A four-dimensional model. *The Personnel and Guidance Journal, 39,* 645-649.

Mathewson, R. H. (1961). School guidance: A four-dimensional model. *The Personnel and Guidance Journal, 39,* 645-649.

McCracken, T. C., & Lamb, H. E. (1923). *Occupational information in the elementary school.* Boston, MA: Houghton Mifflin.

McCreary, W. H., & Miller, G. (1966). Elementary school counselors in California. *The Personnel and Guidance Journal, 44,* 494-498.

McCully, C. H. (1962). The school counselor: Strategy for professionalization. *The Personnel and Guidance Journal, 40,* 681-689.

McDaniel, H. B. (1970). *Youth guidance systems.* Palo Alto, CA: College Entrance Examination Board.

McKinnon, B. E. (1974). *Toward accountability: A report on the Mesa approach to career guidance, counseling, and placement.* Mesa AZ: Mesa Public Schools.

McKinnon, B. E., & Jones, G. B. (1975). Field testing a comprehensive career guidance program: K-12. *The Personnel and Guidance Journal, 53,* 663-667.

Mitchell, A. M. (1978). The design, development, and evaluation of systematic guidance programs. In G. Walz, & L. Benjamin (Eds.), *New imperatives for guidance* (pp. 113-148). Ann Arbor, MI: ERIC Counseling and Personnel Services Clearinghouse.

Mitchell, A. M., & Gysbers, N. C. (1978). Comprehensive school guidance programs. In *The status of guidance and counseling in the nation's schools* (pp. 23-39). Washington, DC: American Personnel and Guidance Association.

Myers, G. E. (1923). A critical review of present developments in vocational guidance with special reference to future prospects. *The Vocational Guidance Magazine, 2,* 139-142.

Myers, G. E. (1941). *Principles and techniques of vocational guidance.* New York: McGraw-Hill.

Nitzschke, D. F. (1965). Preparation programs in elementary school guidance—A status study. *The Personnel and Guidance Journal, 43,* 751-756.

Odell, L. M. (1973). Secondary school counseling: Past, present, and future. *The Personnel and Guidance Journal, 52,* 151-155.

Odell, L.M. (1971). *American School Counselor Association: The historical growth and development of a professional organization 1953-1970*. (Unpublished doctoral dissertation). The George Washington University, Washington, DC.

Patouillet, R. (1968). Organizing for guidance in elementary school. In D. C. Dinkmeyer (Ed.), *Guidance and counseling in the elementary school* (pp. 54-63). New York: Holt, Rinehart, and Winston, Inc.

Patterson, C. H. (1960). Makeshift counselors [a letter to the editor]. *The Personal and Guidance Journal, 39*, 58.

Peterson, M., & Treichel, J. (1978). *Programmatic approach to guidance excellence: PAGE 2* (Rev. ed.). McComb: Western Illinois University, Curriculum Publishing Clearinghouse.

Pierson, G. A. (1965). *An evaluation counselor education in regular session institutes*. Washington, DC: Office of Education, U.S. Department of Health, Education, and Welfare.

Pine, G. J. (1974). Let's give away school counseling. *The School Counselor, 22*, 94-99.

Polmantier, P. C., & Schmidt, L. D. (1960). Areas of preparation for school guidance workers. *The Personnel and Guidance Journal, 39*, 45-46.

Roeber, E. D. (1963). *The school counselor*. Washington, DC: Center for Applied Research in Education.

Roeber, E. D., Walz, G. R., & Smith. G. E. (1969). *A strategy for guidance*. New York: Macmillan.

Ryan, T. A. (1969). Systems techniques for programs of counseling and counselor education. *Educational Technology, 9*, 7-17.

Ryan, T. A., & Zeran, F. R. (1972). *Organization and administration of guidance services*. Danville, IL: Interstate.

Seidman, E., Peterson, M. B., Byrne, R. H., Dayton, C. M., & Boek, J. R. (1970). The child development consultant: An experiment. *The Personnel and Guidance Journal, 49*, 29-34.

Shaw, M. C., & Tuel, L. K. (1966). A focus on public school guidance programs: A model and a proposal. *The Personnel and Guidance Journal, 44*, 824-830.

Shertzer, B., & Stone, S. C. (1963). The school counselor and his public: A problem of role definition. *The Personal and Guidance Journal, 46*, 687-693.

Skovholt, R. (1977). Issues in psychological education. *The Personal and Guidance Journal, 55*, 472-476.

Sprinthall, N. A. (1971). *Guidance for human growth*. New York: Van Nostrand Reinhold.

Stefflre, B. (1964). What price professionalization? *The Personnel and Guidance Journal, 42,* 654-659.

Stevic, R. (1966). A new strategy for assessing counselor role. *The School Counselor, 14,* 94-96.

Stewart, L. H. (1961). Comments. *The Personal and Guidance Journal, 40,* 133-134.

Stone, S. C., & Shertzer, B. (1963). The militant counselor. *The Personal and Guidance Journal, 47,* 342-347.

Stripling, R. O. (1965). Standards for the education of school counselors. In J. W. Loughary (Ed.), *Counseling, a growing profession* (pp. 19-30). Washington DC: American Personnel and Guidance Association.

Stripling, R. O., & Lane, D. (1966). Guidance services. In L. O. Eckerson & H. M. Smith (Eds.), *Scope of pupil personnel services* (pp. 25-35). Washington, DC: U. S. Government Printing Office.

Sullivan, H. J., & O'Hare, R. W. (1971). *Accountability in pupil personnel services: A process guide for the development of objectives.* Fullerton, CA: California Personnel and Guidance Association.

Swan, R. J. (1966). The counselor and the curriculum. *The Personnel and Guidance Journal, 44,* 689-693.

Tennyson, W. W., & Hansen, L. S. (1971). Guidance through the curriculum. In L. C. Deighton (Ed.), *The encyclopedia of education* (pp. 248-254). New York: Macmillan.

Tiedeman, D. V., & Field, F. C. (1962). Guidance: The science of purposeful action applied through education. *Harvard Educational Review, 32,* 483-501.

Townsend, L. G. (1965). *Independent study of the preparation of professional personnel in NDEA short-term counseling and guidance institutes.* Washington, DC: Office of Education, Department of Health, Education, and Welfare.

Tyler, L. E. (1960). *The national defense counseling and guidance training institutes program: A report of the first 50 institutes.* Washington, DC: U.S. Government Printing Office.

Upton, A., Lowery, B., Mitchell, A. M., Varenhorst, B., & Benvenuti, J. (1978). *A planning model for developing career guidance curriculum.* Fullerton: California Personnel and Guidance Association.

Van Hoose, W. H. , & Vafakas, C. M. (1968). Status of guidance and counseling in the elementary school. *The Personal and Guidance Journal, 46,* 536-539.

Van Hoose, W. H., & Carlson, J. (1972). Counselors in the elementary school: 1970-71. *The Personal and Guidance Journal, 50,* 679-682.

Van Hoose, W. H., & Kurtz, M. (1970). Status of guidance in the elementary school: 1968-69. *The Personal and Guidance Journal, 48,* 381-384.

Warner, O. R. (1969). *Pupil personnel services in the 50 states.* Moravia, NY: Chronicle Guidance.

Wellman, F. E. (1968). *Phase I national study of guidance* (OEG 3-6-001147-1147). U.S. Department of Health, Education, and Welfare.

Wells, C. E., & Ritter, K. Y. (1979). Paperwork, pressure and discouragement: Student attitudes toward guidance services and implications for the profession. *The Personnel and Guidance Journal, 58,* 170-175.

Willis, B. C. (1957). The contribution of guidance to the high school educational program. *The Personnel and Guidance Journal, 35,* 489-494.

Wrenn, C. G. (1962). *The counselor in a changing world.* Washington, DC: American Personnel and Guidance Association.

Wrenn, C. G. (1962). *The counselor in a changing world.* Washington, DC: American Personnel and Guidance Association.

Wrenn, C. G. (1979). Proposed changes in counselor attitudes: Toward your job. *The School Counselor, 27,* 81-90.

Zaccaria, J. S. (1965). Developmental tasks: Implications for the goals of guidance. *The Personnel and Guidance Journal, 44,* 372-375.

Zaccaria, J. S. (1966). Developmental guidance: A concept in transition. *The School Counselor, 13,* 226-229.

Zerface, J. P., & Cox, W. H. (1971). School counselors, leave home. *The Personal and Guidance Journal, 49,* 371-375.

CHAPTER 6

Putting Comprehensive Guidance and Counseling Programs into Practice in the 1980s and 1990s

Many of the economic, educational and social forces that were at work in the 1960s and 1970s were at work again in the 1980s and 1990s, only they intensified, expanding and extending their impact on education and on guidance and counseling. The economy of the 1980s caused some school districts to retrench and cut back on their services and personnel including school counselors. School reform was on the minds of our country's leaders too, resulting in the publication of "A Nation at Risk: The Imperatives for Reform" (The National Commission on Excellence in Education, 1983). Later reports on education highlighted the need for educational standards and accountability.

Social forces such as gender equity, multiculturalism, diversity, sexual orientation and social class also played prominent roles in shaping education and guidance and counseling in the 1980s and 1990s. Programs in schools to foster gender equity grew rapidly. So, too, did programs to promote multicultural and diversity awareness and action. To support multicultural awareness and action in the schools and to improve school counselors' diversity training, the Association for Multicultural Counseling and Development published the "Multicultural Counseling Competencies and Standards" (Sue, Arrendondo, & McDavis, 1992).

Then in 1996, the Education Trust, supported by the DeWitt Wallace-Readers Digest Fund, initiated a five-year project to change the preparation of school counselors and the practice of school counseling. The goal was to help low-income and minority youth improve academically. The goal was to close the academic achievement gap for these youth (Martin, 2002).

As these economic, educational and social forces were continuing to shape our society as well as our schools, work in the 1960s and 1970s, on the nature, purposes, organizational structure and practices of guidance and counseling, continued. As the 1970s ended, the traditional way of organizing and managing guidance and counseling in the nation's schools around positions and services began to give way to the concept of developmental, preventive and comprehensive programs that included positions and services. Many articles were written and books published that provided rationales for this approach as well as descriptions of such programs and ways to implement them. The program approach had the support of the American School Counselor Association (ASCA). It was endorsed first in a 1974 position statement "The School Counselor and the Guidance and Counseling Program" and then again in 1978 with a new position statement "The School Counselor and Developmental Guidance." In 1988 ASCA adopted another position statement, "The Professional School Counselor and Comprehensive School Counseling Programs," which was revised in 1993 and again in 1997.

While considerable attention was being given to the program approach in the 1980s and 1990s, other important issues, covered in the literature in earlier decades, continued to be discussed. The role and function issue was one such issue as was the status of guidance and counseling in the schools. In addition, issues such as time-on-task, other duties as assigned and discipline continued to fill the pages of the literature during this time period. And, importantly, elementary guidance and counseling, "the new kid on the block" received a good deal of attention in the literature. Finally, the issue of leadership and supervision continued to be addressed.

Chapter 6 opens focusing on the emergence of comprehensive guidance and counseling programs and the development of many state program models. Particular attention is given to federal legislation that supported guidance and counseling in the schools as well as to discussion concerning the need for political advocacy. Then Chapter 6 examines the continued attention being given to the guidance curriculum and the content to be included. This is followed by a review of the literature on the status of guidance and counseling. The continued debate about school counselor role and function is presented next as is discussion about the terminology issue. The chapter closes with a review of the role and function of elementary school counselors and the literature on leadership and supervision as well as a summary of the major trends and issues in school counseling in the 1980s and 1990s.

Comprehensive Programs Gain Acceptance

The work of putting comprehensive guidance and counseling programs into place in the schools continued throughout the 1980s. Gysbers and Moore (1981) provided a theoretical base as well as a step-by-step process for developing and implementing comprehensive school guidance programs in their book "Improving Guidance Programs." This publication grew out of earlier work (Gysbers & Moore, 1974) in the University of Missouri project to assist states in developing and implementing models or guides for career guidance, counseling and placement. In their book Gysbers and Moore (1981) described a comprehensive guidance and counseling program framework divided into structural components (definition, rationale, assumptions) and program components (guidance curriculum, individual planning, responsive services, system support). Their step-by-step implementation process included getting organized, assessing your current program, selecting and using a program model, and implementing and evaluating the program.

Johnson and Johnson (1982) proposed the development of an approach to guidance and counseling in the schools called *competency-based guidance*. They described this approach as a "shift from process management to product management (i.e., from providing sets of services to managing programs designed to provide sets of student competencies)" (p. 329). Later, Johnson and Johnson (1991) described this approach as the new guidance, a concept they defined as: "a total pupil services program developed with the student as the primary client. The program is designed to guarantee that all students acquire the competencies to become successful in school and to make a successful transition from school to higher education, to employment or to a combination of higher education and work" (p. 6).

Then in 1984 Hargens and Gysbers presented a case study on how one school district (St. Joseph, Mo.) had begun to remodel and revitalize its school guidance and counseling program so it was developmental and comprehensive. At this same time (1984) the state of Missouri launched a major training effort to remodel and revitalize guidance and counseling in all of its school districts K-12. The work done in St. Joseph and the work done earlier at the University of Missouri served as the basis for this initiative in Missouri.

The state of Missouri published a draft version of "Missouri Comprehensive Guidance," (1986) which presented the state's plan to help school districts develop, implement and evaluate comprehensive, systematic school guidance programs begun during the 1984–1985 school year. Wisconsin published "School Counseling Programs: A Resource and Planning Guide" (Wilson, 1986), the result of work begun in 1984 to re-examine the school counselor's role. The National School Boards Association (1986) passed a resolution supporting comprehensive programs of guidance and counseling in the schools. The College Entrance Examination Board (1986) issued "Keeping the Options Open: Recommendations," a report with direct relevance to comprehensive guidance and counseling programs in the schools that was based on work of the Commission on Precollege Guidance and Counseling begun in 1984. Recommendations in the report urged schools to establish comprehensive and developmental guidance programs for K-12. Henderson (1987), in "A Comprehensive School Guidance Program at Work" and "How One District Changed Its Program" (1989), described how a comprehensive guidance program was designed, the program's content, how the program was being implemented in a large school district in Texas and the process used to implement it.

Myrick (1987) added his voice to the increasing attention being devoted to developmental approaches to guidance and counseling in the schools. In his book he described the need for a comprehensive developmental guidance and counseling program. "Times have changed, and there is a need for comprehensive developmental guidance and counseling programs that extend from elementary through high school. In addition, there is a need to reorganize guidance curricula, to retrain school counselors and teachers for new guidance and counseling roles, and to be more account-able in meeting the developmental needs of young people. It does not involve a revolution in education, but it does advance the evolution of guidance and counseling in the schools" (p. 32).

Gysbers and Henderson (1988), building on the work of Gysbers and Moore (1981) and on the work begun by Henderson in Northside Independent School District in Texas in the early 1980s, published their book "Developing and Managing Your School Guidance Program," which presented a program model with structural components (definition, rationale and assumptions) and program components (guidance curriculum, individual planning, responsive services and system support). Included were the steps needed to put the program into place and plan, design, implement and evaluate it. A second edition of the book was published in 1994 (Gysbers & Henderson, 1994).

The American School Counselor Association also became involved in providing guidelines for developmental guidance and counseling programs with the work of Barr, Hoffman, Kaplan and Neukrug (1990). They published a document describing a conceptual model "designed to foster the maximum academic, personal-social and career development of students and to prevent problems from occurring or escalating. They also described the program development process including giving attention to evaluation.

State Program Models Are Developed

In the late 1980s, several states developed and published state guides for comprehensive school guidance programs generally patterned after the organizational framework described in Gysbers and Henderson (1988). Examples include Missouri (Starr & Gysbers, 1986), Alaska (Southeast Regional Resource Center, 1989), Idaho (Idaho Department of Education, 1988), New Hampshire (Carr, Hayslip and Randall, (1988), and Utah (Utah State Office of Education, 1989). The purpose of these guides was to assist local school district counselors and administrators in remodeling and revitalizing their local programs. The work of putting comprehensive guidance and counseling programs into practice, begun in the 1980s, continued into the 1990s. Additional states that developed guides in the early 1990s for local school districts to follow included Nebraska (Nebraska Department of Education, 1990), Nevada (Gribble, 1990), Texas (Texas Education Agency, 1990), Colorado (Developmental Guidance Committee, 1991) and South Dakota (South Dakota Curriculum Center, 1991).

How Missouri, Alaska and New Hampshire, as well as several school districts across the country, undertook the planning, designing, implementing and evaluating phases of installing their guidance and counseling programs was documented in "Comprehensive Guidance Programs That Work" (Gysbers, 1990). Other states developed guides in the 1990s including Alabama (Alabama State Department of Education, 1996) or updated and revised previously published guides later in the 1990s. States updating and revising guides developed in the 1980s included Missouri (Gysbers, Starr, & Magnuson, 1998) and Utah (Utah State Office of Education, 1998).

Many Articles and Books Written

In addition to the development of state models for comprehensive guidance and counseling programs being written, considerable literature was devoted to the design and implementation of comprehensive programs in schools. Allen and James (1990) described a comprehensive developmental guidance program that had been developed and implemented in a small rural school district. It had a developmental guidance curriculum, career planning activities and a support system for the program. Rye and Sparks (1991) wrote about the planning and management of a school counseling program. They highlighted the importance of an advisory committee, statements of philosophy and rationale, doing a needs assessment, the establishment of goals and objectives and evaluation. Wittmer (1993) identified similar implementation strategies as being necessary to develop and implement comprehensive programs in the schools. Developing a comprehensive program approach to guidance and counseling in the schools is challenging but implementing it is even more challenging.

Olson and Perrone (1991) took on the task of helping a school district implement a program. They gathered information about changing to a comprehensive program and found factors for and against change. These for and against factors are listed here because they are representative of what happened in many school districts during this time period.

Factors Favoring Change
- A new superintendent who wanted change
- Existence of a state-approved developmental guidance curriculum
- A central office administrator trusted by everyone
- A sense among guidance staff that "something" had to change
- Support for change from school psychologists and school social workers
- Concerns raised by parents and community mental health workers

Factors Against Change
- A dissatisfied, largely nonsupportive board of education
- An indifferent faculty with a few strong antagonists
- An apathetic student body with few supportive students

- Counselors accustomed to doing their own thing
- An understaffed guidance department
- No elementary school guidance personnel
- Some guidance staff with dated skills
- Personality and ideological differences among guidance staff
- Insufficient guidance resources (budget and materials)
- Declining school population and school budget
- Little political support from community
- Minimal communication among guidance staff within and between buildings
- Hidden agendas among guidance staff and administrators
- Ambiguous and dated counselor role descriptions
- Building-specific "personalities" with unique guidance needs
- Overburdened administrators
- No current information regarding students' guidance needs
- No student follow-up information
- No written guidance philosophy and no written guidance objectives
- A history of "false starts" regarding the establishment of guidance programs (pp. 42-43).]

Olson and Perrone reported that at the end of the first year progress had been made in the realignment of the guidance staff and the development of a new administrative structure for the program.

Newbrug, Barr, Hoffman and Kaplan (1993) also described the development of a developmental school counseling and guidance model local school districts could use. It featured a conceptual model and the steps to develop and implement it. Evaluation of the program was noted as a key part of the process.

In addition, Snyder and Daly (1993) spoke about the task of remodeling guidance and counseling in the schools. They described an effort in Orange County, Fla., schools to restructure guidance and counseling to make it more proactive following Myrick's (1987) model. They developed a time frame describing a process to change guidance and counseling "from a crisis-oriented, information service that was unplanned, unstructured and reactive to one that was developmental, planned, sequential, proactive and goal-oriented" (p. 39).

One of the challenges in comprehensive guidance and counseling program development and implementation was overcoming resistance. Nagierkowski and Parsons (1995) noted this challenge, saying, "It is sad that there has been very little attention paid to teaching counselors how to implement these desired programs within resistant realities experienced by many school counselors" (p. 364). They went on to suggest the following principles including keeping the program in line with the culture and values of the system, focusing on people, aligning the program with opinion leaders and demonstrating the value of the program to the system.

Paisley and Peace (1995) called attention to the need to focus on developmental principles in designing school counseling programs. They stated that developmental school counseling programs are based on theory and relevant research, are committed to a particular philosophy and use program planning strategies grounded in human growth and development theory and practice. They suggested that a cognitive developmental approach was a useful approach to guide program development and implementation.

The ERIC Counseling and Student Services Clearinghouse published two books on comprehensive guidance programs. The first described a visit to the comprehensive guidance program at Northside Independent School District from the school counselors' point of view (Bailey, Henderson, Krueger, & Williams, 1995), and the second ("Comprehensive Guidance Programs That Work-II"; Gysbers and Henderson, 1997) featured the work of 10 school districts across the country as well as four states.

As the 1990s ended, comprehensive guidance and counseling programs increasingly were being developed and put into operation as a result of the work of guidance leaders at the state level and the work of counselors, administrators and boards of education at the local level. Gysbers, Lapan and Blair (1999) reported on a statewide study in Missouri indicating progress was being made in implementing comprehensive guidance programs in the schools of Missouri. It was noted that the performance of nonguidance tasks continued to be a barrier to full program implementation.

A nationwide survey conducted by Sink and MacDonald (1998) revealed that approximately one half of the states had developed models for comprehensive guidance and counseling programs, and the authors speculated that by the end of the 1990s this number would increase to 34 or more states. With the increased recognition of guidance as a unique program within schools and the advancement of supervision and administration in the counseling field, new models for providing leadership to school guidance programs and counselors were evolving (Gysbers & Henderson, 1994; Gysbers & Henderson, 1997; Henderson & Gysbers, 1998).

The Importance of Legislation

As described previously, in the 1940s and 1950s, Congress passed the Vocational Education Act of 1946 (P.L. 586) and the National Defense Education Act of 1958 (P. L. 85-864). Each of these acts had substantial, long-lasting impact on the nature, structure and availability of guidance and counseling in the schools. In addition to these two earlier pieces of legislation, the 1960s witnessed the passage of the Elementary and Secondary Education Act of 1965 and the amendment to that act in 1969, both of which provided some funding for school guidance and counseling (Herr, 2003).

Vocational education (career and technical education) legislation has continued to provide support for guidance and counseling in the schools through the reauthorization of such legislation in the 1930s, 1940s, 1950s, 1960s, and 1970s. Beginning in the 1980s, this legislation was named after Carl D. Perkins, a legislator from Kentucky, and was called the Carl D. Perkins Vocational Education Act of 1984 (P.L. 98-524). Subsequent reauthorizations occurred in 1990 (Carl D. Perkins Vocational Education and Applied Technology Education Act of 1990; P.L. 101-392). This act contained the following definition of career guidance and counseling: "(5) The term 'career guidance and counseling' means programs, (a) which pertain to the body of subject matter and related techniques and methods organized for the development in individuals of career awareness, career planning, career decision-making, placement skills, and knowledge and understanding of local, state and national occupational, educational and labor market needs, trends and opportunities; and (b) which assist such individuals in making and implementing informed educational and occupational choices."

Several other federal laws are worth noting. In 1994, the School-to-Work Opportunities Act of 1994 (P.L. 103-239) was passed. It had the same definition of guidance and counseling as the 1990 Carl D. Perkins Act (P.L. 101-392). The same year the Elementary School Counseling Demonstration Act of 1994 (P.L. 103-382) was passed and provided funds for guidance and counseling in the schools.

Then in 1998 the Carl D. Perkins Vocational Technical Act Amendments of 1998 (P.L. 105-332) were passed. It is interesting to note that a dramatic shift in definition of career guidance and counseling occurred. Now it was called career guidance and academic counseling and was defined as follows: "(4) Career Guidance and Academic Counseling – The term 'career guidance and academic counseling' means providing access to information regarding career awareness and planning with respect to an individual's occupational and academic future that shall involve guidance and counseling with respect to career options, financial aid and postsecondary options.

Political Advocacy Emphasized

In the 1980s political action was on school counselors' minds. Articles were being written exhorting school counselors to become politically active. For example, a special issue of *The Personnel and Guidance Journal* was devoted to this topic in 1982 (Solomon, 1982). In it articles were written on topics such as the case for political action, the need for political awareness and case studies in political action. Of particular interest is an article by Robinson (1982) stressing the need for school counselors to be politically active in light of what he called new conservative challenges, particularly classroom guidance or consultation activities "that utilize techniques or processes drawn from behavior modification, client-centered therapy, decision making, human relations, group dynamics, magic circle or values clarification ..." (p. 601). He recommended the following actions be taken.

"It behooves each of us to examine the basic tenets of our profession, check current abuses that lend credence to the cries of the critics and begin to act positively and responsibly in containing the current political realignment in order to ensure that the self-serving "politics of resentment" noted by Crawford (1980) are not legitimized under the current conservative climate (p. 602).

Kaplan (1996), writing on the same topic, felt it was important for school counselors to consider the concerns parents have whether they are outrageous or legitimate. Among the parental concerns she addressed were different values and practices in school counseling and confidentially. She felt it was important to separate outrageous concerns from legitimate ones, listen respectfully and bring parents into the program. Writing later, Kaplan (1997) stressed the need to listen and work with parents. She stated that although some parents' rights advocates will not be satisfied no matter what is done, it is important to work with all parents. "Parents who have challenging and unanswered questions about their children's education and safety put school counselors at risk. Effectively addressing student achievement, communication and research may not satisfy parents' rights advocates whose values oppose public education in general and school counseling in particular. It may, however, reassure and enlist other parents whose implicit rights are equally valid. School counselors need not barricade against parents' rights but can better listen to each parent's interests and support his or her efforts to raise healthy, well-educated children" (p. 342).

As developmental, comprehensive guidance and counseling programs were being implemented increasingly across the United States, some groups of citizens began raising questions about some of the activities being used as noted by Robinson (1982). Brigman and Moore (1994) stated that "Censorship is on the rise and threatens the progress made in expanding developmental counseling programs" (p. 3).

Among the activities being questions, the following types of counseling or counseling-related programs have been most frequently challenged:

- **Developmental counseling:** Especially the preventive, classroom guidance component, which includes most, if not all, of the categories below.
- **Self-esteem programs:** Most prevention programs such as Quest and Project Charlie, as well as the programs listed below under Affective Education, including a self-esteem component. All developmental counseling programs include a self-esteem focus.
- **Affective education:** This is a broad category, including social-emotional development programs such as DUSO, PUMSY, Positive Action and TAD.
- **Relaxation and imagery:** These two are frequently cited as the most objectional parts of the programs challenged.
- **Thinking skills and cooperative learning:** Programs teaching children to think critically, make decisions, solve problems and which involve small-group discussion are seen by some as undermining parental authority (p. 5).

Gysbers and Henderson (1994) also called attention to the issue of censorship. They described individuals who saw the work of school counselors as an invasion of privacy, an attempt to undermine family values or anti-spiritual as critical constituents. They described a number of ways to work with such constituents including developing policies and procedures to handle complaints and, most importantly, being proactive in responding to challenges and concerns.

The American School Counselor Association (ASCA) also was directly involved in dealing with censorship. In 1985, the association issued a position statement titled "The School Counselor and Censorship." In 1990 ASCA issued another position statement, "The School Counselor and Developmental Guidance."

Interest in the Guidance Curriculum Continued

Interest in a curriculum for guidance and counseling continued in the 1980s and 1990s. Martin (1983) noted that in the 1980s school counselors faced a number of problems including high counselor-student ratios, an emphasis on remedial versus preventive/developmental programs and school counselors being seen as frills. To respond to problems such as these Martin proposed a three-pronged solution:

- A clear recognition that counseling is a form of instruction and that counselors must function as curriculum developers if they are to be effective and efficient in discharging their instructional roles in today's schools;
- The development, field-testing and implementation of counseling curricula in regularly scheduled, academic periods in schools; and
- Changes in the areas of counselor education, research in counseling, and implementation (p. 407).

Morgan (1984) described the importance of moving guidance from a "frill" to becoming part of the mandated curriculum of the school. As a mandated curriculum it would be taught to all students K-6. The curriculum was based on the following premises:

- Guidance is a curricular program with goals, objectives and specific methods (including guidance media and material and particular student activities), and it should incorporate an evaluation process.
- The scope and sequence of the guidance curriculum can be described.
- Students are entitled to instruction in the guidance and affective areas, and this instruction is essential if students are to learn efficiently.
- Teachers are competent to implement and conduct such a program when they are provided with inservice training and support (p. 467-468).

Morgan went on to provide a definition for guidance as well as suggest goals for a guidance curriculum. The guidance definition states that guidance and counseling is that part of the school program enabling students to understand themselves, understand their relationship with others, and acquire the ability to make decisions leading to productive and enriched living. Curriculum goals included:

- Students will develop their personal selves to the fullest.
- Students will exhibit effective interpersonal skills
- Students will take responsibility for giving direction to their lives (p. 468).

Aubrey (1985) was concerned about the lack of school counselor involvement in what he called the mainstream of education. He had reviewed various educational reform documents and found few even mentioned school counseling. He felt school counselors were partly to blame for this because they have chosen "not to be an integral part of the mainstream of education" and "not to enter the school curriculum or 'teach' content to students" (p. 95). He urged school counselors to "enter and 'own' some of this turf, for they have unique skills and knowledge to impart to students" (p. 97).

Nicoll (1994) stressed the need for classroom guidance to be developed within a conceptual framework. He recommended that Adlerian psychology could provide that framework. He then outlined a five-state framework around which to develop a classroom guidance curriculum. He felt the goal of such a curriculum was to assist "teachers to develop more personally effective students and more effective classroom environments, thereby increasing the effectiveness of classroom instruction" (p. 364).

Interest in the content for guidance and counseling (knowledge and skills, sometimes called competencies) continued in the 1980s and 1990s. ASCA assumed an active role in identifying student outcomes. In "Counseling Paints a Bright Future," student competencies were identified and organized around the domains of personal/social, educational and career. Then in 1997 national standards for student competencies were published (Campbell & Dahir, 1997). These standards used the domains of academic, career and personal/social development to group nine standards, three in each domain. The next year Dahir, Sheldon, and Valiga (1998) published "Vision into Action," which described the process to implement these standards.

The Status of Guidance and Counseling

Even as the details of the nature and structure of the program approach to guidance and counseling were beginning to emerge and evolve as a way to solidify the place of guidance and counseling in education and provide a way to clarify the role and function of school counselors, some writers were continuing to express concern about the status of guidance and counseling in the schools and the role and function of school counselors. Aubrey (1982), in a major article on the topic, described the evolution of guidance and counseling in the schools. His analysis, he stated, "reveals a house divided by diversity and contradictions" (p. 198).

"Diversity and contradiction within the field of school guidance and counseling have not stemmed solely from contending internal ideologies. The guidance movement has also been characterized by a series of competing methodologies (Stefflre & Grant, 1972). As these competing counseling methodologies proliferated, they tended to focus the attention of counselors on technique and process and away from consideration of objectives and content. This is important historically because alterations in counseling methodology sometimes triggered changes in the substance and priority of school guidance programs" (p. 199).

Aubrey went on to state that because of this diversity and these contradictions guidance and counseling remained outside of the mainstream of education. "As a consequence, students and teacher alike continued to view guidance and counseling as a supportive, supplementary and ancillary activity in public schools. Irrespective of lofty myths and a greatly improved technology, guidance and counseling remained on the periphery of American education, desirous of eminence and influence but hesitant and uncertain" (p. 203).

The status of the United States economy and the potential for cutbacks in education in general and guidance and counseling specifically in the 1980s were also of concern to the profession. As mentioned previously, a similar situation occurred in the 1930s. Atkinson, Skipworth and Stevens (1983) described what happened in a school district in California when a decision was made to eliminate school counselors and replace them with administrators called deans of student services. In their article they described how school and community resources were brought together as advocates with the result that the plan to eliminate school counselors was withdrawn. Berger's (1983) article described unique problems school counselors face in years of declining budgets. He shared four survival strategies including becoming a friendly adversary, building coalitions, reviewing budgets and being strategically political.

During the 1980s a number of reports were issued addressing the condition of education. Aubrey (1984) reviewed four such reports in detail and found that guidance and counseling with a few exceptions was notable because of its absence. Herr (1984) summed up his review of these national reports as follows:

"If the national reports have done nothing else, they have made it clear that school counselors must increase their efforts to acquaint policy makers with the contributions they make to the educational priorities of states and the nation. They must ensure that policy makers do not consider counselors as specialists of the past, professionals whose skills are obsolete in the contemporary world of advanced technology. In addition, the omissions in the national reports remind school counselors that they have an important role to play in advocating to policy makers that student learners are not abstract pawns to be moved hither and yon as international political and economic conditions change. Rather, students are developing as individually unique human beings whose intellectual and emotional lives are interactive parts of a dynamic whole; educational reform of any kind must recognize both this reality and the complexity of its implications for change. Finally, school counselors must be assertive about the record of empirical successes on which their practice rests and the direct relevance these areas of demonstrated competency hold for the achievement of educational reform. If such results should ensue from the national reports, all of the effort they represent would be worth the expenditures" (p. 219).

One of the concerns affecting the status of school counseling is what one author called "the privatization of school counseling" (p. 29) (Dykeman, 1995). Dykeman pointed to the growing movement toward the privatization of public education in the 1990s. He was particularly concerned about the movement to privatize counseling. He conducted a study in the state of Washington and found that 26 percent of all counseling in the public schools was contracted to outside agencies. He called for more research on this movement to ascertain its effectiveness and its impact on the work of school counselors.

The Continuing Debate about Role and Function

Concern about the identity of school counselors and their role and function that had been voiced in earlier decades continued in the 1980s and 1990s. Various opinions were expressed about the focus of the work of school counselors. Hays (1980) for example, felt the field needed to transform itself to meet the challenges of the future with school counselors becoming human development specialists. Podemski and Childers (1980) called for school counselors to become change agents. Boy and Pine (1980) wondered if negotiating a behavioral contract with principals would clarify the role and function issue for school counselors. Schmidt (1984) was concerned about this issue as well. He felt the survival of the profession required the following:

"First, members of the profession should have consensus about their role and function, as well as the training and education needed to perform their professional responsibilities. Second, the consumers of the profession's services should have a common understanding of what to expect. They should also be confident that the professional's level of skill can meet their expectations. Finally, a profession must demonstrate effectiveness – either short-term, long-term or both. In our society, few movements, products or services survive without "demand," and counseling in schools will not survive unless the public and the school system recognizes its benefits and have faith in professional counselors" (p. 391).

A popular approach to determine school counselor role and function during the 1980s and 1990s was to survey counselors, administrators and teachers. Hutchinson, Barrick, and Groves (1986) surveyed 56 secondary school counselors in Indiana. They found that:

"In most cases, counselors reported actually doing what they thought they should be doing. Group counseling, career and life planning and classroom guidance activities, however, were functions for which counselors found less time than they believed they should. Scheduling, testing, record keeping and noncounseling activities required more counselor time and attention than counselors believed was warranted" (p. 90).

Miller (1988) sent a survey to 666 excellent public schools across the country identified by the U.S. Department of Education. A total of 419 were used in the study. The survey of 34 items was factor-analyzed, producing eight factors. A rauls ordering of these factors for elementary, middle and high school counselors was completed with the following results:

"For elementary school counselors, the rankings were as follows:
(1) Counseling and Consulting
(2) Coordinating
(3) Professional Development
(4) Career Assistance
(5) Organization
(6) Educational Planning
(7) Assessment
(8) Discipline
The middle school counselors had the following rankings:
(1) Counseling and Consultation
(2) Coordination
(3) Career Assistance
(4) Professional Development
(5) Organization
(6) Educational Planning
(7) Assessment
(8) Discipline
At the high school level, the counselors' rankings were:
(1) Counseling/Consultation
(2) Career Assistance
(3) Coordination
(4) Professional Development
(5) Educational Planning
(6) Organization
(7) Assessment
(8) Discipline (pp. 91-92).

Then in 1989, *The School Counselor* devoted an entire issue to the role and function debate. It was edited by Ponzo (1989). In the introduction he challenged school counselors to go beyond perseverating about role and function and to take action. He stated that the authors of the special issue realized it was imperative that the profession take a stand on the role and function issue, advocate for it and work to implement it.

Parsley and Borders (1995) spoke about school counseling as an evolving specialty and identified specific issues they felt school counseling faced. One issue they identified was control over the profession. Another issue focused on school counselors' role and the nature of supervision they received. They stated that the question of what is counseling in the schools continues to be asked particularly focusing around the issue of whether or not school counselors should be doing "therapy."

During the 1990s concern was expressed by some about meeting the mental health needs of at-risk youth. Keys, Bemak and Lockhart (1998), writing on this topic, felt that although school counselors have an important role to play in working with at-risk youth, they thought the structure of the currently proposed developmental guidance and counseling programs was inadequate to provide appropriate services to these youth. They proposed a three-part transformed model to respond to the needs of at-risk youth. First, in the program organization and planning phase, school counselors would provide "leadership within the school for an alliance with school-based mental health professionals and help to establish school-based mechanisms to support a variety of collaborative efforts" (p. 384). Second, the functions of coordination, consultation and counseling would be redefined to meet the needs of at-risk youth. Third, they recommended a list of skills and expertise for school counselors to acquire to include understanding differences between normal and abnormal development, command of systems theory, multicultural counseling techniques, and direct and indirect services.

The issue of school counselor time-on-tasks was a frequently researched and discussed topic in the 1980s and 1990s. In a study conducted in Ohio, Partin (1993) found that although school counselors do spend time in individual and small-group counseling, they would like to spend more time doing these activities. As has been documented in previous studies, Tennyson, Miller, Skovolt and Williams (1989) found that other duties as assigned were pervasive and were "time robbers."

"Particularly for senior high counselors, paper work, scheduling and administrative tasks are seen as significant time robbers that deter counselors from allotting more time for individual and group counseling. In many schools the counselor's role has evolved into that of an assistant principal. If not on paper, at least by default, the counselor's job description has grown to encompass a vast array of non-counseling duties, from supervising restrooms to conducting school fundraising drives. This seems to be less the case with elementary counselors, although they are asked to substitute for absent teachers more often than middle school-junior high or senior high teachers" (pp. 279-280).

The Terminology Issue Again

The terminology issue for school counselors' work remained an issue in the 1980s and 1990s. Myrick (1987) stated that the term guidance had always presented a problem to users. "It is a term in education that has flip-flopped with the word 'counseling' for more than 50 years" (p. 3). He went on to point out that traditionally the word guidance was an "umbrella" term that organized a grouping of services while counseling was used to describe a helping process. To make matters worse, he said, the terms guidance and counseling are sometimes used interchangeably. For his purpose he decided to use school guidance as the title of a grouping of services with counseling being one of those services.

Hoyt (1993) surveyed ASCA leadership and found that they favored the use of the word counseling rather than guidance to label their work. Hence the program would be called counseling rather than guidance. Hoyt disagreed strongly with this point-of-view.

"In my opinion, *guidance* is not a dirty word; counseling is a proper new name for guidance; and counseling is one of the functions of [guidance]— not vice versa" (p. 273).

Hoyt (1993) also weighed in on whether or not counselors were educators first and then counselors. In his opinion, school counselors were educators first. As we know the issue of title and orientation continues today with discussion focusing on, "Is it guidance? Is it counseling? Is it both? Are school counselors educators who counsel or vice versa?"

Work on the Role and Function of Elementary School Counselors Continues

The debate about elementary school counselors' role and function continued to take center stage in the literature in the 1980s and 1990s. This literature offered a variety of opinions as to their role and function.

Kameen, Robinson and Rotter, (1985) were concerned about the coordination role. They surveyed elementary and middle school counselors in 12 southeastern states. The data they presented "strongly suggest that systematic coordination of guidance programs is paramount to effective delivery of services" (p. 102). They went on to recommend the coordination skills school counselors require including "managerial skills, interpersonal skills, decision-making skills, team-building skills, program-planning skills and evaluation skills" (p. 102).

Wilgus and Shelley (1988) found, "As the counselor's role evolves, a continual redefining of priority functions finds direct counseling services, staff consultation and parent consultation to be our 'laison d'etre'" (p. 265). Humes and Hohenshil (1987) stressed the need for elementary school counselors to provide developmental and prevention programs. Bauer and Sapona (1988) urged elementary school counselors to collaborate closely with teachers.

In a discussion with ASCA leaders (Bailey, Deery, Gehrke, Perry & Whitledge, 1989) there was agreement "that the major focus of elementary counseling programs should be to create a positive school environment for students through a comprehensive developmental approach to guidance and counseling" (p. 6). They agreed that the three C's of counseling, coordination, and consultation were critical strategies. To the three C's they added the fourth C of curriculum.

Myrick (1989) agreed developmental guidance and counseling was a good idea at the elementary level. Within a developmental program designed to provide services to all students, he stressed the need for an organized guidance curriculum. While perhaps integrated into the total educational process, there also would be stand-alone guidance units focusing on personal and social development. He also stressed the need for teacher involvement as well as careful management of elementary counselor time built around six basic interventions.

"There are six basic counselor interventions around which counselors can build their schedules: individual counseling (e.g., four to six cases); small-group counseling (four to six groups seen twice a week); large-group guidance (two to four classrooms, once or twice a week); peer facilitator training (one to two hours a week); consultation with teachers and parents (one hour a day); and coordination of guidance activities" (p. 19).

Casting the elementary guidance and counseling program as a developmental program was popular during the 1980s and 1990s. So was the use of the term preventive program. Gibson (1989), in a survey of 114 elementary schools, found 85 percent of them had an emphasis in prevention compared with 12 percent with an emphasis in crisis work.

Consultation as a role for elementary school counselors also continued to be popular. For example, Dustin and Ehly (1992) stressed the importance of the consultation role. They described four models most relevant for elementary counselors, namely, "the mental health model, the behavioral model, the Adlerian model and the advocacy model" (p. 166). They then described the processes involved in consultation as well as what they thought the future of consultation would be in the 21st century. They predicted that the consultation role would continue to grow.

Hall and Liu (1994) stated that consultation was "one of the primary responsibilities of the school counselor" (p. 16). They described an integrative consultation model that provided a theory-based, systematic and eclectic approach. They identified a framework for consultation that included consultation goal, consulting, relationship, consultant role, consultee role, consultation process and consultant communication skills. They also identified stages of consultation including entry, diagnosis, implementation and disengagement.

In a study of 95 elementary school counselors in the state of Connecticut, Carroll (1993) found they supported the traditional roles of consultant, coordinator and counselor. They also supported delivering classroom guidance units but were not able to do much of this because of a lack of time. They also felt they lacked training in needs assessment and program evaluation.

Do elementary school counselors have a role to play in school discipline? Benshoff, Poidevant, and Cashwell (1994) stated that school counselors "may need to assume a more prominent role [in schools' discipline programs] by (a) educating school personnel about discipline models and their potential impact on students and (b) influencing schoolwide decisions about adoption of these programs" (pp. 163-164). They saw school counselors as internal consultants to administrators and other school staff on discipline policies and procedures.

An interesting topic that appeared in the 1990s was the issue of role conflict among elementary school counselors. Coll and Freeman (1997) reported that 525 elementary school counselors in their sample reported higher levels of role conflict than middle (468) and high school counselors (417) did. For elementary school counselors role conflict centered around not having the appropriate structure or the resources to do what they were asked to do. They also experienced more role overload (too many roles) and incongruency of roles (working with groups with different expectations) than did their peers in middle and high school.

One of the issues facing elementary school counseling was advocacy or as one author put it "image-building." Green (1988) stated the need for "image building" as follows:

"Elementary counselors need to create and maintain the image of a specialist. Counselors should be aware, however, that once an image is created, people will demand the delivery of services commensurate with professional expertise. Overselling oneself or creating an image that exceeds a level of credibility can tarnish and eventually destroy professional image" (p. 190).

In a similar fashion, Holcomb and Niffenegger (1992) recommended using educational reform as a springboard for advocacy for elementary guidance and counseling. They emphasized the need for an effective, systematic marketing plan linking the work of elementary school counselors to the goals of educational reform.

The training of elementary school counselors also was of concern in the 1980s and 1990s. Concern was expressed, for example about the similarity of training for elementary and secondary school counselors. Hosie and Mackey (1985) conducted a survey of counselor preparation programs that graduate both elementary and secondary school counselors. They found "that little progress has been made since 1973 in differentiating between elementary training programs" (p. 289), and this was a cause for concern.

Finally, an interesting development occurred in the 1970s in Oregon when the state legislature authorized a new elementary specialist, a child development specialist (CDS). The services of the CDS "were designed to *recognize, define, preserve* and *promote* a child's strengths" (Sheldon & Morgan, 1984, p. 471). Sheldon and Morgan described the role of this new professional as follows:

- Observing and analyzing behaviors in social systems using concepts such as attitude change, interpersonal relations, social stratification, group dynamics, leadership, stereotypes and physical development of the individual child;
- Establishing counseling and supporting relationships that help children and adults deal with school-related problems;
- Explaining the functions of the following types of measurements: achievement tests, intelligence tests, behavioral observations, sociometric tests and rating scales;

- Communicating the results of assessment (in cooperation with specialists) to children, parents and teachers;
- Working effectively in schools, agencies and the community.
- Identifying resources and making appropriate referrals;
- Planning, coordinating and consulting with others to provide educational programs in areas such as human relations, student records, test interpretation, parent conferences, child development and parenting skills;
- Using interpersonal skills such as leadership, working with groups, family counseling and individual counseling;
- Developing and implementing an organizational plan;
- Recognizing and developing the strengths and positive characteristics of primary age children; and
- Identifying and using teacher materials dealing with the affective domain (p. 472).

Leadership and Supervision Concerns Continue

Concerns about the need for leadership and supervision of school counselors continued to be expressed in the 1980s and 1990s.

Henderson (1986) found building-based guidance program department heads needed and wanted to provide better leadership of school counselors. They recognized their staff members' needs for assistance, but they lacked supervisory skill and program vision and were somewhat lacking in commitment to the counseling profession. They were not applying the scientific approaches of instructional supervision. They observed school counselors without recording what they saw, and they did not use formal mechanisms for providing feedback. In turn, district-level guidance program staff leaders did not provide effective supervision to the building-based leaders either.

Yet, as with the counseling profession as a whole, training for fulfilling supervisory roles was not readily available. Barret and Schmidt (1986) wrote that "in the specialty area of school counseling little has been done to generate a consensus about certification standards or supervision expectations" (p. 50). Henderson (1986) found that building-level guidance program staff leaders were selected "because they were for some external reason – money, prestige – motivated to seek the position. Also, they were selected because principals felt they had earned the respect of their colleagues for professional leadership" (p. 42). On the other hand, as had been well-described earlier, school counselors were "often supervised primarily by principals and other administrative personnel who have little or no training in counseling" (Barret & Schmidt, 1986, p. 52).

For school counselors directly supervised by their building principals, Lampe (1985) found the vast majority of principal training programs didn't require their students to take a separate course in school guidance: a few do, most offer it as an elective, a few include the content in other courses and very few do not include it at all. Often, if they wanted to fulfill a legitimate supervisory role, principals had attempted to modify models of instructional supervision developed for use with teachers to apply to counselors (Childers & Podemski, 1985).

Barret and Schmidt (1986) proposed a solution that made sense in the context of the 1980s for the provision of effective assistance for school counselor performance improvement. It integrated the needed approaches to supervision and suggested ways to make appropriate use of the leadership talent available:

"Should counselor supervision be categorized as a threefold process: administrative (performed by principals with a focus on employee attendance, punctuality, staff relations, outreach to parents); clinical (performed by properly trained and certified counseling supervisors with a focus on direct service delivery); and developmental (performed by program coordinators with a focus on program development, in-service training and other systemwide concerns)?" (p. 53)

A primary obstacle in the 1980s and 1990s was the insufficient number of individuals who were competent in school counseling and in school administration or supervision. Thus, often different individuals fulfilled different roles, but their respective roles and responsibilities were not clarified. The building principals could provide useful administrative supervision, but it is unlikely that they were current in the clinical functions of counseling.

By the 1990s, however, some consensus was emerging as to what staff leadership efforts were required to help school counselors carry out their work most effectively. For example, Henderson and Gysbers (1998) described a model for building and district guidance program leadership. In the model are descriptions of the essential work of guidance program staff leaders at the building and district levels. Tasks such as defining school counselors' roles and responsibilities with a program, assessing their individual levels of professionalism, providing supervision, evaluating their competence, team building for effective program implementation and advocating for school counselors were fully described in their book.

Major Trends and Issues

The 1980s and 1990s witnessed progress being made in defining and describing guidance and counseling in the schools. It was a time of increased professional activity. Many books and articles were published on all aspects of guidance and counseling.

The concept of a program of guidance and counseling, talked about since the 1970s, began to take form in the 1960s and 1970s and then became a major way to organize and manage guidance and counseling in the schools in the 1980s and 1990s. The work of individuals such as Gysbers and Moore (1974; 1981), Gysbers and Henderson (1988; 1994), Johnson and Johnson (1982; 1991) and Myrick (1987) served as the foundation for the program concept and provided ideas for its framework. Their work also helped identify and describe the steps necessary to implement and manage guidance and counseling programs as well as provided ideas about how to evaluate these programs.

As the 1980s and 1990s unfolded states began the process of developing state models for guidance and counseling programs. Many states and local school districts initiated training programs to help personnel in school districts plan, design and implement comprehensive school guidance and counseling programs. Work was also underway to develop ways to evaluate school counselors and the programs in which they worked.

The importance of legislation supporting comprehensive guidance and counseling programs also received attention. A number of articles emphasized the importance of political advocacy focusing on state and federal legislation. ASCA and the American Counseling Association became increasingly active.

A curriculum for guidance and counseling, an idea that has been part of guidance and counseling since the beginning of the movement, received a great deal of attention in the literature. This attention caused the field to focus on what some writers called the "content" for guidance. It became increasingly common to use the domains of academic, career and personal-social to organize this content, although the titles of these domains were by no means consistent across the country. It is interesting to note that what had once been types of guidance (educational-academic, vocational-career and personal-social) were now the titles of the "content" for guidance and counseling.

The status of guidance and counseling in society and in the educational system continued to be of concern to some writers. During this time period a number of major reports about education were issued. Their focus was on the need for educational reform. It was noted that these reports failed to mention guidance and counseling as having a role in educational reform.

Guidance and counseling in the schools also received some attention that was unwelcome. Some groups were highly critical of the work of school counselors, feeling that the roles of parents were being undermined. The term critical constituents was used to describe these individuals. This led to ASCA's position statement on censorship.

The role and function issue for school counselors was of great concern during this time period. Some writers advocated the role of human development specialist, other writers recommended the role of change agent. Predominating roles were coordinating, counseling and consulting, with other duties frequently added that had nothing to do with guidance and counseling. Tied to the role and function issue was the terminology issue. Is it guidance, guidance and counseling or counseling?

The new "kid on the block," elementary guidance and counseling, also received a great deal of attention. Surveys were done to examine elementary school counselor role and function. Emphasis in the literature was given to developmental preventive programs in which elementary school counselors would counsel, coordinate, consult and collaborate. The curriculum was also emphasized as a major vehicle for elementary school counselors.

Finally, by the 1990s, the need for effective leadership and supervision of school counselors had been well-established. There was recognition that building and district leaders were required to bring school counselors together to develop, implement and manage school counseling programs. There also was recognition that building and district leaders needed to be well-trained with the necessary knowledge and skills to carry out the essential work of leaders.

References

Alabama State Department of Education (1996). *The revised comprehensive counseling and guidance state model for Alabama's public schools* (Bulletin 1996, No. 27). Montgomery, AL: Author.

Allen, S., & James, R. (1990). A developmental guidance program for the rural schoolhouse. *The School Counselor, 37,* 184-191.

American School Counselor Association (1974). *The school counselor and the guidance and counseling program.* Alexandria, VA: Author.

American School Counselor Association (1978). *The school counselor and developmental guidance.* Alexandria, VA: Author.

American School Counselor Association (1985). *The school counselor and censorship, position statement.* Alexandria, VA: Author.

American School Counselor Association (1988; 1993; 1997). *The professional school counselor and comprehensive school counseling programs.* Alexandria, VA: Author.

American School Counselor Association (1990). *The school counselor and developmental guidance, position statement.* Alexandria, VA: Author.

American School Counselor Association (n.d.). *Counseling points a bright future.* Alexandria, VA: Author.

Atkinson, D. R., Skipworth, D., & Stevens, F. (1983). Inundating the school board with support for counselors: An eleventh hour strategy for saving an endangered species. *The Personnel and Guidance Journal, 61,* 387-389.

Aubrey, R. F. (1982). A house divided: Guidance and counseling in 20th Century America. *The Personnel and Guidance Journal, 61,* 198-204.

Aubrey, R. F. (1984). Reform in schooling: Four proposals on a educational quest. *Journal of Counseling and Development, 63,* 204-213.

Aubrey, R. F. (1985). A counseling perspective on the recent educational reform reports. *The School Counselor, 33,* 91-99.

Bailey, M., Henderson, P., Krueger, D., & Williams, L. (1995). *A visit to a comprehensive guidance program that works.* Greensboro, NC: ERIC Counseling and Student Services Clearinghouse.

Bailey, W. R., Deery, N. K., Gehrke, M., Perry, N., & Whitledge, J. (1989). Issues in elementary school counseling: Discussion with American School Counselor Association leaders. *Elementary School Guidance and Counseling, 24,* 4-13.

Barr, C. G., Hoffman, L. R., Kaplan, L. S., & Neubrug, E. S. (1990). *ASCA guidelines for developing a developmental school counseling and guidance program* (mimeograph copy).

Barret, R. L., & Schmidt, J. J. (1986). School counselor certification and supervision: Overlooked professional issues. *Counselor Education and Supervision, 26,* 50-55.

Bauer, A. M. & Sapona, R. H. (1988). Facilitation and problem solving: A framework for collaboration between counselors and teachers. *Elementary School Guidance and Counseling, 23,* 5-9.

Benshoff, J. M., Poidevant, J. M., & Cashwell, C. S. (1994). *Elementary School Guidance and Counseling, 28,* 163-169.

Berger, M. A. (1983). The preservation of counseling in an Era of cutback management. *The Personnel and Guidance Journal, 62,* 170-173.

Boy, A. V., & Pine, G. J. (1980). A new approach to defining the counselor's role. *The School Counselor, 27,* 156-157.

Brigman, G., & Moore, P. (1994). *School counselors and censorship: Facing the challenge.* Alexandria, VA: American School Counselor Association.

Campbell, C. A., & Dahir, C. A. (1997). *Sharing the Vision? The national standards for school counseling programs.* Alexandria, VA: American School Counselor Association.

Carr, J. V., Hayslip, J., & Randall, J. (1988). *New Hampshire comprehensive guidance and counseling program: A guide to an approved model for program development.* Plymouth, NH: Plymouth State College.

Carroll, B. W. (1993). Perceived roles and preparation experiences of elementary counselors: Suggestions for change. *Elementary School Guidance and Counseling, 27,* 216-226.

Childers, J. H., & Podemski, R. (1985). Developing and supervising the counselor role. *TACD Journal, 13,* 29-36.

Coll, K. M., & Freeman, B. (1997). Role conflict among elementary school counselors: A national comparison with middle and secondary school counselors. *Elementary School Guidance and Counseling, 31,* 251-261.

College Entrance Examination Board (1986). *Keeping the options open: Recommendations.* New York: Author.

Dahir, C. A., Sheldon, C. B., & Valiga, M. J. (1998). *Vision into action.* Alexandria, VA: American School Counselor Association.

Developmental Guidance Committee (1991). *A team approach to guiding students to excellence: A comprehensive school guidance program at work in Colorado.* Denver, CO: Colorado School Counselor Association.

Dustin, D., & Ehly, S. (1992). School consultation in the 1990s. *Elementary School Guidance and Counseling, 26,* 165-175.

Dykeman, C. (1995). The privatization of school counseling. *The School Counselor, 43*, 29-34.

Gibson, R. L. (1989). Prevention and the elementary school counselor. *Elementary School Guidance and Counseling, 24*, 30-36.

Green, R. L. (1988). Image-building activities for the elementary school counselor. *Elementary School Guidance and Counseling, 22*, 186-191.

Gribble, C. (1990). *Nevada school and counseling: Grades K-12.* Carson City, Nevada State Department of Education.

Gysbers N. C., & Henderson, P. (1994). *Developing and managing your school guidance program* (2nd Ed.). Alexandria, VA: American Counseling Association.

Gysbers N. C., & Henderson, P. (1997). *Comprehensive guidance programs that work—II.* Greensboro, NC: ERIC Counseling and student Services Clearinghouse.

Gysbers, N. C., & Henderson, P. (1988). *Developing and managing your school guidance program.* Alexandra, VA: American Counseling Association.

Gysbers, N. C., & Henderson, P. (1994). *Developing and managing your school guidance program* (2nd Ed.). Alexandria, VA: American Counseling Association.

Gysbers, N. C., & Moore, E. J. (1981). *Improving guidance programs.* Englewood Cliffs, NJ: Prentice-Hall.

Gysbers, N. C., & Moore, E. J. (Eds.) (1974). *Career guidance counseling and placement: Elements of an illustrative program guide.* Columbia: University of Missouri.

Gysbers, N. C., Lapan, R. T., & Blair, M (1999). Closing in on the statewide implementation of a comprehensive guidance program model. *Professional School Counseling, 2*, 357-366.

Gysbers, N. C., Starr, M. F., & Magnuson, C. S. (1998). *Missouri comprehensive guidance: A model for program development and implementation* (Rev. ed.). Jefferson City: Missouri Department of Elementary and Secondary Education.

Gysbers, N. C., with Guidance Program Field Writers (1990). *Comprehensive guidance programs that work.* Ann Arbor, MI: ERIC Counseling and Personnel Services Clearinghouse.

Hall, A. S., & Lin, M. J. (1994). An integrative consultation framework: A practical tool for elementary school counselors. *Elementary School Guidance and Counseling, 29*, 16-27.

Hargens, M., & Gysbers, N. C. (1984). How to remodel a guidance program while living in it: A case study. *The School Counselor, 32*, 119-125.

Hays, D. G. (1980). The buffalo, the dodo bird, and the whooping crane. *The School Counselor, 27,* 255-262.

Henderson, P. (1987). A comprehensive school guidance program at work. *Texas Association for Counseling and Development Journal, 10,* 25-37.

Henderson, P. (1989). How one district changed its program. *The School Counselor, 37,* 31-40.

Henderson, P. G. (1986). *Improving the high school guidance program by improving the performance of the counseling staff through staff development, inservice education, supervision and evaluation.* Unpublished doctoral dissertation, Nova University, Fort Lauderdale, FL.

Henderson, P., & Gysbers, N. C., (1998). *Leading and managing your school guidance program staff.* Alexandria, VA: American Counseling Association.

Herr, E. L. (1979). *Guidance and counseling in the schools: The past, present, and future.* Washington, DC: American Personnel and Guidance Association.

Herr, E. L. (1984). The national reports on reform in schooling: Some missing ingredients. *Journal of Counseling and Development, 63,* 217-220.

Holcomb, T. F., & Niffernegger, P. B. (1992). Elementary school counselors: A plan for marketing their services under the new education reform. *Elementary School Guidance and Counseling, 27,* 56-63.

Hosie, T. W., & Mackey, J. A. (1985). Elementary and secondary school counselor preparation programs: How different are they? *Counselor Education and Supervision, 24,* 283-290.

Hoyt, K. B. (1993). Guidance is not a dirty word. *The School Counselor, 40,* 267-273.

Humes, C. W., & Hohenshil, T. H. (1987). Elementary counselors, school psychologists, school social workers: Who does what? *Elementary School Guidance and Counseling, 22,* 37-45.

Hutchinson, R. L., Barrick, A. L., & Groves, M. (1986). Functions of secondary school counselors in public schools: Ideal and actual. *The School Counselor, 34,* 87-91.

Idaho Department of Education (1988). *Idaho comprehensive guidance and counseling program model.* Boise, ID: Author.

Johnson, C. D., & Johnson, S. K. (1982). *Competency-based training of career development specialists or "let's get off the calf path".* Vocational Guidance Quarterly, 30, 327-335.

Johnson, S. K., & Johnson, C. D. (1991). The new guidance: A system approach to pupil personnel programs. *CACD Journal, 11,* 5-14.

Kameen, M. C., Robinson, E. H., & Rotter, J. C. (1985). Coordination activities: A study of perceptions of elementary and middle school counselors. *Elementary School Guidance and Counseling, 20,* 97-104.

Kaplan, L. S. (1996). Outrageous or legitimate concerns: What some parents are saying about school counseling. *The School Counselor, 43,* 165-170.

Kaplan. L. S. (1997). Parents' rights: Are school counselors at risk? *The School Counselor, 44,* 334-343.

Keys, S. G., Bemak, F., & Lockhart, E. J. (1998). Transforming school counseling to serve the mental health needs of at-risk youth. *Journal of Counseling & Development, 76,* 381-388.

Lampe, R. E. (1985). Principals' training in counseling and development: A national survey. *Counselor Education and Supervision, 25,* 44-47.

Martin, J. (1983). Curriculum development in school counseling. *The Personnel and Guidance Journal, 61,* 406-409.

Martin, P. J. (2002). Transforming school counseling: A national perspective. *Theory into Practice, 41,* 148-153.

Massachusetts School Counselor Association (1991). *Comprehensive developmental guidance and counseling curriculum guide and role statement revision.* Fitchburg, MA: Author.

Miller, G. M. (1988). Counselor functions in excellent schools: Elementary through secondary. *The School Counselor, 36,* 88-93.

Missouri Comprehensive Guidance (1986). *The Counseling Interviewer, 18,* 6-17.

Morgan, C. (1984). A curricular approach to primary prevention. *The Personnel and Guidance Journal, 62,* 467-469.

Myrick, R. D. (1987). *Developmental guidance and counseling: A practical approach.* Minneapolis, MN: Educational Media Corporation.

Myrick, R. D. (1989). Developmental guidance: Practical considerations. *Elementary School Guidance and Counseling, 24,* 14-20.

Napierkowski, C. M., & Parsons, R. D. (1995). Diffusion of innovation: Implementing changes in school counselor roles and functions. *The School Counselor, 42,* 364-369.

National Commission on Excellence in Education (1983). A nation at risk: The imperatives for educational reform.

National School Boards Association (1986). *Resolution on guidance and counseling.* Alexandria, VA: Author.

Nebraska Department of Education (1990). *Nebraska school counseling program guide for planning and program improvement.* Lincoln, NE: Author.

Neukrug, E. S., Barr, C. G., Hoffman, L. R., & Kaplan, L. S. (1993). Developmental counseling and guidance: A model for use in your school. *The School Counselor, 40,* 356-362.

Nicoll, W. G. (1994). Developing effective classroom guidance programs: An integrative framework. *The School Counselor, 41,* 360-364.

Olson, M. J., & Perrone, P. A. (1991). Changing to a developmental guidance program. *The School Counselor, 39,* 41-46.

Paisley, P. O., & Peace, S. D. (1995). Developmental principles: A framework for school counseling programs. *Elementary School Guidance & Counseling, 30,* 85-93.

Paisley, P. O., & Borders, L. D. (1995). School counseling: An evolving specialty. *Journal of Counseling and Development, 74,* 150-153.

Partin, R. L., (1993). School counselors' time: Where does it go? *The School Counselor, 40,* 274-281.

Podemski, R. S., & Childers, Jr., J. H. (1980). The counselor as change agent: An organizational analysis. *The School Counselor, 27,* 168-174.

Ponzo, Z. (Ed.) (1989). Beyond role debate to role implementation [Special issue]. *The School Counselor, 37*(1).

Robinson, E. H. (1982). The counselor and the new conservatism: Challenges in the 1980s. *The Personnel and Guidance Journal, 60,* 598-602.

Rye, D. R., & Sparks, R. (1991). The School Counselor, 38, 263-267.

Schmidt, J. J. (1984). School counseling: Professional directions for the future. *The School Counselor, 31,* 385-392.

Sheldon, C., & Morgan, C. D. (1984). The child development specialist: A prevention program. *The Personnel and Guidance Journal, 62,* 470-474.

Sink, C.A., & MacDonald, G. (1998). The status of comprehensive guidance and counseling in the United States. *Professional School Counseling, 2,* 88-94.

Snyder, B. A., & Daly, T. P. (1993). Restructuring guidance and counseling programs. *The School Counselor, 41,* 36-42.

Solomon, C. (Ed.) (1982). Political action [Special issue]. *The Personnel and Guidance Journal, 60*(10).

South Dakota Curriculum Center (1991). *South Dakota comprehensive guidance and counseling program model* (working document, 1st draft). Pierre, SD: South Dakota Department of Education and Cultural Affairs.

Southeast Regional Resource Center (1989). *Alaska school counseling program guide.* Juneau, AK: Author.

Starr, M., & Gysbers, N. C. (1986). *Missouri comprehensive guidance: A model for program development, implementation, and evaluation.* Jefferson City, MO: Missouri Department of Elementary and Secondary Education.

Stefflre, B., & Grant, W. H. (1972). *Theories of counseling.* New York: McGraw-Hill.

Sue, D. W., Arrendondo, P., & McDavis, R. J. (1992). Multicultural counseling competencies and standards: A call to the profession. *Journal of Counseling & Development, 70,* 477-486.

Tennyson, W. W., Miller, G. D., Skovolt, T. G., & Williams, R. C. (1989). Secondary school counselors: What do they do? What is important? *The School Counselor, 36,* 253-259.

Texas Education Agency (1990). *The comprehensive guidance program for Texas public schools: A guide for program development, pre-K-12th grade.* Austin, TX: Author.

Utah State Office of Education (1989). *Utah comprehensive counseling and guidance program: A proposed model for program development.* Salt Lake City, UT: Author.

Utah State Office of Education (1998). *Model for comprehensive counseling and guidance programs* (Rev. ed.). Salt Lake City, UT: Author.

Wilgus, E., & Shelley, V. (1988). The role of the elementary-school counselor: Teacher perceptions, expectations, and actual functions. *The School Counseling, 35,* 259-266.

Wilson, P. J. (1986). *School counseling programs: A resource and planning guide.* Madison: Wisconsin Department of Public Instruction.

Wittmer, J. (1993). Implementing a comprehensive developmental school counseling program. in J. Wittmer, *Managing your school counseling program: K-12 developmental strategies* (pp. 12-30). Minneapolis, MN: Educational Media Corporation.

Comprehensive Guidance and Counseling Programs Continue to Evolve

In the first decade of the 21st century, economic and social forces, already at work over the past decades, continued to shape education in general and school counseling specifically. Work and workplaces became more global, characterized by technological change moving at near light speed. Social structures and social and personal values also continued to change as our nation's population became increasingly diverse. Our society had become multiracial, multilingual and multicultural in this decade. Women entered the labor force in record numbers and men were questioning traditionally held beliefs about their roles.

In addition, public education received considerable attention. School reform efforts intensified, focusing on the need to reduce dropout rates and increase graduation rates, all of which took place in the context of increasing students' academic achievement. With the passage of the No Child Left Behind Act (Pub. L. 107-10) in 2001, academic achievement became the priority in education. Closing the academic achievement gap of low-income students and minority students became a focal point for all of education but particularly for school counseling.

As these forces were at work challenging and changing our economic, social and educational institutions as well as the values and beliefs individuals hold about themselves, about others and about the world, what was the impact on school counseling during this decade? The evolution of school counseling continued in this decade, but the pace of evolution increased substantially.

In the first decade of the 21st century work continued on developing, implementing and evaluating comprehensive guidance and counseling programs in our nation's schools. The professional literature during this time period contained many references to the need for and importance of these programs as well as to how these programs should be structured, organized, implemented and evaluated. Various opinions were offered in the literature concerning what a program should consist of, how it should be structured and organized and what student outcomes should be emphasized. Debate was ongoing on these points but particularly on what role school counselors should assume in these programs. In addition, issues from past decades continued to be discussed as well. These issues included the terminology issue, the need for teaching experience, educational reform, principal-counselor relationships, legislation and advocacy, standards for the preparation of school counselors, leadership and supervision and school counselor assignments and ratios.

Chapter 7 begins by describing the continuing debate about the familiar topics of school counselor and program identity, program purposes and school counselor role. Then work on the development and implementation of comprehensive guidance and counseling programs undertaken during the first decade of the 21st century is presented. Particular attention in the next section of the chapter is paid to differing opinions in the literature concerning the purposes of comprehensive guidance and counseling programs and the work of school counselors within these programs. Next suggestions for improvement of comprehensive programs are described followed by a presentation of what school counselors had to say about their work in comprehensive programs. The current status of comprehensive programs is described next. Following this is discussion of a continuing topic of concern, namely, should school counselors have teaching certificates and experience? Then the importance of principal-school counselor relationships is discussed. The chapter closes with a presentation of federal and state legislation, discussion focusing on the Education Trust proposals to transform school counseling preparation and practices, discussion of leadership supervision and school counselor assignments and ratios.

Identity, Purposes and Role: The Debate Continues

The debate about the identity of school counseling, the purposes of school counseling and the role of school counselors, begun in the last century, continued into the first decade of the 21st century. Should school counselors emphasize academic achievement? What about student career and personal-social development? Should school counselors focus more on student mental health issues? Should school counselors provide direct services to all students or should they emphasize indirect services through a focus on leadership and collaboration? Are school counselors primarily advocates and change agents? Are school counselors primarily "systems analysts" collecting and analyzing data particularly focusing on issues such as closing academic achievement gaps?

Johnson (2000) described how school counseling and school counselors were still struggling with identity issues and role definition. She stated that for school counseling "to achieve a viable professional identity ... it must be seen as an integral component of the educational enterprise and understood as a primary player in the central academic mission of the school" (p. 33). She went on to point out that there was no need to pit academic achievement against mental health. Rather school counseling should be focusing on personal/social, career and educational development. To promote the identity of school counseling she suggested the need to build consensus around program goals, prepare plans of action and inform and promote the program.

Bemak (2000) called for school counselors to be leaders and change agents focusing on school, community and family collaboration. He called for school counselors to "de-expertize" so that they could more effectively lead collaborative efforts. He also called for school counselors to be referred to as school counselors, not guidance counselors. He stated this represents a change from traditional vocational guidance to the future of school counseling.

To help shape the identity of school counseling Gysbers, Lapan and Jones (2000) felt the need to address school board policies for guidance and counseling. They found that in an analysis of 24 state school board association policies for guidance and counseling, these policies had not kept pace with current program conceptions. They stressed the need to have school board policies written from a comprehensive program perspective.

Discussion also continued concerning whether or not school counseling should be mental-health-oriented or focused on closing the academic achievement gap. House and Hayes (2002) advocated for a major effort to close the achievement gap for poor students and students of color. They proposed a new vision for school counselors, moving them from a mental health, clinical, deficit model with a primary emphasis on personal/social issues to an emphasis on student academic achievement with school counselor being leaders, collaborators and advocates focusing on districtwide concerns. They also recommended school counselors become agents of change using data to effect change as well as be brokers of community and school resources for parents and students.

In the first article of a special section of *Professional School Counseling, Volume 10, Number 4,* Hipolito-Delgado and Lee (2007) expressed concern about the marginalization for groups of students and the perpetuation of what they called oppression in schools. They stated that for school counselors to address the achievement gap, they needed a theoretical perspective to practice that would be more empowering for students in marginalized groups. They recommended the use of empowerment theory. They offered the following conclusion as they closed their article.

"Oppression is a reality faced by students of marginalized communities. It causes negative psychological and sociopolitical effects. These negative effects permeate the school system and serve as barriers to the advancement of marginalized communities. The school counseling profession in partnership with oppressed students and communities can play a pivotal role in facilitating the empowerment of such groups. Through the adoption of empowerment theory as a guide for social advocacy, professional school counselors can be active in facilitating the empowerment of their students" (p. 331).

While discussion was ongoing concerning whether or not school counseling should emphasize academic achievement or personal-social (mental health) development, voices were also heard expressing a need to pay more attention to career development, the original heritage of the field. Barker and Satcher (2000) stressed the need to provide students with workplace skills and career development competencies. Feller (2003) emphasized the need for school counseling programs and school counselors to prepare students "for a life-time of learning and work transitions" (p. 269). Dykeman, Wood, Ingram, Pehrsson, Mandsager, & Herr (2003) reported on the development of a career development interventions taxonomy. They pointed out that the taxonomy "enhances the school counselor's ability to comprehensively and systematically evaluate and monitor their career development efforts" (p. 278). Gysbers and Lapan (2009) presented a strengths-based model of career development for school guidance and counseling programs. They emphasized that a strengths-based model was critical to assist students in their transitions within school and from school to work and college and then on to work or more education.

School counselor identity was on the minds of Lambie and Williamson (2004) when they wrote about the need to change from guidance counselor to professional school counselor. They stressed the need to "shift away from school counselors being perceived as 'assistant administrators' (guidance counselors) to become school counseling professionals with clearly defined roles and responsibilities ..." (p. 129). Colbert, Vernon-Jones and Pransky (2006) recommended that school counselors shift their focus from individual students and their families to a focus on schoolwide concerns, from a "responsive service orientation to counseling partnerships that are proactive and developmental" (p. 74) and to shift from working primarily with individuals to working with groups in "developing professional teams or communities" (p. 74).

Work Continues on Program Models

Gysbers & Henderson (2000) published the third edition of their book, "Developing and Managing Your School Guidance Program." In it they expanded and extended their original description of a comprehensive program and the steps to implement and manage it. They also described the needed evaluation system for these programs, the personnel involved and the expected student outcomes using the formula Program + Personnel = Results. They closed the evaluation loop by describing the enhancement phase that featured using data from the evaluation system to enhance the program to more effectively meet student needs and address school improvement plan goals. In doing so, they stressed the need for data-driven decision making. Gysbers and Henderson (2006) further refined their model in the fourth edition of their book published in 2006.

Johnson and Johnson (2003) updated work they had published in 1991 and 1996 in an article focusing on results-based guidance or what they called new guidance. Their "approach focuses on the student as the primary client, not on the services being provided" (p. 184). They identified 13 interrelated and interdependent program elements. Student support teams including school psychologists, social workers, attendance professionals and health professionals are featured. "The one common focus is the need to ensure that all student gain specific competencies they need to be successful students and to become successful adults. In 2006 they published a book "Building a Results-Based Student Support Program" (Johnson, Johnson, & Downs, 2006) that further elaborated upon their model and provided a detailed process for the implementation of the model.

Myrick (2003), in the fourth edition of his book "Developmental Guidance and Counseling: A Practical Approach," described six basic counselor interventions. They included individual counseling, small-group counseling, large-group guidance, peer facilitator training and projects, consultation and coordination of guidance services. He also described a management system emphasizing priority-setting and the use of weekly counselor calendars. Then he described in detail the six interventions. He emphasized the importance of accountability and outlined some ways school counselors can be accountable.

In March 2001, the American School Counselor Association Governing Board decided a national school counseling program model was a needed next step to build on The National Standards that had been developed in the late 1990s. To develop a national model, leaders in the field met several times over the next two years to discuss and decide on its nature, structure and organization. In 2003 "The ASCA National Model: A Framework for School Counseling Programs" was published. The ASCA National Model was based on the work of Gysbers and Henderson (2000), Myrick (2003) and Johnson and Johnson (2001). With the ASCA National Model's publication, the National Standards became the content standards for student academic, career and personal/social development. "The ASCA National Standards are for students, not programs" (American School Counselor Association, 2003). The ASCA National Model contains four elements including foundation, delivery system, management system and accountability. It is comprehensive in scope, preventive in design, developmental in nature and is an integral part of the total educational program. It is implemented by certificated school counselors. Conducted in collaboration, it monitors student progress and is driven by data. A workbook was published in 2004 (American School Counselor Association, 2004) and a second edition of the ASCA National Model was published in 2005 (American School Counselor Association, 2005).

In the second edition of the ASCA National Model, Henderson (2005) added a section titled "The Theory b\Behind the ASCA National Model." In it she defined what constituted a theory and presented a brief history of school counseling theory. Then she outlined seven questions to be answered by theory. She answered them by presenting 27 major principles and 15 subprinciples to represent the theory base of the ASCA National Model.

The publication of the ASCA National Model served to further stimulate the movement begun in the 1970s to develop, implement and evaluate comprehensive guidance and counseling programs in all of the states and school districts in the United States. Its publication resulted in some state, which previously didn't have statewide models, developing them. It also resulted in those states that already had state models aligning them with the ASCA National Model.

Some Challenges and Differing Opinions

In the first part of the first decade of the 21st century three special issues of Professional School Counseling were devoted to challenges faced in implementing comprehensive guidance and counseling programs. They also contained articles presenting differing opinions concerning the purposes of these programs and the role of school counselors within them, continuing the debate about purposes and role that had been taking place over the past century.

Some Challenges: The first special issue, *Professional School Counseling, Volume 4, Number 4*, published in April 2001 was titled "Comprehensive Guidance and Counseling programs: Theory, Policy, Practice and Research." Lapan (2001), the guest editor, stated that the purpose of the special issue was to provide discussion of some of the challenges faced in implementing effective comprehensive guidance and counseling programs.

In the opening article of this special issue Herr (2001) stated that the work of school counselors will continually be affected and challenged by national policies, economics and school reform. As a result, he felt, "… school counselors will likely be continuously required to hone their planning skills, take a comprehensive perspective on the needs for their services and their roles in the schools and be prepared to demonstrate that they achieve results consistent with the outcomes for which they have been assigned accountability in a particular school district. The model used to respond to such issues will be that of comprehensive guidance programs" (p. 244).

Gysbers and Henderson (2001) then provided a brief overview of the history of guidance and counseling in the schools and identified a number of strengths of comprehensive programs that would enhance school counselors' work, helping them meet the challenges of the 21st century. "The program's organizational structure not only provides the means and a common language for ensuring guidance for all students and counseling for the students that need it, it also provides a foundation for the accountable use of an ever-broadening spectrum of resources. It provides the means for matching school counselors' talents with the needs of students to help them achieve results desired by a school-community. The program supports accountability for content priorities through evaluation of student results, for program relevance through continuous reconsideration of the contents of the structural and program components, for program delivery through evaluation in light of locally established program standards and for school counselors' performance through assessment of their use of time and evaluation of their competence based on professional school counseling standards" (p. 256).

Writing in this same issue, Lee (2001) stated that "among the issues facing contemporary school counselors, addressing the developmental needs of a growing number of students from culturally diverse backgrounds is, perhaps, the most challenging" (p. 257). He felt that culturally responsive counselors needed to be facilitators of and advocates for students and their development. He ended his article by stating that comprehensive programs "have the potential to be on the cutting edge of promoting access, equity and educational justice" (p. 261).

Paisley (2001), in this same issue, emphasized the challenge of creating and maintaining a developmental focus for comprehensive guidance and counseling programs. She felt that too often developmental principles that undergird these programs are often ignored. She also stated that:

"School counselors and school counselor educators will also have to become more systematic in collecting data showing promoting development in these domains [academic, personal/social and career] also supports the main mission of the school and meets the needs of those children and adolescents often underserved by the system" (p. 276).

Finally, in the special issue, Sink and Yillik-Downer (2001) reported on school counselors' perceptions of comprehensive guidance and counseling programs. The data from their survey suggested that the more school counselors value comprehensive guidance and counseling programs, they will be more engaged in the development and implementation of these programs. Related to this finding the data also suggested that as school counselors become more involved, their level of concern and anxiety about completing the tasks of putting these programs in place tends to decrease. Finally, the data indicated that high school counselors reported higher task concerns than did elementary school counselors. Sink and Yillik-Downer stated this made sense since high school counselors spend more of their time performing clerical-type duties than elementary school counselors.

Differing opinions: The focus of the next special issue was on School Counseling Past, Present and Future, Volume 5, Number 2, December 2001. In it Baker (2001) described his journey in the field from school counselor to counselor educator and journal editor. He raised the questions "Is the glass half empty?" "Is the glass half full?" He concluded that it is half full concerning the promise of guidance and counseling in schools. Green and Keys (2001) offered a number of recommendations for transforming school counseling. Among them, they recommended a shift toward an indirect services model, more collaboration and the use of evidence-based practices and outcome-based evaluation. They stressed the importance of taking into account contextual factors that may hinder or promote healthy student development. Gysbers (2001) presented his vision for guidance and counseling in the 21st century by stating that he hoped there would be fully implemented comprehensive guidance and counseling programs in every school district in the United States. In the final article Paisley and McMahon (2001) presented a snapshot of the ideal school counselor as follows:

"In sum, they would intentionally and collaboratively design responsive school counseling programs. They would hold themselves accountable rather than wait for someone else to. They would evaluate their programs and share the results with the school community and use the results to enhance the programs to more effectively meet student needs and support student learning" (p. 114).

In the last special issue in this series (Volume 5, Number 3, February 2002), a number of individuals were asked to react to the articles in Volume 5, Number 2, December 2001. Whiston (2002), in her reaction article, identified a number of issues from the past that were still of concern, including school counselors being pulled in different directions due to multiple expectations and role definition. She stated: "It may be that school counselors continue to be torn between two or more 'lovers' (e.g., education versus guidance, guidance versus counseling, vocational health versus mental health)" (p. 150). As we have seen in previous chapters, what Whiston described is a continuation of the debate that has taken place over the last 100 years concerning what the focus and purpose of guidance and counseling in schools should be.

Whiston also commented on several points in the Paisley and McMahon (2001) article and the article by Green and Keys (2001). She noted that Paisley and McMahon had advocated for the importance of collaboration while Green and Keys had also promoted collaboration as well as the need for more indirect services in the work of school counselors. She expressed concern about this by stating:

"My concerns about the increasing focus on collaboration should not be construed as being uncooperative or opposed to collaborative activities. However, I am concerned that some of the systemic problems in school counseling cannot be addressed through typical collaborative activities. Some collaborative efforts are short-lived and fade away after the initial excitement dissipates, or there are personnel changes within the cooperating organizations. My concern is with students and the belief that unrealistic caseloads keep school counselors from providing the assistance students need. Although collaboration can often be an important activity, it may be time for the field to place more emphasis on increasing the number of school counselors and providing more effective programs to students rather than on initiating collaborative programs" (p. 152).

Sink (2002) summed up what he thought he and the authors of the articles in the previous special. "To sum up, the authors and I seem to be encouraging school counselors to remain focused on:

- Developing and updating the skills needed to serve all students
- Exploring innovations in educational and counseling theory and practice
- Advocating for themselves and their programs
- Implementing well-designed comprehensive programs
- Collaborating with one another, other school personnel and with community agencies and programs
- Measuring student and program accomplishments and needs
- Creating a sense of community in their schools

■ Demonstrating a high degree of professionalism" (p. 161)

Finally Sears and Granello (2002), in their reaction article, stressed the need for practicing school counselors to establish a clearer professional identity and for counselor education to change its training to provide school counselors "with the skills to lead change in systems, to collaborate with key stakeholders, to coordinate programs designed to improve student achievement, to use data and technology to promote change and to advocate for all students" (p. 170).

Model Limitations: Suggestions for Improvement

Even as comprehensive guidance and counseling programs continued to be developed and implemented in increasing numbers, stimulated in part by the publication of the ASCA National Model, some writers were expressing concern about what they called model limitations. Galassi and Akas (2004) reviewed contemporary school counseling models and noted what they called model limitations. They were concerned about their developmental nature and their comprehensiveness. They recommended that the current models could be improved by focusing on what they called developmental advocacy. "In developmental advocacy the focus is on promotion of development rather than on prevention and remediation ..." (p. 152). School counselors' primary role is the optimal development of all students.

Some writers focused on offering ideas to improve aspects of program models. Eschenauer & Chen-Hayes (2005) suggested reconceptualizing individual counseling using what they called The Transformative Individual Counseling Model. They called for a shift from mental health to a school and academic perspective using functional behavioral assessment to identify a problem. Then, using a single-case research design, individual counseling could be evaluated.

The guidance curriculum component of a comprehensive program also received attention. Rowley, Stroh and Sink (2005) conducted a survey of 102 school districts in 12 states. The survey was mailed to 193 school counselors; 86 surveys were returned. The major finding was that

"... the study tentatively shows that school counselors see the guidance curriculum component as a teaching-learning process that aids in meeting programmatic goals as well as helps students attain developmental competencies" (p. 302).

Akos, Cockman and Strickland (2007) stressed the importance of what they called differential planning and delivery of classroom guidance. They recommended paying attention to student readiness and interests and then differentiating the content and processes of delivery accordingly. In closing their article they wondered about the training school counselors receive to deliver guidance curriculum in light of the fact that most states have done away with teaching certificates and experience.

Brown and Trusty (2005) wondered if school counselors were posing more than they could deliver. In their article, they concluded that there is little research support for the idea that comprehensive school counseling programs (CSCP) improve student achievement. As a result they supported the use of what they called "strategic interventions" such as study skills groups to improve student achievement. They ended their article by suggesting "that it may not be prudent to tout the impact of CSCPs on achievement until more and better research evidence is produced." Sink (2005), in a rejoiner to Brown and Trusty, suggested otherwise:

"Despite the fact that direct causal links are not realistic possibilities in CSCP research, given fairly strict adherence to certain methodological caveats, causal inferences can still be tentatively offered" (p. 11).

Since the publication of the ASCA National Model in 2003 many articles appeared in the literature. As we have seen, some articles offered ideas about how to expand models. Other articles offered ways to improve various program components. Still others cautioned readers concerning the actual impact of these programs with the suggestion that additional research was needed. An article by Dimmitt and Carey (2007) used the ASCA National Model to show how it could address student transitions. They stated:

"With a planned, comprehensive school counseling program in place that adheres to the standards set forth by the ASCA National Model, student transitions from grade to grade and from school into the world of college and work can be even more successful" (p. 231).

What School Counselors Say

About Comprehensive Guidance and Counseling Programs

As comprehensive guidance and counseling programs were being implemented increasingly, particularly since the publication of the ASCA National Model, articles began appearing assessing school counselors' beliefs about and their satisfaction with their roles within these programs. Two studies appearing in 2006, one by Baggerly and Osborn (2006) and one by Rayle (2006), both indicated that job satisfaction was high when school counselors were performing preferred duties. However, when school counselors were performing inappropriate duties they expressed less job satisfaction and were more frustrated.

Walsh, Barrett and DePaul (2007) reviewed the activity time logs of elementary school counselors in four Boston public elementary schools. The results indicated that the activities of these elementary school counselors were aligned with the delivery system of the ASCA National Model. In terms of time, "... the guidance curriculum represented 32 percent of school counselor activities, individual planning represented 17 percent of their activities, responsive services represented 34 percent of their activities, and system support represented 17 percent of school counselor activities" (p. 374).

They also found that when these elementary school counselors practiced according to the ACSA National Model guidelines, they earned the support of school principals.

Hatch and Chen-Hayes (2008) conducted a survey of school counselors (3,000 were sent, 1,279 surveys were returned, 43 percent return rate) using the School Counseling Program Component Scale. Four factors were found including use of data for program planning, use of data for accountability, administrator support and mission, goals and competencies. The results of the study indicated:

"While school counselors reported the use of data as at least moderately important, the results suggested that the sample of school counselors in this study had stronger beliefs about the importance of program foundation components (e.g. mission, goals) and administrative support (e.g., favorable student-to-counselor ratios and reductions in noncounseling activities) than about the importance of using data" (p. 40).

Scarborough and Luke (2008) conducted a qualitative study exploring the personal perspectives of eight school counselors who had success in implementing comprehensive school counseling programs. All participants expressed the importance of implementing comprehensive programs. They understood the system in which they worked and they believed in their ability to implement a program. Finally they understood the political and structural contexts in which they worked.

Poynton, Schumacher and Wilczenski (2008) explored school counselors' attitudes regarding the implementation of a statewide comprehensive guidance program model. Ten percent of the membership of the Massachusetts School Counselor Association (MASCA) responded to a survey using the Concern-Based Adoption Model (CBAM). Five stages of concern are identified including awareness, personal, management, impact and collaboration. Findings indicated that the respondents were mostly in the personal stage. This suggests that the Massachusetts school counselors who responded were in the early stages of model adoption.

Dahir, Burnham and Stone (2009) surveyed school counselors in Alabama. Seventy-four percent of the 1,691 school counselors returned completed surveys designed to assess school counselor needs for professional development and to measure school counselor readiness and progress toward the implementation of comprehensive programs. Survey results indicated:

"… elementary school counselors' commitment to emphasize strong personal-social growth for students and the intent to implement a classroom guidance curriculum. Additional distinctive conclusions for elementary school counselors also revealed a strong commitment to program management, less emphasis on academic development priorities and little or no involvement in career development …

"Middle school counselors, who bridge the worlds of childhood and adolescence, identified priorities that bring balance to academic, career and personal-social development as well as adhere to the belief that comprehensive school counseling programs are an integral component to every student's school success …

"Compared to counselors at other school levels, high school counselors placed significantly higher priority on academic development and career and postsecondary development …

"This study reaffirmed their traditional practice priorities of individual counseling, educational and career planning and preparing for postsecondary opportunities" (p. 190).

Finally, an article by Kolodinsky, Draves, Lindsey and Zlatev (2009), described levels of satisfaction and frustration of Arizona school counselors. A total of 155 Arizona school counselors returned a survey designed to measure school counselor satisfaction with their job and any frustrations they had. The respondents reported being satisfied with their work but expressed frustration with being overwhelmed with off-task duties that often are classified as non-school-counseling duties. The subtitle of this article captures a major finding of the study: A desire for greater connections with students in a data-driven era. When asked, the school counselors in the survey responded that their greatest area of job satisfaction came from directly serving students.

Although the ASCA National Model points to an increase in accountability, data collection and program evaluation by school counselors (Dollarhide & Saginak, 2008; Poynton & Carey, 2006), it is interesting to note that the vast majority of respondents in this study reported that their greatest feeling of job satisfaction came in interactions where they had greater freedom to directly serve and interact with students (p. 198).

The Current Status of Program Models: Progress and Problems

Progress: The development and implementation of comprehensive guidance and counseling programs has been underway since the 1970s. In 1998 Sink and Mac Donald (1998) found that 24 states had models for comprehensive guidance and counseling programs. What is the status of model development and implementation today? Martin, Carey and DeCosler (2009) found that "17 states have established models, 24 are progressing in model implementation, and 10 states are at a beginning stage of model development" (p. 378). Thus all 50 states and the District of Columbia are at some stage of program development and implementation. In their article they went on to explore why states are where they are. They found that state leadership for guidance and counseling, state school counselor leadership, state legislation, policy and rules, efforts to evaluate programs and local control all played a part in program development, implementation and evaluation.

Problems: There are many issues affecting the full implementation of comprehensive guidance and counseling programs in the schools. One of those issues is school counselor time on task – spending 100 percent time carrying out the tasks of developing, implementing and evaluating comprehensive programs with at least 80 percent time in direct service to students and their parents. How serious is the problem?

In a three-year study conducted in Arizona (Vandegrift, 1999), the question was asked, "Are Arizona public schools making the best use of school counselors?" The study revealed that school counselors in Arizona were spending up to 15 percent of their time in performing "non-guidance" activities. To put this percentage into perspective, Vandegrift (1999) conducted a cost-benefit analysis based on 1996 median salaries: "A simple cost-benefit analysis helps in beginning to answer these questions. The median counselor salary in Arizona is $27,000. The median salary of a school secretary is $20,600. Fifteen percent of a counselor's wages is $4,050, while 15 percent of a secretary's wages is $3,909 – a difference of nearly $1,000. If all 1,327 Arizona public school counselors (who comprise the state's counselor directory) are spending an average of 15 percent of their time on non-guidance activities, this represents an investment of some $5 million. Assuming non-guidance activities such as class scheduling could be performed by secretarial staff, Arizona taxpayers currently are paying 100 times more (or over $1 million) for these services to be performed by master's-degreed professionals. Moreover, time spent on non-guidance activities clearly is time not spend working with students, faculty and staff" (p. 5).

In a similar study conducted in Texas (Rylander, 2002), the study revealed that, "school counselors spend only about 60 percent of their time exclusively on counseling. A good portion of their time is spent on other administrative tasks. Counselors acknowledge they should not be relieved entirely of administrative duties, because all school staff must assume some measure of administrative responsibility. Most clamed, however, that excessive administrative duties hampered their effectiveness and their availability to students. One particular area of concern among counselors was their role in administering statewide tests. While counselors believe they have a role in test assessment, they argued that the role of coordinator of TAAS [Texas Assessment of Academic Skills] testing took too much time away from counseling. Many recommend shifting most or all of those duties to other staff" (Executive summary).

Two studies conducted by the Joyce Ivy Foundation in 2008 and 2009 indicated the problem of counselor time off task continues to be a major problem. In their study in Michigan (Joyce Ivy Foundation, 2008) of school counselor time, 406 Michigan high school counselors from more than 350 high schools reported that 30 percent of their time was "absorbed with administration and paperwork, much of it attributable to their increasing role and duties in administering tests and curriculum changes" (p. 9). In a similar study in Ohio (Joyce Ivy Foundation, 2009), 630 Ohio school counselors spent 34 percent of their time off-task "performing administrative work, such as scheduling, test management, maintaining student records and signing tardy slips."

Teaching vs Non-Teaching Backgrounds

A continuing issue being discussed over the past decades has been about whether or not teaching certificates and experience were necessary for school counselors. Please remember that the first school counselors were teachers and administrators who assumed counseling roles along with their teaching and administration roles. Then as the field matured more and more full-time school counselors were appointed. Teaching certificates and experience were still seen by most professionals as important. Gradually, over the last decades, that changed so that now most states do not require teaching certificates and teaching experience as necessary prerequisites to become school counselors.

Counselor educators were surveyed as to their perceptions of whether or not teaching experience was necessary for school counselors by Smith, Crutchfield and Culbreth (2001). The majority of counselor educators surveyed (75 percent) felt teaching experience was not necessary while the remainder (25 percent) felt it was. What were the beliefs of these two groups?

"Counselor educators who maintained that teaching experience is not needed cited reasons such as students' personal characteristics and skills as measures of effectiveness, the lack of research evidence that supports the need for teaching experience and their ability to teach school counselors to be successful in the school environment through field work and coursework. Those who endorsed the teaching requirement cited reasons such as employability, needed skills in classroom management and guidance, increased credibility with teachers, provision of career opportunities for schoolteachers and increased understanding of problems that are unique to schools"(p. 221).

In a study of the personal and professional adjustments of school counseling interns with and without teaching experience Peterson, Goodman,

Keller and McCauley (2004) found that both groups were challenged. Those without teaching experience were challenged by adjusting to the school culture and to classroom management issues. Those with teaching experience were also challenged. They found that the transition from previous roles involved in teaching to the new roles of school counseling was also a challenge.

In their study of whether or not teaching experience was needed, Bringman and Lee (2008) found that although teaching experience was helpful, it was not necessary in conducting guidance curriculum classroom units. They also found that "most important for self-perceived competence in developmental classroom lessons is school counseling experience" (p. 384). They did point out that students without teaching experience would benefit from conducting classroom units during their practicum experience.

Akos, Cockman and Strickland (2007) focused on the need for differentiated classroom guidance to meet students' developmental needs and levels. They went on to state that a teaching background would influence a school counselor's ability to teach classroom guidance lessons. They ended their article with the following words:

"If classroom guidance is to remain an important and central part of school counselor practice (25 percent-45 percent in the ASCA National Model), it would be prudent to teach, document and replicate best practices, such as differentiation, in classroom guidance. Further, before more roles and services are suggested for school counselor practice (an apparently never-ending list with no discussion of what services are less important), the practice of classroom guidance should be investigated and enhanced thoroughly" (p. 462).

Principal-Counselor Relationships

A topic that has received considerable attention over the past decades is the importance of principal-counselor relationships. Interest in this topic during this decade continued to be high. Louis and Gordon (2006) argued for the inclusion of student support staff including school counselors in the school reform movement to improve student learning. They pointed out that it is the responsibility of principals to work with school counselors to help them become active participants to improve student learning. In their book they suggested guidelines for principals to accomplish this task.

Two documents published in 2009 (Hale, 2009; Finkelstein, 2009) described the importance of the principal-counselor relationship. Finkelstein (2009) reported on a survey of principals and counselors concerning the principal-counselor relationship and found that:

- Principals and counselors both ranked communication and respect as the two most important elements in the principal-counselor relationship.
- Principals and counselors both saw time as being the biggest barrier to collaboration between them.
- Principals had a better match between their perceptions of how important an element is to a successful principal-counselor relationship and the extent to which they saw that element as being present in the principal-counselor relationships within their own schools. When elements were rated as important, principals tended to rate them as being more present that did counselors.
- When asked what one thing they would change that would lead to an improved principal-counselor relationship within their own schools, both principals and counselors most frequently mentioned communication, followed by respect/understanding.
- Principals and counselors agreed that the most important activities for a counselor to engage in to improve student outcomes are helping to promote student personal growth and social development and helping students with career planning.
- While both principals and counselors agreed that supportive administrative tasks are less important for counselors to engage in to improve student outcomes, principals saw these tasks as taking up less of counselors' time than counselors said they took.
- Both principals and counselors saw state test scores as the area where gaps between subgroups most needed to be addressed in their schools.
- When asked about the roles of principals and counselors in education reform efforts, both principals and counselors most often said that the role of the principals is to be a leader and the role of the counselor is to be an advocate (p. 12).

Hale (2009) provided examples of how effective principal-counselor relationships can lead to success for all students. He described these relationships in seven schools. In summarizing the lessons learned he stated that often the principal creates the environment that allows the expertise of school counselors to be used and valued. In turn he also emphasized that school counselors needed to provide principals with information they needed that was backed up with data.

At the same time, Martin, Lopez and Carey (2009) provided guidelines for principals to consider in the organization and management of school counseling programs. They focused on topics such as the number of school counselors needed to operate a program, effective staffing patterns, hiring school counselors and school counselor leaders, school counselor supervision and program accountability. In the same book Janson and Stone (2009) focused on helping principals see the value of comprehensive programs in their schools. They provided principals with specific examples of schools with such programs showing how they contributed to student success.

Perusse, Haas, Lally and Mische (2009) pointed to the importance of the role of principals in supporting the work of school counselors. They also pointed out that principal preparation programs did little to prepare principals to work effectively with school counselors to incorporate them into the school reform and improvement processes.
"We contend that principal preparation programs should more explicitly prepare pre-service principals on how to include school counselors in the school improvement process" (p. 39).

Federal and State Legislation

In 2001, the U.S. Congress reauthorized the Elementary and Secondary Act of 1965 (Pub. L 89-10, 79 Stat. 27, 20 U.S.C. ch 70) as the No Child Left Behind Act (Pub. L. 107-10). In it, Part D, Subpart 2, Section 5421 titled "Elementary and Secondary School Counseling Programs" provided grants to local educational agencies to establish or expand elementary and secondary school counseling programs. The legislation specified that the programs be comprehensive, addressing the counseling and educational needs of all students. It also specified the use of a developmental, preventive approach to counseling.

Aside from Part D, Subpart 2, Section 5421, it is important to consider the overall impact this federal law has on school counselors. Dollarhide and Lemberger (2006) conducted a national survey examining the effects of the No Child Left Behind legislation; 210 school counselors responded to the survey. According to their survey, the school counselors who responded stated they were informed about the law and that the law had had a substantial impact on school counseling programs. A major finding was that the high-stakes testing required by the law "has magnified the already skewed perspective of counselors as test administrators" (p. 303). The authors went on to say, "Within the context of this study, there is a concern that holistic school counseling programs might be eroded, which, ironically, may lead to many children being left behind" (p. 303).

Then in 2006, The Carl D. Perkins Vocational and Technical Education Act of 1998 was amended to become The Carl D. Perkins Career and Technical Education Improvement Act of 2006 (Pub. L. 109-270). The definition for career guidance/school guidance and counseling in the 2006 act, Section 3, changed from a program definition in previous versions of the act to the following information-giving focus:

"(7) Career Guidance and Academic Counseling: The term 'career guidance and academic counseling' means guidance and counseling that –

- provides access for students (and parents, as appropriate) to information regarding career awareness and planning with respect to an individual's occupational and academic future; and
- provides information with respect to career options, financial aid and postsecondary options, including baccalaureate degree programs."

At the same time, later in Section 118c of the 2006 act, career guidance and academic counseling are described as being "programs designed to promote career and education decision making by students (and parents, as appropriate) regarding education (including postsecondary education) and training options and preparations for high-skill, high-wage or high-demand occupations and non-traditional fields." Note that in the first definition the word program does not appear, and yet, in a later section it does.

A number of states also have been active in passing legislation or rules for guidance and counseling in the schools. For example, Utah's State Board of Education passed a rule (R277-462) defining a comprehensive guidance program as well as providing qualification criteria by which to distribute Comprehensive Guidance Funds. In another example, the Texas Legislature enacted SB 518, which made Education Code Sections 33.003-33.006 applicable to all school districts ("An Act Relating to Public School Counselors," 2001). These sections stated that Texas school counselors shall plan, implement and evaluate developmental guidance and counseling programs. Similarly, in West Virginia, the Board of Education enacted a legislative rule for comprehensive developmental guidance and counseling in 2002. Finally, as a last example, the state of Florida enacted a bill titled "An Act Relating to Career Education" in 2004. In Section 5, Section 1006.025, it states each district school board shall annually submit a district guidance report to the commissioner of education that includes the degree to which a district has adopted or implemented a guidance model program.

The Preparation of School Counselors

As you have seen much has been written about the preparation of school counselors going back to the beginning of guidance and counseling in the early 1900s. Discussion has focused on what school counselors need to know, when they need to know it and how the course work should be structured so they can gain the knowledge and skills they require. The Association for Counselor Education and Supervision (ACES) and the counselor education and supervisor groups that preceded ACES all had been working on the preparation of school counselors. Then in 1981 the Council for Accreditation of Counseling and Related Educational Programs (CACREP) was founded. Over the years that followed standards for the preparation of counselors including school counselors were published, with the most recent set of standards being published in 2009.

In 1996 a new effort to change the way school counselors were prepared was initiated. "The Education Trust, a Washington, D.C.-based nonprofit organization, with support from the DeWitt Wallace-Reader's Digest Fund, launched a five-year, multistage national initiative for transforming school counseling" (Martin, 2002, p. 148). The goal of The Transforming School Counseling Initiative (TSCI) was to change the way school counselors were prepared and practiced in the schools. More specifically the initiative focused on moving school counselors away from the status quo to become social action advocates, from being ancillary to becoming critical players in schools and from a mental health focus to a focus on academic achievement (Martin, 2002).

Seashore, Jones and Seppanen (2001) conducted an evaluation of TSCI with a grant from the Wallace-Reader's Digest Fund. In their report they described the progress and difficulties of changing the preparation of school counselors. They offered six lessons to guide program change in school counselor preparation programs.

- Negotiate your institutional context and the politics of program change.

- Use "Guerilla Partnering'"Tactics to strengthen local support for reformed counselor roles.
- Bring practitioners into an on-going dialogue about changing counselor roles.
- Use resources to support local conditions for change
- Focus on the basics: curriculum, recruitment and field experiences.
- Link schools counseling to critical priorities (pp. 40-42).

What does TSCI recommend concerning the preparation of school counselors? House and Sears (2002) described a mission-driven model with eight essential elements to revise the curriculum for school counselor preparation. The eight elements included attention to the selection of candidates, curricular content, structure and sequence of courses, methods of instruction and induction into the profession.

To carry out the mission of the Education Trust Initiative, The Education Trust and the MetLife Foundation established the National Center for Transforming School Counseling (NCTSC) in June 2003. The goal of this organization was to ensure school counselors are trained and ready to help all groups of students reach high academic standards. School counselors are seen as assertive advocates, leaders and team members to help each student succeed.

Galassi and Akos (2004) reviewed current school counseling models including the one being proposed by the National Initiative for Transforming School Counseling. They pointed out that this initiative was a shift from a mental health focus to an academic achievement focus. They expressed concern about this as follows:

"The Transforming School Counseling Initiative, in response to educational reform, has focused almost entirely on academic achievement and narrowing the minority achievement gap. Although these are laudable goals, they seem to minimize the role of the other developmental needs (personal and social) in academic achievement and career development in the lives of twenty-first century youth" (p. 149).

More on Leadership and Supervision

In the first decade of this century, there was growing recognition that effective leadership of school counseling programs and effective supervision of school counselors are required if school counselors are to carry out their work within the framework of these programs. Also, during this time period more and more school counseling leaders were identified at the building and district levels and are now serving as directors or supervisors (Gysbers & Henderson, 2006). The importance of these appointments to these positions was stressed by a number of authors including Lieberman (2004) and Schwallie-Giddis, ter Maat and Pak (2003).

Henderson and Gysbers (2002) edited a book addressing 10 critical issues in leadership. Twenty guidance leaders from around the country were chosen to show how effective leadership could be responsive to these critical issues. It was clear from their responses that the key to success was effective leadership.

Then in 2009, Henderson's book "The New Handbook of Administrative Supervision in Counseling" was published. In it she described administrative supervisors' responsibilities and the knowledge and skills they need to do their work effectively. She drew upon the experiences of administrative supervisors as well as the theory and research of counseling leadership and supervision and related disciplines.

School Counselor Assignments and Ratios

An interesting issue that received attention in this decade was the way secondary school counselors are assigned students. Akos, Schuldt and Walendin (2009) surveyed all school counselors in a large Southeastern school district. Of the 196 potential respondents, 146 completed the survey. They found that the traditional ways of assigning students by grade-level and/or alphabet were used most frequently. Four percent were assigned by the domains of academic, career and personal-social. The authors concluded that more research was necessary on this topic. They also pointed out that each school should examine the way assignments are made.

"It seems necessary for each school and school counselor to thoughtfully examine the school counselor assignment currently in use and determine what advantages and challenges exist. Effectiveness, efficiency and equity in services to students and families are important considerations school counselors should evaluate. With these data in mind, professional school counselors can negotiate the optimal school counselor assignment in management agreements with administration" (p. 28).

What should be the student-to-counselor ratio? You will recall that Hoyt (1955) raised the question about what the ratio should be. In his opening words in the article he stated that nobody knows. He then went on to analyze the work of school counselors and suggested a 400-to-one ratio was appropriate. Later the American School Counselor Association (2005) recommended a ratio of 250-to-one. In 2009 the state of Utah adopted a rule requiring school districts and charter schools in Utah to have a ratio of one counselor for every 350 students (Utah State Board of Education, 2009). Carrell and Carrell (2006) reported that in 2003 the national average was 478 students per counselor "with California having the highest ratio of 951 followed by Minnesota at 797" (p. 1).

Do student-to-counselor ratios make a difference in student outcomes? There is an absence of research on this topic so Carrell and Carrell (2006) took on this task by examining elementary schools in Alachua County, Fla. Their results indicated that lower student-to-counselor ratios decreased both the recurrence of disciplinary problems and the share of students involved in discipline incidents. Of importance is the fact that these effects were greater for minority and low-income students. They found that if one additional counselor were added to the elementary schools in the study it would reduce the student-to-counselor ratio from 544 to 272. "Our models estimate that doing so would result in a total of 257 to 984 fewer students, per year, involved in at least one disciplinary incident" (p. 13). What difference would that make? Carrell and Carrell quoted a study by Figlio (2005) that suggested one additional disruptive student in a classroom results in reduced peer mathematics test scores of 2.2 national percentiles.

Major Trends and Issues

While substantial progress has been made in developing, implementing and evaluating comprehensive school counseling programs in this first decade of the 21st century, debate continued about program focus, purposes and the work of school counselors. The program focus issue continued a debate begun in the early 1900s. Should the focus be educational (academic), vocational (career) or personal-social (mental health)? Some writers urged practitioners to focus on academic achievement and perhaps career but not personal-social or mental health. Other writers urged the opposite with mental health issues needing more attention. A few writers urged the adoption of a holistic approach emphasizing attention to academic, career and personal social concerns of students.

There was also debate about program purposes and school counselors' roles. Some writers emphasized an advocacy change agent focus. Others talked about the need to emphasize collaboration. Still others recommended school counselors do more indirect work and less direct work with students. Finally there was a movement for school counselors to become more data-oriented, using data to identify school concerns and student needs. Interesting, there was push back on this from practicing school counselors who wanted to spend most of their time working directly with students and their parents (Kolodinsky, Draves, & Schroder, 2009).

The development and implementation of comprehensive school counseling programs across the country grew, stimulated by the development of the American School Counselor Association National Model and its adoption by many school districts and states. A major challenge of the decade then became the implementation issue or the implementation gap. Many written programs existed; fewer were implemented.

The issue of the requirement of teaching certificates and experience for school counselors continued to be debated too. The number of states requiring teaching certificates and experiences grew smaller indicating the belief that school counselors needed teaching certificates and experience was changing. The majority of states and most leaders of the school counseling movement agreed that teaching certificates and experience were no longer necessary to be a school counselor.

The debate about the nature, structure and content of school counselor preparation continued as well. Led by the Association for Counselor Education and Supervision (ACES), the American School Counselor Association (ASCA), the Council for Accreditation of Counseling and Related Educational Programs (CACREP) all prepared or collaborated in preparing standards for the preparation of school counselors. The National Center for Transforming School Counseling, working with a number of school counselor preparation programs, focused on training school counselors to become social action advocates focusing on closing the achievement gap for low-income and minority students.

The chapter also continued a review of the literature dealing with leadership and supervision. This literature continued to stress the importance of the position of building and district-level leaders and the supervision they provide to practicing counselors. It closed with a presentation of two studies dealing with school counselor assignments and the impact of student-to-counselor ratio.

References

Akos, P. Schuldt, H., & Walendin, M. (2009). School Counselor assignment in secondary schools. *Professional School Counseling, 13,* 23-29.

American School Counselor Association (2003). *The ASCA National Model: A framework for school counseling programs.* Alexandria, VA: Author.

American School Counselor Association (2004). *The ASCA National Model Workbook.* Alexandria, VA: Author.

American School Counselor Association (2005). *The ASCA National Model: A framework for school counseling programs* (2nd Ed.). Alexandria, VA: Author.

An Act Relating to Career Education, Florida H.B. 0769 (2004).

An Act Relating to Public School Counselors, SB518, Amends Texas Education Code, Sections 33.001, 33.005-33.006 (2001).

Baggerly, J., & Osborn, D. (2006). School counselors' career satisfaction and commitment: Correlates and predictors. *Professional School Counseling, 9,* 197-205.

Baker, S. B. (2001). Reflections on forty years in the school counseling profession: Is the glass half-full or half-empty? *Professional School Counseling, 5,* 75-83.

Barker, J., & Satcher, J. (2000). School counselors' perceptions of required workplace skills and career development competencies. *Professional School Counseling, 4,* 134-139.

Bemak, F. (2000). Transforming the role of the counselor to provide leadership in educational reform through collaboration. *Professional School Counseling, 3,* 323-331.

Bringman, N., & Lee, S. M. (2008). Middle school counselors' competence in conducting developmental classroom lessons: Is teaching experience necessary? *Professional School Counseling, 11,* 380-385.

Brown, D., & Trusty, J. (2005). School counselors, comprehensive school counseling programs and academic achievement: Are school counselors promising more than they can deliver? *Professional School Counseling,*

9, 1-8.

Carrell, S. & Carrell, S. (2006). Do lower student-to-counselor ratios reduce school disciplinary problems? Contributions to Economic Analysis & Policy, 5, 1-23.

Colbert, R. D., Vernon-Jones, R., & Pransky, K. (2006). The school change feedback process: Creating a new role for counselors in education reform. Journal of Counseling and Development, 84, 72-82.

Dahir, C. A., Burnham, J. J., & Stone, C. (2009). Listen to the voices: School counselors and comprehensive school counseling programs. Professional School Counseling, 12, 182-192.

Dimmitt, C., & Carey, J. (2007). Using the ASCA National Model to facilitate school transitions. Professional School Counseling, 10, 227-232.

Dollarhide, C. T., & Lemberger, M. E. (2006). "No child left behind": Implications for school counselors. Professional School Counseling, 9, 295-304.

Dollarhide, C. T., & Saginak, K. A. (2008). Comprehensive school counseling programs: K-12 delivery systems in action. Boston, MA: Pearson-Allyn and Bacon.

Dykeman, C., Wood, C., Ingram, M. A., Pehrsson, D., Mandsager, N., & Herr, E. L. (2003). The structure of school career development interventions: Implications for school counseling. Professional School Counseling, 6, 272-278.

Eschenauer, R., & Chen-Hayes, S. F. (2005). The transformative individual school counseling model: An accountability model for urban school counselors. Professional School Counseling, 8, 244-248.

Feller, R. W. (2003). Aligning school counseling, the changing workplace and career development assumptions. Professional School Counseling, 6, 262-271.

Feller, R. W. (2003). Special issue: Career development and the changing workplace. Professional School Counseling, 6.

Figlio, D. N. (2005). Boys named Sue: Disruptive children and their peers. NBER Working Paper w11277.

Finkelstein, D. (2009). A closer look at the principal-counselor relationship: A survey of principals and counselors. Washington DC: The College Board, American School Counselor Association, National Association of Secondary School Principals.

Galassi, J. P., & Akos, P. (2004). Developmental advocacy: Twenty-first century school counseling. Journal of Counseling & Development, 82, 146-157.

Galassi, J. P., & Akos, P. (2004). Developmental advocacy: Twenty-first century school counseling. *Journal of Counseling and Development, 82,* 146-157.

Green, A., & Keys, S. (2001). Expanding the developmental school counseling paradigm: Meeting the needs of the 21st century student. *Professional School Counseling, 5,* 84-95.

Gysbers, N. C., & Henderson, P. (2000). *Developing and managing your school guidance program* (3rd Ed.). Alexandria, VA: American Counseling Association.

Gysbers, N. C., & Henderson, P. (2001). Comprehensive guidance and counseling programs: A rich history and a bright future. *Professional School Counseling, 4,* 246-256.

Gysbers, N. C., & Henderson, P. (2006). *Developing and managing your school guidance and counseling program* (4th Ed.). Alexandria, VA: American Counseling Association.

Gysbers, N. C., & Lapan, R. T. (2009). *Strengths-based career development for school guidance and counseling programs.* Ann Arbor, MI: Counseling Outfitters.

Gysbers, N. C., (2001). School guidance and counseling in the 21st century: Remember the past into the future. *Professional School Counseling, 5,* 96-105.

Gysbers, N. C., Lapan, R. T., & Jones, B. A. (2000). School board policies for guidance and counseling: A call to action. *Professional School Counseling, 3,* 349-353.

Hale, J. (2009). *Finding a way: Practical examples of how an effective principal-counselor relationship can lead to success for all students.* Washington DC: The College Board, American School Counselor Association, National Association of Secondary School Principals.

Hatch, T., & Chen-Hayes, S. F. (2008). School counselor beliefs about ASCA National Model School Counseling Program Components Using the SCPCS. *Professional School Counseling, 12,* 34-42.

Henderson, P. (2005). The theory behind the ASCA National Model. In American School Counselor Association, *The ASCA National Model* (pp. 79-101). Alexandria, VA: Author.

Henderson, P. G. (2009). *The new handbook of administrative supervision in counseling.* New York: Routledge.

Henderson, P., & Gysbers, N. C. (Eds.) (2002). *Implementing comprehensive school guidance programs: Critical leadership issues and successful responses.* Greensboro, NC: ERIC/CASS.

Herr, E. L. (2001). The impact of national policies, economics and school reform on comprehensive guidance programs. *Professional School Counseling, 4,* 236-245.

Hipalito-Delgado, C. P., & Lee, C. C. (2007). Empowerment theory for the professional school counselor: A manifesto for what really matters. *Professional School Counseling, 10*, 327-332.

House, R. M., & Hayes, R. L. (2002). School counselors: Becoming key players in school reform. *Professional School Counseling, 5*, 249-256.

House, R. M., & Sears, S. J. (2002). Preparing school counselors to be leaders and advocates: A critical need in the new millennium. *Theory Into Practice, 41*, 154-162.

Hoyt, K. B. (1955). What should be the pupil load for the school counselor? *Personnel and Guidance Journal, 34*, 86-88.

Janson, C., & Stone, C. (2009). What works in the field: Comprehensive school counseling programs. In F. Connolly, & N. Protheroe (Eds.), *Principals and Counselors Partnering for Student Success*. Washington, DC: Educational Research Service and Naviance, Inc.

Johnson, C. D., & Johnson, S. K. (2001). *Results-based student support programs: Leadership academy workbook*. San Juan Capistrano, CA: Professional Update.

Johnson, L. S. (2000). Promoting professional identity in an era of educational reform. *Professional School Counseling, 4*, 31-40.

Johnson, S., & Johnson, C. D. (2003). Results-based guidance: A systems approach to student support programs. *Professional School Counseling, 6*, 180-184.

Johnson, S., & Johnson, C. D., & Downs, L. (2006). Building a results-based student support program. Boston, MA: Lahaska Press, Houghton Mifflin Company.

Joyce Ivy Foundation. *Converting high school achievement into adult opportunity: 2009 Ohio high school counselor report*. Ann Arbor, MI: Author.

Joyce Ivy Foundation. *The eleven-month challenge: 2008 Michigan high school counselor report*. Ann Arbor, MI: Author.

Kolodinsky, P., Draves, P., Schroder, V., Lindsay, C., & Zlatev, M. (2009). Reported levels of satisfaction and frustration by Arizona school counselors: A desire for greater connections with students in a data-driven era. *Professional School Counseling, 12*, 193-199.

Lambie, G. W., & Williamson, L. L. (2004). The challenge to change from guidance counseling to professional school counseling: A historical proposition. *Professional School Counseling, 8*, 124-131.

Lapan, R. T. (2001). Special issue: Comprehensive guidance and counseling programs: Theory, policy, practice and research. *Professional School Counseling, 4*, iv-v.

Lee, C. C. (2001). Culturally responsive school counselors and programs: Addressing the needs of all students. *Professional School Counseling, 4,* 257-261.

Lieberman, A. (2004). Confusion regarding school counselor functions: School leadership impacts role clarity. *Education, 124,* 522-529.

Louis, K. S., & Gordon, M. F. (2006). *Aligning student support with achievement goals: The secondary principal's guide.* Thousand Oaks, CA: Corwin Press.

Martin, I., Carey, J., & DeCoster, K. (2009). A National study of the current status of state school counseling models. *Professional School Counseling, 12,* 378-386.

Martin, I., Lopez, H., & Carey, J. C. (2009). A principal's guide to practical considerations in the organization and management of the school counseling program. In F. Connolly, & N. Protheroe (Eds.), *Principals and Counselors Partnering for Student Success.* Washington, DC: Educational Research Service and Naviance, Inc.

Martin, P. J. (2002). Transforming school counseling: A national perspective. *Theory Into Practice, 41,* 148-153.

Myrick, R. D. (2003). *Developmental guidance and counseling: A practical approach* (4th Ed.). Minneapolis, MN: Educational Media Corporation.

Myrick, R. D. (2003). *Developmental guidance and counseling: A practical approach* (4th Ed.). Minneapolis, MN: Educational Media Corporation.

Paisley, P. O. (2001). Maintaining and enhancing the developmental focus in school counseling programs. *Professional School Counseling, 4,* 271-277.

Paisley, P. O., & McMahon, H. G. (2001). School counseling for the 21st century: Challenges and opportunities. *Professional School Counseling, 5,* 106-115.

Perusse, R., Haas, E., Lally, I., & Mische, S. (2009). Preparing future principals to work with school counselors. *AASA Journal of Scholarship and Practice, 5,* 39-48.

Peterson, J. S., Goodman, R., Keller, T., & McCauley, A. (2004). Teachers and non-teachers as school counselors: Reflection on the internship experience. *Professional School Counseling, 7,* 246-255.

Poynton, T. A., & Carey, J. C. (2006). An integrative model of data-based decision making for school counseling. *Professional School Counseling, 10,* 121-130.

Poynton, T. A., Schumacher, R. A., & Wilczenski, F. L. (2008). School counselors' attitudes regarding statewide comprehensive developmental guidance model implementation. *Professional School Counseling, 11,*

417-422.

Rayle, A. D. (2006). Do school counselors matter? Mattering as a moderator between job stress and job satisfaction. *Professional School Counseling, 9*, 206-215.

Rowley, W. J., Stroh, H. R., & Sink, C. A. (2005). Comprehensive guidance and counseling programs use of guidance curricula materials: A survey of national trends. *Professional School Counseling, 8*, 296-304.

Rylander, C. K. (2002). *Guiding our children toward success: How Texas school counselors spend their time.* Austin, TX: Texas Comptroller of Public Accounts.

Scarborough, J. L., & Luke, M. (2008). School counselors walking the talk and talking the talk: A grounded theory of effective program implementation. *Professional School Counseling, 11*, 404-416.

Schwallie-Giddis, P., ter Maat, M., &Pak, M. (2003). Initiating leadership by introducing and implementing the ASCA National Model. *Professional School Counseling, 6*, 170-174.

Sears, S. J., & Granello, D. H. (2002). School counseling now and in the future: A reaction. *Professional School Counseling, 5*, 164-171.

Seashore, K. R., Jones, L. M., & Seppanen, P. (2001). *Transforming school counseling.* Minneapolis, MN: Center for Applied Research and Educational Improvement. University of Minnesota.

Sink, C. A. (2002). In search of the profession's finest hour: A critique of four views of 21st century school counseling. *Professional School Counseling, 5*, 156-163.

Sink, C. A. (2005). Comprehensive school counseling programs and academic achievement—A rejoinder to Brown and Trusty. *Professional School Counseling, 9*, 9-12.

Sink, C. A., & MacDonald, G. (1998). The status of comprehensive guidance and counseling programs in the United States. *Professional School Counseling, 2*, 88-94.

Sink, C. A., & Yillik-Downer, A. (2001). School counselors' perceptions of comprehensive guidance and counseling programs: A National survey. *Professional School Counseling, 4*, 278-286.

Smith, S. L., Crutchfield, L. B., & Culbreth, J. R. (2001). Teaching experience for school counselors: Counselor educators' perceptions. *Professional School Counseling, 4*, 216-224.

Utah State Board of Education Rule R277-462, *Comprehensive Guidance Program*, 1997.

Utah State Board of Education Rule R277-462, *Comprehensive Guidance Program*, 2009.

Vandergrift, J. A. (1999). *Are Arizona public schools making the best use*

of school counselors? Results of a 3-year study of counselors' time use.
Phoenix, AZ: Morrison Institute for Public Policy.

Walsh, M. E., Barrett, J. G., & DePaul, J. (2007). Day-to-day activities of
school counselors: Alignment with new directions in the field and the
ASCA National Model. *Professional School Counseling, 10,* 370-378.

West Virginia Board of Education Legislative Rule, Series 67,
Comprehensive Developmental Guidance and Counseling (2315), 2002.

Whiston, S.C. (2002). Response to the past, present, and future of school
counseling: Raising some issues. *Professional School Counseling, 5,*
148-155.

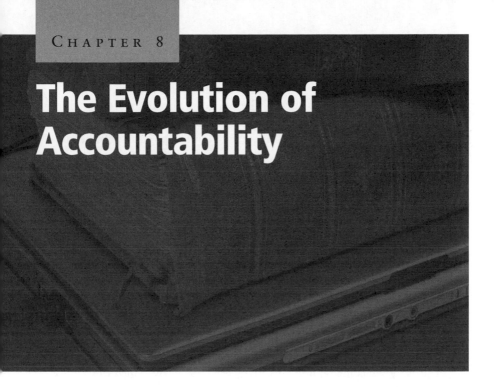

CHAPTER 8

The Evolution of Accountability

Today the issue of accountability is in the forefront of professional dialogue (Gysbers & Henderson, 2006; Gysbers & Lapan, 2009; Stone & Dahir, 2007; Whiston & Quinby, 2009). School counselors, working within the framework of comprehensive school counseling programs, increasingly are being asked to demonstrate their work contributes to student success, particularly student academic achievement. Not only are school counselors being asked to tell what they do, they also are being asked to demonstrate how what they do and the program in which they work makes a difference in students' lives.

Is the focus on accountability a new phenomenon or has our profession always been concerned about assessing the effects of school counselors' work? This chapter's purpose is to answer this question by tracing the evolution of accountability as documented in professional literature. The story begins in the 1920s soon after guidance and counseling was introduced in the schools as vocational guidance in the early 1900s. A sampling of literature in each decade from 1920 through 2009 was reviewed, first for evidence of expressions of concern about the need for accountability and then, for articles describing evaluation studies on the impact of guidance and counseling programs on student outcomes. Articles describing studies on the impact of specific guidance and counseling activities, techniques and methods, while important, were not included. The last part of the chapter identifies several themes from the literature describing necessary prerequisite conditions for accountability to occur including the importance of school counselors and school counselor educators becoming accountability leaders.

(Parts of this chapter appeared in an article titled "Comprehensive Guidance and Counseling Programs: The Evolution of Accountability" by Norman C. Gysbers published in *Professional School Counseling, 8*, 1-14. Used with permission.)

Accountability Over the Decades

THE 1920s

Before the 1920s, the work of professionals focused on establishing guidance and counseling (then called vocational guidance) in the schools. Rapid progress was made, and this progress carried over into the 1920s. By the 1920s, however, concern about accountability was beginning to be expressed in the literature as indicated by this statement by Payne (1924):

"What method do we have of checking the results of our guidance? For particular groups was it guidance, misguidance or merely a contributing experience? We simply must work out some definite method of testing and checking the results of our work. If we do not, some other group will, with possibly disastrous results for our work" (p. 63).

During the same year, Edgerton and Herr (1924) described the efforts of school districts in 143 cities across the United States to provide organized educational and vocational guidance activities in their respective school systems. They did not describe any studies assessing the impact of these activities, but they did identify some outcomes they thought were achieved.

"As an outcome of these serious endeavors to meet current and changing demands for purposeful instruction and systematic guidance, it is found that marked increases in interest, ambition and school attendance often follow the inauguration and development of suitable courses of study and their accompanying guidance programs" (p. 5).

Much of the work on accountability in the 1920s focused on establishing standards for judging whether or not a guidance and counseling program was complete. Myers (1926) was one of the first to suggest such standards. He identified four, including completeness as measured by the number of guidance and counseling activities, distribution of emphasis as shown by the time devoted to each activity, thoroughness as revealed by the kinds and quality of the work completed and consistency of organization. Later Edgerton (1929) presented data indicating a vocational guidance program needed to contain seven guidance activities to be claimed as complete.

THE 1930s

The 1930s witnessed intensive work on the issue of accountability picking up on efforts begun in the 1920s. One line of investigation focused on the work of Myers (1926) and Edgerton (1929) to establish standards to judge which guidance and counseling activities, when brought together, would constitute a complete program. The need to develop standards to judge the completeness of a program arose because of the wide array of activities being conducted under the banner of guidance and counseling by this time. Proctor (1930) made this point as follows:

"One of the great needs in the field of guidance is some fairly objective means of comparing the guidance activities of one secondary school system with that of another. It is only in this manner that we shall ever arrive at an estimate of what constitutes a standard setup for the carrying out of a guidance program" (p. 58).

To respond to this concern Proctor (1930) developed a score card system designed to assess whether or not certain guidance and counseling activities were in place and functioning the way they should. This system was the forerunner of today's concept of program evaluation (program audit). References to this aspect of accountability continued to appear in the literature in the 1930s. It was important work because of the need to develop a generally accepted notion of what constituted a complete program of guidance and counseling in the schools.

While work continued on establishing standards to measure the completeness of guidance and counseling programs, several writers began expressing the need to also focus on results. Hedge and Hutson (1931), for example, worried that individuals involved in guidance work were "still so occupied with the establishment of procedures of guidance that we have not yet attained the critical attitude which engenders attempts at objective measurement of results" (p. 508). This focus on results caused a number of writers to begin identifying what they felt were the desirable outcomes of guidance and counseling programs. For example, Christy, Stewart and Rosecrance (1930), Hinderman (1930) and Rosecrance (1930) identified the following student outcomes:

- Fewer pupils dropping out of school
- Increase in the standard of scholarship
- Better morale in the student body
- Better all-round school life
- Fewer student failures and subject withdrawals
- Young people better informed about the future
- Satisfactory adjustment of graduates to community life and vocation and to a college or university
- Fewer disciplinary cases
- Fewer absences
- More intelligent selection of subjects
- Better study habits

A focus on results was also on the mind of Smith (1931). He stated that the field should give increasing attention to the product of the vocational guidance process, to checking the results. "We are not so much concerned about the completeness of the set-up of the testing department of a guidance program, the classes in occupations or the placement office as we are about the effect actually produced within the individual" (p. 293).

Other writers, picking up on the results theme, began to explore what might be involved in measuring results. In a series of articles from 1932 to 1934, Kefauver and his colleagues (Kefauver, 1932; Kefauver & Davis, 1933; Kefauver & Hand, 1932, 1934; Kefauver, Hand, & Block, 1934) described possible outcomes for guidance. They also presented different approaches to conducting evaluation studies. Later, Hutson (1935) stated that the need for measuring the results of guidance was beginning to receive recognition. "These are days ... when all school activities are subject to the sharpest scrutiny, and the administrator is called upon to justify every expenditure of time and money in the operation of the school" (p. 21).

In fall 1934 Kefauver and Hand (1941) undertook a study involving junior high school students over a three-year period, supported by a grant from the Carnegie Foundation for the Advancement of Teaching. The study focused on two junior high schools from Oakland, Calif., and two junior high schools from Pasadena, Calif. Students entering seventh grade in fall 1934 served as the subjects. One school in each city was chosen as an experimental school while the second was chosen as a control school. Kefauver and Hand developed six tests and two inventories to administer to the experimental and control group students at the beginning and end of the study.

Before highlighting some of the findings, it is important to share the researchers' use of the words *experimental* and *control*.

"It may be desirable to caution against interpreting the use of the term 'control' as referring to groups or schools without any guidance service. One cannot find a school without some form of guidance. The comparisons between experimental and control groups are actually comparisons between schools with different forms of guidance service and different amounts of emphasis on guidance. The added emphasis on guidance in the two so-called experimental schools took the form, for the most part, of an increase in the amount of school time given to guidance activities by students, increase in staff time for guidance work and extension in the amount of material and tests over and above that generally employed in the regular guidance programs in the two cities. The comparisons reported in the study, then, do not purport to show how students develop with or without guidance. Instead, they indicate some of the major outcomes yielded by the two 'plus' programs" (Kefauver & Hand, 1941, p. 168).

Kefauver and Hand (1941) reported there were small beneficial effects in favor of the experimental schools in providing educational, recreational and social-civic guidance information. Larger beneficial effects were noted in health guidance information. Even larger beneficial effects were noted in imparting vocational guidance information and information about false guidance. Of particular interest to us today was that "students in the experimental schools typically made slightly greater gains in mean scores on the Stanford Achievement Test than did the students (1) in the corresponding control situations or (2) those who had been graduated by the two experimental schools prior to the three-year period during which the study reported in this section of the volume was conducted" (Kefauver & Hand), 1941, p. 215).

The six tests and two inventories used in this study were published by World Book Company in 1937 (Kefauver & Hand, 1937). The six tests were Educational Guidance Test, Health Guidance Test, Recreational Guidance Test, Social-Civic Guidance Test, Vocational Guidance Test and Student-Judgment Guidance Test. The first five tests measured the extent to which students possessed knowledge in the areas the tests measured. The sixth test "was constructed to determine the extent to which students recognize the limitations of the various methods used by those who gave false guidance" (Kefauver & Hand, 1937). The first inventory was a measure of student's self-ratings of abilities while the second was an inventory of the plans students had for the future. The development and use of these standardized tests and inventories were important because it marked the first time tests and inventories had been developed and used to provide a measure of student knowledge and self-estimates resulting from their participation in a guidance program.

Another major study of guidance began in the school year 1936-1937 in Arlington, Mass., (Rothney & Roens, 1950). Eighth-graders were divided into a guided group (experimentals) and an unguided group (controls). At the beginning of the study there were 129 students in each group. The experimental group received intensive assistance by counselors while the control group received no assistance other than routine help in selecting courses and making educational and vocational plans that had been available previously.

Comparisons were made between the two groups at the end of the senior year (June 1941). There were 81 students in the guided group and 90 students in the unguided group at graduation time in June 1941. The comparisons were made on the following criteria: dropouts, subject failures, grade failures, curriculum changes, graduation standing (an overall estimate of school achievement) and college admission. The findings were as follows:

- The dropout incidence in the two groups was approximately the same. Guidance apparently had no effect with respect to the retention of students.
- The rate of subject failures and the average number of failures per subject decreased faster in the guided group than in the unguided group.
- The rate of grade failure was higher in the unguided group in grade 10, the critical first year of senior high school. It seems reasonable to assume that the lower rate of the guided group was partly the result of guidance.
- Fewer students in the guided group made curriculum changes, and the total number of changes they made was less than in the unguided group. More of the guided students who were in the college curriculum remained in it. The relatively more permanent decisions made by the guided group may be attributed in part to guidance.

- The mean scholastic rating of the guided group was higher than that of the unguided group by a statistically reliable margin.
- A significantly larger percent of the guided group than of the unguided group was admitted to institutions of higher learning (Rothney & Roens, 1950, pp. 216-217).

Additional results from this study were gathered by comparing the answers to questions administered to the guided and unguided students during their senior year (85 guided and 94 unguided) and eight months later (85 guided and 82 unguided). The questions dealt with education and employment. The responses indicated that students in the guided group were better equipped with information about their goals, better adjusted and more confident, more familiar with community agencies, more secure about their future and more satisfied with their choice of school or employment.

Treacy (1937) offered a series of questions for administrators to use to review their guidance programs. One of the questions was, "Is there a constant effort to evaluate the effectiveness of the guidance program?" (p. 30). Alstetter (1938) stated that no program in schools was more difficult to evaluate than the guidance service. Finally, Becker (1937) listed a number of criteria that could be used to judge the effectiveness of guidance. She also identified a number of ways these criteria could be measured.

THE 1940s

The literature of the 1940s continued to emphasize the need for the evaluation of guidance. Wrenn (1940), substituting the phrase student personnel work for guidance, urged that more studies were needed. He recommended, "Let us have more developmental studies that will follow over a period of years counseled students and students exposed to certain personnel procedures, that will use control groups matched upon the more intangible aspects of personality as well as upon such objective measures as test scores and grades, that will evaluate the success of the work done with students in terms of broad areas of life adjustment and that will indicate the extent to which the assistance the student receives is effective in an after-institutional environment as well as within the school walls" (p. 414).

Schultz (1941) reviewed the literature on guidance in five educational magazines covering the period 1934 to 1939. He replicated a similar study conducted by Kefauver and Davis (1933) covering the time period

1927 to 1932. He found that in these five magazines for the time period covered there were no articles based on investigations which involved "the projection of as complete a program of guidance as possible, following a group of students through this service and making a careful measure of the results" (p. 494).

In the 1940s, the issue of what kind of training school counselors should have was receiving increasing attention. Jager (1948) pointed out that little or no mention of training in the evaluation of guidance programs can be found in the literature. He indicated that such training in evaluation should take two forms: "that of the program as a whole and of the techniques, staff and administrative provisions with which it operates and that of its results as evidenced in the counselees" (p. 481).

A landmark document on evaluation appeared in the 1940s authored by Froehlich (1949). He reviewed and classified 173 studies according to the following system:

- External criteria, the "do-you-do-this?" method.
- Follow-up, the "what-happened-then?" method.
- Client opinion, the "what-do-you-think?" method.
- Expert opinion, the "information, please" method.
- Specific techniques, the little-little method.
- Within-group changes, the before-and-after method.
- Between-group changes, the "what's-the-difference?" method (p. 2).

Froehlich (1949) concluded his review by stating that much more work on evaluation was needed. He was concerned about the lack of suitable evaluation criteria and the need for methods that met acceptable research standards but yet could be used by practitioners.

"Since its inception the guidance movement has been concerned primarily with the establishment of philosophies, the development of instruments and techniques and the organization of programs – to the exclusion of the evaluation of results" (Wilson, 1945, p. 1). This was the opening sentence in Wilson's book, "Procedures in Evaluating a Guidance Program." The remainder of her book focused on different evaluation procedures, including the use of surveys, questionnaires, interviews, observations and self-evaluations. She provided detailed discussions concerning the design and uses of each of these procedures.

Later in the 1940s, Wrenn (1947) again spoke to the need for evaluating personnel services. In this article Wrenn was using the words personnel services synonymously with the word guidance. He stated, "Neither they [personnel workers] nor the public have been aware of the needs for evaluation, but as the public becomes more intelligent about what we are doing it will demand proof of value, and we must be prepared to supply it" (p. 512).

One final article is worth noting from the 1940s. Travers (1949), in a lengthy article reviewing a number of issues surrounding the evaluation of guidance, stated, "Progress will be slow until guidance workers come to recognize guidance as a learning situation which can be investigated by the methods developed for investigating other learning situations. These methods involve the specification of the objectives of learning that are to be achieved, the specification of the means of achieving these objectives, the selection of criteria for determining whether the learning objectives have been achieved and provision for the control of relevant variables. Until more studies of guidance are undertaken following these steps, there will be very little certain knowledge of what guidance is actually accomplishing" (p. 223).

THE 1950s

Interest in the evaluation of school guidance and counseling programs continued unabated during the 1950s. Calls for more and better evaluation of guidance programs continued to be heard (Cottle, 1957; Jones, 1951; Mahoney, 1950). Such calls stressed the need to establish better criteria for measuring the results of guidance in schools.

Guidance and counseling activities in the 1950s were reviewed three times in the *Review of Educational Research*. Wagner, Arbuckle & Carnes (1951) noted that while there had been an increase in the number of studies of guidance over the three years of their review period, the focus of these studies had been limited to specific parts of guidance. They stressed the need "to evaluate total programs as well as specific or isolated phases" (p. 106). Later, McDaniel (1954), in his review of three years of literature, pointed out that the research conducted during that period had been mainly on the process aspects of guidance programs and that more research was needed on the effectiveness of various organizational structures for guidance. Kelley (1955) also expressed concern about school counselors focusing on process rather than outcomes. "Are guidance counselors not too often concerned with *how many* come to a counselor's office rather than with *how many have changed their behavior* as a result of the visit" (p. 364). Finally Cottle (1957) reported on several studies that indicated total programs of guidance in the schools had had an impact on students' lives.

The major study of the 1950s, concerning the effects of guidance in the schools, occurred in Wisconsin. It is known as the Wisconsin Counseling Study (Rothney, 1958). The full details of the study were published in his book "Guidance Practices and Results." All 870 sophomores in the schools of the four communities in Wisconsin were placed in either an experimental group or a control group. The experimental group received an intensive guidance program while the controls did not.

Since the control and experimental subjects attended the same school in the same city, questions were raised about contamination. Rothney (1958) acknowledged that contamination probably occurred, but given the fact that this was a natural setting, it could not be avoided. He stated that he had "even observed an experimental boy with his arm around a control-group girl while off on an evening's excursion and it was assumed that some 'contamination' might have resulted" (p. 61).

On graduation day in June 1951 there were 690 graduates. Three follow-ups took place: one six months after high school graduation, one two and one half years after graduation and one five years after graduation in 1956. One hundred percent of the students (685) who were living participated in the final follow-up.

Here are the findings of this landmark study. Students who received counseling:

- Achieved slightly higher academic records in high school and post-high school education;
- Indicated more realism about their own strengths and weaknesses at the time they were graduated from high school;
- Were less dissatisfied with their high school experiences;
- Had different vocational aspirations;
- Were more consistent in expression of, entering into, and remaining in their vocational choices, classified by areas;
- Made more progress in employment during the five-year period following high school graduation;
- Were more likely to go on to higher education, to remain to graduate and to plan for continuation of higher education;

- Were more satisfied with their post-high school education;
- Expressed greater satisfaction with their status five years after high school and were more satisfied in retrospect with their post-high school experiences;
- Participated in more self-improvement activities after completing high school;
- Looked back more favorable on the counseling they had obtained (Rothney, 1958, pp. 479-480).

Rothney (1950) offered the following conclusion to the study: "When so many small and a few large differences in the directions hypothesized by guidance workers can be obtained under representative high school counseling conditions, it seems likely that greater differences would appear if counseling were done under more ideal circumstances. Such circumstances would seem to require more acceptance of counseling as a regular part of secondary school experience, more enthusiastic support by parents and school personnel and better techniques of evaluation" (pp. 482-483).

THE 1960s

In 1958, the National Defense Education Act (NDEA) became law. Not since the passage of the Vocational Education Act of 1946 (often referred to as the George-Barden Act) did a federal law have as much impact on the field of guidance and counseling. NDEA provided funding for state supervisors of guidance, statewide testing programs and training for individuals to become school counselors through summer and yearlong institutes. Propelled by NDEA, the 1960s began a period of rapid expansion for guidance in schools, particularly at the elementary level.

The 1960s also witnessed the emergence of the accountability movement in education. As education was being held accountable for its outcomes, so too was guidance. It was clear that it would be necessary for school counselors to state guidance objectives in measurable terms and then show how these objectives related to the goals of education. It was also clear that the value of guidance programs was increasingly going to be judged based on their impact on students.

In 1961, Wellman and Twiford prepared a bulletin for the U.S. Office of Education (USOE) titled "Guidance Counseling and Testing Program Evaluation." This bulletin was a response to a requirement in Title V-A of NDEA that required states to review and evaluate annually local programs of guidance and counseling. The bulletin summarized the recommendations of the participants of a series of workshops held in 1959 concerning the evaluation of school guidance programs. It provided some desired student outcomes of guidance programs, offered suggestions for data collection and presented suggested procedural methods that could be used in studies of students. The student outcomes identified were:

- Do students develop greater understanding of their abilities, aptitudes and interests?
- Are students, and their parents, fully aware of opportunities and requirements for education and careers?
- Do students select courses, and achieve in them, in line with their abilities, aptitudes, interests and opportunities?
- Do those students who are able to do so finish secondary school?
- Do those students, who are capable of doing so continue education beyond the secondary school?
- Are those students who continue their education beyond the secondary school successful in their educational pursuits?
- Are significant numbers of the especially able students getting more extensive background in mathematics, science and the foreign languages? (Wellman & Twiford, 1961, p. 26)

The USOE continued its interest in the evaluation of guidance and counseling by sponsoring research seminars at the University of Georgia in 1961 and at the University of Michigan in 1962. The focus of these seminars was on problems in evaluating the effectiveness of guidance. In 1963, the USOE initiated a request for a proposal to evaluate the effectiveness of guidance focusing on outcomes using the recommendations from these seminars. Charles Neidt (1965) was awarded a contract to develop the research design while Fred Proff (1965) was awarded a contract to do a literature review.

In his report Neidt (1965) recommended that the purpose of the proposed National Study of Guidance should be "to identify factors of the guidance process that are uniquely related to changes in the behavior of students" (p. 2). As reported in Wellman and Moore (1975) the research design Neidt suggested had four phases:

- The development of taxonomies and operational definitions of variables to be included in each of the four variable domains, i.e., process, criterion, student and situational
- Instrumentation and field testing of instruments
- Sample selection

■ Data collection and analysis (p. 5)

Only phase one of the proposed National Study was completed, with the work being done at the University of Missouri-Columbia between 1966 and 1968 (Wellman & Moore, 1975).

One result of the work of Wellman and his colleagues was the development of a systems model for evaluation accompanied by a taxonomy of guidance objectives classified in the three domains of educational, vocational and social development. This model and its companion taxonomy of objectives served as a basis for a number of evaluation models that began appearing in the late 1960s and early 1970s. "A Process Guide for the Development of Objectives," originally published by the California State Department of Education in 1970 and later by the California Personnel and Guidance Association (Sullivan & O'Hare, 1971), was an example of one such model.

In a series of reviews of the evaluation of guidance and counseling published in the 1960s in the *Review of Educational Research* by Rothney and Farwell (1960), Patterson (1963), Strowig and Farwell (1966), and Gelatt (1969), discussion centered on the need for evaluation and the lack of evidence that it was occurring. Rothney and Farwell stated that "Guidance services, like many others in education, are still offered largely on the basis of hope and faith" (p. 168). Strowig and Farwell (1966) were particularly concerned about the lack of total program research. Gelatt (1969), repeating the concerns of previous writers over the years, expressed his concern about the confusion and vagueness that existed concerning guidance objectives and outcomes.

In a report of research conducted in Minnesota, Tamminen and Miller (1968) discussed the lack of attention to outcomes research. To Rothney and Farwell's comment about accepting guidance in the schools based on hope and faith, Tamminen and Miller added charity. "Faith, hope and charity have characterized the American attitude toward guidance programs – faith in their effectiveness, hope that they can meet important if not always clearly specified need and charity in not demanding more evaluative evidence that the faith and hope are justified" (p. 3).

THE 1970s

In the early 1970s the accountability movement intensified. Concurrently, interest in the development of comprehensive systematic approaches to guidance program development and management continued to increase. The convergence of these movements in the 1970s served as a stimulus to continue the task of defining guidance developmentally in measurable individual outcome terms – as a program in its own right rather than as services ancillary to other programs.

On the West Coast, McDaniel (1970) proposed a model for guidance called Youth Guidance Systems. It was organized around goals, objectives, programs, implementation plans and designs for evaluation. Hayes (1970) edited a workbook to provide practitioners with a guide to identify program goals and objectives in measurable terms. Then in 1971, O'Hare and Lasser (1971) and Sullivan and O'Hare (1971) prepared monographs for the California Personnel and Guidance Association that presented systematic evaluation strategies. Sullivan and O'Hare (1971) stated the importance of evaluation as follows. Notice they used the title pupil personnel services rather than school counselors and guidance and counseling programs.

"The development and implementation of programs for achieving specific student outcomes will be among the most important and progressive work in pupil personnel services during the 1970s. Current thinking in education espouses the development of objectives-based programs because they facilitate both effective planning and evaluation of educational experiences. In addition, increasing pressure has been placed upon the schools in recent years to provide evidence that various educational programs, including programs in pupil personnel services, produce desirable changes in student performance."

The Comprehensive Career Guidance System (CCGS) developed by personnel at the American Institutes for Research (Jones, Helliwell, Ganschow, & Hamilton, 1971; Jones, Hamilton, Ganschow, Helliwell, & Wolff, 1972) was designed to systematically plan, implement and evaluate guidance programs. At about the same time, personnel at the National Center for Vocational and Technical Education designed a behavioral model for career guidance based on a systems approach focusing on evaluation (Campbell et al., 1971). Later, the American College Testing Program (1976) created the River City Guidance Model, which also stressed evaluating program results.

In addition to these approaches, a systematic approach to guidance was being advocated in the Program of Learning in Accordance with Needs (PLAN) System of Individualized Education at about the same time

(Dunn, 1972). Guidance was seen as a major component of PLAN and was treated as an integral part of the regular instructional program. According to Dunn (1972) the guidance program in PLAN "to be effective, must be predicated on empirical evidence" (p. 8).

Concurrent with these efforts, a national effort was begun to assist the states in developing and implementing state models or guides for career guidance, counseling and placement. In 1971, the University of Missouri-Columbia was awarded a U.S. Office of Education grant to assist each state, the District of Columbia and Puerto Rico in developing models or guides for implementing and evaluating career guidance, counseling and placement programs in local schools. This project was the next step in a program of work begun as a result of a previous project at the university, a project that conducted a national conference on career guidance, counseling and placement in October 1969 and regional conferences across the country during spring 1970. All 50 states, the District of Columbia and Puerto Rico were involved in the 1971 project, and by the time the project ended in 1974, 44 states had developed some type of guide or model for career guidance, counseling and placement.

As a part of the assistance provided to the states, project staff conducted a national conference in January 1972 and developed a manual (Gysbers & Moore, 1974) to be used by the states as they developed their own guides. The manual described how to develop, implement and evaluate a comprehensive guidance program. The program concept described in the manual was evaluation-based focusing both on process and outcome evaluation. Four questions were asked. What do we want to accomplish? What kind of delivery system is needed? What did we provide and do? What was the impact?

As the movement toward planning and implementing systematic developmental and accountable guidance programs in the early 1970s became more sophisticated, theoretical models began to be translated into practical, workable models to be implemented in the schools. One example of this occurred in Mesa, Ariz. The guidance staff in the Mesa Public Schools felt the need to reorient the guidance program to make it more accountable.

"Our main objective was, briefly stated, to reduce the size of our "universe" down to manageable size and then – within the parameters of this "new" definition of guidance – be responsible i.e., accountable. We were committed to move toward a model of accountability, based not only upon what counselors did but rather based on results or outcomes in terms of observable student behaviors. (McKinnon, n.d., p.iii)

In 1974, the American Institutes for Research began work on bringing together program planning efforts previously undertaken by the Pupil Personnel Division of the California State Department of Education and its own Youth Development Research Program in Mesa, Ariz., and elsewhere (Jones, Helliwell, & Ganschow, 1975). This resulted in the development of 12 competency-based staff development modules on developing comprehensive career guidance programs K-12. Module 3, titled "Assessing Desired Outcomes" (Dayton, n.d.), focused on the need for programs to be accountable by starting with desired student outcomes spelled out in "concrete, measurable terms, not vague statements" (Dayton, p. 7).

In addition to these local, state and national efforts to establish guidance as a program and make it accountable, there was substantial discussion of these issues in professional literature. For example, in a book titled "Research and the School Counselor," Cramer, Herr, Morris and Frantz (1970), devoted a chapter to the evaluation of guidance programs. They pointed to the "increasing pressure on school counselors to document and justify the efficacy of their services" (p. 87). They described possible methodology to accomplish the task whether the focus was on total guidance program evaluation or only on specific aspects of the program.

Another example of attention to the topic of accountability occurred when one journal, Measurement and Evaluation in Guidance, devoted an entire issue (Volume 8, Number 3, October, 1975) to evaluation. Pine (1975), writing in this issue, opened his article with this statement: "In this age of accountability the evaluation of school counseling is of paramount concern to all counselors regardless of their theoretical and philosophical biases" (p. 136).

Pine went on in his article to identify criteria typically used to establish that behavior change in students has occurred at the elementary school level as a result of being involved in counseling.

- Academic achievement
- Increase in grade-point average
- Improvement in reading
- Peer relations

- Personal adjustment
- School attendance
- School adjustment
- School attitudes
- School anxiety
- Self-concept
- Self-esteem
- Self-understanding
- Teacher-pupil relationships
- Reduction of inappropriate behavior
- Intelligence test scores
- Setting realistic goals (p. 138)

Pine also identified methods typically used for evaluating the effectiveness of elementary school counseling programs. These were:

- The experimental approach: the "after-only" design, the "before-and-after" design and the "before-and-after-with-control-group design
- The tabulation approach: the number of clients, the number of counseling sessions, the nature and kinds of problems discussed, the number of parental contacts
- The follow-up approach
- The expert opinion: the "information-please" method, a subjective evaluation by experts
- The client opinion: ("what-do-you-think" method) characterized by opinion surveys of counselees
- The external criteria: the "do you do this?" method; the first step is to set up standards against which the program to be evaluated is compared.
- Opinion surveys of teachers, parents and employers
- The descriptive approach: counseling practices are analyzed and described
- The case-study approach: a longitudinal view of each client (p. 139)

The other writers in this special issue of Measurement and Evaluation in Guidance echoed the need for guidance and counseling program evaluation focusing on outcomes. They presented various evaluation procedures and talked about minimizing measurement concerns in guidance program evaluation (Bardo & Cody, 1975; Buckner, 1975; Hilliwell & Jones, 1975; Lasser, 1975; & Miller & Grisdale, 1975; O'Connor & Wigtel, 1975).

Wellman and Moore (1975) reported on a three-year longitudinal evaluation project in Cobb County, Ga. The design of the study and the results are reported below because this is one of only a few experimental control studies done in the 1970s.

"The evaluation design included (1) four experimental schools where the comprehensive PPS were implemented, (2) four control schools where no PPS were provided and (3) an independent control group that was drawn from other schools in the county for some of the achievement comparisons. The primary outcome measures were the Metropolitan Achievement Tests (MAT); and the Behavior Maturity Scale (MBS), a teacher rating of each pupil's academic, social and emotional behavior. The MAT was administered in April of each year as a post-test measure, and the BMS was administered in October and April for gain analysis, as well as comparisons with the control pupils. Additionally, differential effectiveness of the PPS was analyzed with respect to sex and diagnostic classification of the pupils. The diagnostic types included (1) average, (2) slow maturing, (3) slow learner, (4) environmentally disadvantaged, (5) accelerated learner, (6) emotionally disturbed, (7) neurologically handicapped and (8) educable mentally retarded. Comparisons were made among these subgroups where the number of pupils was adequate. More than 1,000 experimental pupils and a comparable number of control pupils provided the data for this evaluation, with data for the full three-year period from 250 experimental pupils and 290 control pupils. The principal outcome analyses involved comparisons between the experimental and control pupils with respect to growth and academic achievement. Statistical significance at the .05 level was required to accept differences on all gain and group comparisons."

The results from this evaluation showed rather conclusively that comprehensive PPS do make a difference in the development of pupils in the primary grades. The major findings included the following:

- The educational achievement of pupils in the experimental schools was better than that of concurrent controls and baseline criterion groups. The experimental pupils excelled over the control pupils in 66 percent of all comparisons of educational achievement during the three years, and the controls failed to excel in a single comparison. Also, the superior achievement attained by the experimental pupils during the first year was maintained through the following two years.
- Differential effectiveness of the PPS program was found with regard to areas of educational achievement, sex and type of the pupils. The

impact of the program was greater in the area of verbal achievement than in numeral achievement; the boys showed substantially greater achievement differences over their control counterparts than did the girls; and the slow learning and environmentally disadvantaged pupils achieved significantly higher than the control pupils much more often than did the average or accelerated pupils. Thus the evidence supported the effectiveness of the PPS program for improving verbal achievement with boys and with pupils who might be expected to have learning difficulties more than with girls and with the average or superior pupils.

- The experimental pupils had slightly better gains in task-oriented, social and emotional behaviors than did the control group, but these differences were not as consistent as in the area of educational achievement. (pp. 10-11)

As we have seen, the 1970s witnessed considerable interest in evaluation. In addition to the sources quoted so far, there were many other articles focusing on evaluation. Most of them highlighted the need for accountability in all of education including guidance and counseling because of increasing competition for tax dollars and the need to show the public that guidance and counseling in schools can contribute to student success (Atkinson, Furlong, & Janoff, 1979; Bardo, Cody, & Bryson, 1978; Burck & Peterson, 1975; Carr, 1977; Crabbs & Crabbs, 1977; Gamsky, 1970; Gerler, 1976; Gubser, 1974; Humes, 1972; Knapper, 1978; Krumboltz, 1974; Thompson & Borsari, 1978).

Wellman and Gysbers (1971) in the title of their article asked the question that many others had asked previously, "Did the program make a difference?" They asked this question because they pointed out that federal and state funding for guidance placed responsibility on professionals to demonstrate program effectiveness. They contended that outcomes must be stated in behavioral terms that would permit measurement. Finally, they suggested a variety of designs for outcome evaluation including baseline comparison group, within group design and experimental design.

Campbell (1978), Herr (1978) and Mitchell (1978) writing in *New Imperatives for Guidance* all stressed the need for and importance of accountability for guidance. Campbell pointed out that simply demonstrating that a guidance program is needed is not enough, that decision-makers want documentation of the results. Herr reviewed definitions of the terms *research*, *evaluation* and *accountability*. He focused his attention mainly on the issue of research examining the need for research and how research forms that basis for accountability. Mitchell emphasized the importance of prioritizing student needs and being accountable for student outcomes based on those needs. In her discussion of the evaluation of guidance Mitchell made an interesting observation concerning the nature of such studies.

"Evaluation studies need not be exhaustive, scientifically oriented, statistically embellished. On the other hand, they should be something more than "warm-puppy studies." Warm-puppy studies focus on how happy everyone is with the program, how much they like it. Such studies, although helpful for ego-deficient program leaders, do little to identify the strengths and weaknesses of the program or to suggest direction for change in order to enhance the likelihood of effectiveness (p. 127).

In the mid-1970s the College Entrance Examination Board (1978) developed the Career Skills Assessment Program. John Krumboltz was the principal consultant and author. Six content modules consisting of an exercise booklet, self-scorable and machine-scorable response sheets and a self-instructional guide were created as follows:

- Self-Evaluation and Development Skills
- Career Awareness Skills
- Career Decision-Making Skills
- Employment-Seeking Skills
- Work Effectiveness Skills
- Personal Economics Skills

In the Career Skills Assessment Program manual (College Entrance Examination Board, 1978), Section IV described various uses of the instruments including conducting evaluation and research studies of career guidance programs. The point was made that few evaluation tools existed to measure student achievement in career guidance programs. It was suggested that the instruments could help assess program effectiveness from both a formative and summative basis.

THE 1980s

The concern about accountability did not lessen in the 1980s, rather it increased. Due to budget cuts at federal, state and local levels, the theme that school counselor survival depended upon accountability was prevalent (Hayden & Pohlmann, 1981; Shay, 1981; Wiggins, 1981). Shay quoting Thurow (1980) said, "The theme for the 1980s will be: All stress, much strain" (p. 74).

As a result of these conditions numerous articles were written about the need for accountability in guidance and the lack of work being done to make programs accountable (Huber, 1980; Froehle & Fuqua, 1981; Wilson & Rotter, 1982; Wilson, 1985). A number of other writers during the 1980s provided ideas about how to do program evaluation (Lewis, 1983; Lombana, 1985; Pine, 1981; Wheeler & Loesch, 1981).

Two special issues of the *Personnel and Guidance Journal* were published in April and May 1981. The first one was edited by Minor (1981), and the second one was edited by Remer (1981). Both special issues dealt with research and evaluation issues and practices for counseling in general and school counseling specifically.

In 1981, the California State Department of Education published "Guidelines for Developing Comprehensive Guidance Programs in California Public Schools: Kindergarten Through Adult School." In this document formative and summative evaluation were described using product data, process data and context data. It was stated that formative evaluation answers the question, "How are we doing?" while summative evaluation answers the question "How did we do?"

Do elementary school counselors make a contribution to student learning? Gerler (1985) reviewed the research published in *Elementary School Guidance & Counseling* from 1974 to 1984 to explore this question. Based on his review he concluded, "This review of more than a decade of research on elementary school counseling establishes that counseling programs can positively influence the affective, behavioral and interpersonal domains of children's lives and, as a result, can affect children's achievement positively" (p. 48).

Wilson (1985) lamented the lack of research conducted by school counselors. In her article she described a number of reasons for this. She concluded that whatever the obstacles school counselors face in conducting research, it is important that they get involved. If they don't they "run the risk of having outside evaluation forced on them" (p. 118). She went on to say that research activity must be part of school counselors' role and not to do it is "at worst dangerous" (p. 118).

Fairchild and Zins (1986) reported on a national survey of accountability practices. Of the 239 respondents (239 out of 500), 55 percent indicated they were collecting accountability data. The remainder stated they lacked knowledge of accountability procedures, and time was a major problem for them.

THE 1990s

Continued expressions about the lack of research concerning the impact of guidance and counseling were apparent as the decade of the 1990s began. Campbell and Deck (1990) edited a special issue of Elementary School Guidance & Counseling on this topic. Lee and Workman (1992) noted, "Compared to other areas of the profession, school counseling seems to have little empirical evidence to support claims that it has a significant impact on the development of children and adolescents" (p. 15). Fairchild (1993) stated that while there had been an increase in work on accountability by school counselors since the survey Fairchild and Zins (1986) had conducted earlier, there were still many practitioners who did not collect accountability data.

Ways of proceeding with school guidance program evaluation were also described in the 1990s. Johnson and Whitfield (1991) presented an overall plan to evaluate school guidance programs. In the opening sentence of the introduction to their edited monograph they said, "Evaluation is an integral part of every program and when considered during the program development state, assures clear, measurable goals" (p. 1).

Gysbers, Hughey, Starr and Lapan (1992) described the overall evaluation framework that guided Missouri's efforts to evaluate comprehensive school guidance programs. Two of the five questions guiding the evaluation process focused on the measurement of students' mastery of guidance competencies and the possible impact of the program on the school's climate and goals.

During this same period, Borders and Drury (1992) described components of effective programs. One of the components was program evaluation. In this component it was suggested that "evaluation plans should focus on program results rather than program services" (p. 493). They suggested an evaluation plan that would focus on results as well as a variety of evaluation methods that could be used to accomplish this task.

Later in the 1990s, Whiston (1996) outlined a number of approaches to research that could be used in many settings including schools. She pointed out that school counselors were encountering increased pressure to be accountable and, therefore, needed to be more active in outcome research. Then in 1998, Whiston and Sexton (1998) presented a review of school counseling outcome research published between 1988 and 1995. In their opening sentence they said, "In this era of accountability, school counselors increasingly are asked to provide information to parents, administrators and legislators on the effectiveness of school counseling activities" (p. 412).

Two studies conducted in the late 1990s provide evidence of the contribution of comprehensive guidance and counseling programs to important markers of student success. Lapan, Gysbers and Sun (1997) compared students in Missouri high schools with more fully implemented guidance and counseling programs with students in less fully implemented programs. They found that students in high schools with more fully implemented programs reported they had earned higher grades, their education was better preparing them for the future and their schools had a more positive climate.

In Utah, Nelson, Gardner and Fox (1998) also compared students in high schools with more fully implemented guidance and counseling programs with students in less fully implemented programs. They found that students in high schools with more fully implemented programs took more advanced math and science courses, took more vocational/technical courses and had higher ACT scores on every scale of the test.

One of the challenges in evaluating the impact of comprehensive guidance and counseling programs is finding reliable and valid instruments to measure student outcomes. As you will recall, the work of Kefauver and Hand (1937) and the work of Krumboltz (College Entrance Examination Board, 1978) were attempts to respond to this challenge. Lapan, Gysbers, Multon and Pike (1997) reported on work done in Missouri to develop guidance competency self-efficacy surveys for high school and middle school students. The surveys were developed by using the three guidance content areas (standards) Missouri used in the 1980s and 1990s, namely Career Planning and Exploration, Knowledge of Self and Others, and Educational and Vocational Development. This work resulted in the publication of two surveys, one for grades 9-12 and one for grades 6-9.

2000

The emphasis on accountability that began in the 1920s continued with renewed vigor in the first decade of the 21st century. Trevisan and Hubert (2001) reiterated statements made over the past 20 years concerning the importance of program evaluation and of obtaining accountability data regarding student results. Foster, Watson, Meeks and Young (2002) also reiterated the need for accountability for school counselors and offered the single-subject research design as a way to demonstrate effectiveness. The use of single-subject design was also advocated by Foster, Watson, Meeks and Young (2002). Lapan (2001) stressed the importance of comprehensive programs of guidance and counseling "conceptualized as results-based systems" (p. 289). In his article he described a framework for guidance program planning and evaluation. Hughes and James (2001) noted the importance of using accountability data with site-based management teams and other school personnel. In addition, articles by Myrick (2003), Johnson and Johnson (2003), and Dahir and Stone (2003) in the February 2003 issue of *Professional School Counseling* all emphasized the need for accountability.

Two more studies, one in Missouri and one in the state of Washington, shed light on the contribution of comprehensive guidance and counseling programs to student success. Lapan, Gysbers and Petroski (2001) compared selected outcomes for middle school students in schools with more fully implemented programs with middle school students in schools with less fully implemented programs. Middle school students in schools with more fully implemented programs reported they earned higher grades, schools were more relevant, they had positive relationships with teachers, they were more satisfied with their education and they felt safer in school.

Sink and Stroh (2003) conducted a similar study only with elementary students. They compared elementary students enrolled in well-established guidance and counseling programs with students who were enrolled in schools with less-well-established programs. They found that elementary students (grades three and four) enrolled in schools with a comprehensive school counseling program produced higher achievement test scores on the Iowa Tests of Basic Skills–Form M and the Washington Assessment of Student Learning.

Many writers in this decade have discussed the importance of evaluation of comprehensive guidance and counseling programs. Other writers have presented data showing the impact of these programs on student success.

Trevisan (2002) stated that what has been missing in the accountability dialogue has been attention to something he called evaluation capacity. In his article he used the Milstein and Colton (2000) evaluation capacity framework to describe the contextual factors and system characteristics that have an impact on the evaluation capacity of school guidance and counseling programs. The framework contains the following categories:

- *Forces:* Policies, tacit expectations and incentives that drive an organization toward evaluation
- *Organizational environment:* Properties of the agency in which evaluation is conducted
- *Workforce and professional development:* The knowledge and skills of those who conduct evaluation
- *Resources and supports:* Funding, models and methods, for example, that an evaluator uses to ensure evaluations are effective and efficient
- *Learning from experience:* Lessons learned during and after evaluation activities that can positively impact future evaluation work (Trevisan, 2002, p. 292).

Tevisan suggested that this framework can serve as a way to inventory factors that may influence the evaluation process and, having that inventory, plans to strengthen evaluation capacity can be developed.

In January 2003 The Center for School Counseling Outcome Research (CSCOR) was founded (Carey & Dimmitt, 2006). This was important because now there was an active center to provide leadership in promoting quality research and provide school counselors and counselor educators with relevant research to help them make informed program decisions. It also sponsored the National Panel for School Counseling Evidence-Based Practice, a panel whose work will be discussed later in this chapter.

Stone and Dahir (2004) took up the challenge of school counselor accountability by developing an evaluation decision-making model called MEASURE. It describes six steps in the evaluation process including mission; elements; analyze, stakeholders-unite; reanalyze, reflect and revise; and educate. This model stressed the need to focus directly on outcome data, on how students are different as a result of program interventions. A second edition of their book was published in 2007.

One of the challenges school counselors face as they respond to the call for accountability of their work is selecting an appropriate decision-making model. Poynton and Carrey (2006) described five commonly used models. They compared and contrasted these five models concerning the steps and tasks involved. They then synthesized these models into a new five-stage model, the IDEAS model, which they explain in detail in the article. They did express concern about the use of the IDEAS model because of the skills schools would need to implement it. They recommended that CACREP should include the needed competencies for these models into any revision of the standards for the preparation of school counselors.

Concern about school counselors' willingness and ability to evaluate the programs in which they work and ways to respond to this concern was the topic of a number of articles. Bauman (2004) pointed to the need to train and reward school counselors who conduct research. Brott (2006) spoke about the need for counselor educators to train school counselors to be accountable for their work. Gysbers, Lapan and Stanley (2006) described how the state of Missouri (Department of Elementary and Secondary Education, Missouri School Counselor Association and Missouri counselor educators) began the training of school counselors to conduct results-based evaluation. While professional development activities continued, counselor education programs in Missouri incorporated the evaluation model into the training of school counselors. Finally, Holcomb-McCoy, Gonzalez and Johnston (2009) explored school counselor self-efficacy concerning evaluation. They found that counselor self-efficacy influenced data usage. They concluded their article by stating that more research was needed "on the process of developing more school counselors who use and integrate data throughout their school counseling programs" (p. 351).

In 2006 a special issue of *Professional School Counseling* edited by Sink (2006) was published. It covered a wide range of research-related topics and issues. Its publication by ASCA continued to illustrate the high interest in and the need for research and evaluation activities for school counselors. Another issue of *Professional School Counseling* edited by Milsom (2009) picked up on the need for more research, this time, focusing on action research.

Concern about models to guide the process of program evaluation continued to be of concern too. Astromovich and Coker (2007) described a model they endorsed called the Accountability Bridge Model. This model described a way to organize and carry out program evaluation. They called for counselor educators to provide training on how to carry out program evaluation.

Statewide studies of the impact of comprehensive guidance and counseling programs continued to be conducted in the last half of this decade. Three studies in particular are presented. One study was conducted in Missouri, one in Utah and one in Washington.

Lapan, Gysbers and Kayson (2006) found that when school counselors in Missouri work in schools with more fully implemented programs, they make contributions to overall student success including student academic achievement. More specifically they found that students in schools with more fully implemented programs had higher 10th-grade Missouri Assessment Program (MAP) mathematics scores and higher 11th-grade MAP communication arts scores. They also found more students in these schools were likely to attend school, fewer had discipline problems, fewer received out-of-school suspensions.

Nelson, Fox, Haslam and Gardner (2007) conducted the fourth major study of Utah's comprehensive counseling and guidance program. Four major findings were:

- Comprehensive counseling and guidance has fostered more targeted course selection for students and has resulted in more students taking a greater number of higher-level English, science, math and technology-oriented courses.
- The percentage of students who describe their own program of study as "general" has fallen precipitously in the nine years between evaluations.
- Students in high-implementing comprehensive counseling and guidance schools achieve higher levels of academic achievement and make better decisions about education and career planning than do students in matched lower-implementing schools. The importance of this finding cannot be overstressed. Even more powerful is the fact that this same pattern of results was evident in both the 1997 Utah evaluation and the most recent study reported here.
- These studies show that the comprehensive counseling and guidance program is more effectively implemented with adequate counselor-to-student ratios in Utah's schools, whether urban, suburban or rural (p. 2).

Another book dealing with accountability was published in 2006 and was titled "Building a Results-Based Student Support Program" by Johnson, Johnson and Downs (2006). As the title implies, this book stressed the importance of results and outlined a process to develop and implement programs that obtained results data. A year later another book on accountability titled "Evidence-Based School Counseling" by Hatch, Carey and Dimmitt (2007) was published. It focused on how to use data to design, implement and evaluate school counseling programs and interventions.

In a study in Washington state by Sink, Akos, Turnbull and Mvududu (2008) that compared middle school students' academic achievement in schools with at least five years of comprehensive school counseling program implementation versus students in non-program schools found:

"When CSCP versus non-CSCP schools were compared, there were largely nonsignificant mean differences on Grade 6 ITBS and Grade 7 WASL scores. Only grade 7 WASL math scores showed significant group differences, favoring the non-CSCP students. However, high-CSCP-implementation schools significantly outperformed non-CSCP schools on Grade 6 ITBS language, math and core total scores and on Grade 7 reading and math WASL scores. Additionally, students in the high-SCSP-implementation schools tended to perform better than their peers in the low-CSCP-implementation group" (pp. 49-50).

They ended their article by stating that the empirical results from their study provided "provisional evidence for the linkage between long-term CSCPs and the educational development of middle school students" (p. 51).

Instrument development to measure the effects of comprehensive guidance and counseling programs continued to be of interest in the first decades of the 21st century. Whiston and Aricok (2008) developed a 64-item instrument designed to correspond to the National Standards for school counseling programs (Campbell & Dahir, 1997). Whiston and Aricok stated they developed the instrument to provide school counselors with a way to collect data and to provide an outcome assessment instrument to be used in school counseling research. While work still needs to be done to determine whether or not the instrument is reliable, preliminary investigation seems positive.

In a comprehensive review of school counseling research Whiston and Quinby (2009) focused on the effectiveness of school counseling interventions. They concluded that, "Preliminary studies indicate that schools with more fully implemented programs have better student outcomes than schools with a less programmatic approach to school counseling" (p. 271).

One of the important outcomes of the accountability movement in the first decade of the 21st century was the establishment of The National Panel for School Counseling Evidence-Based Practice in 2003. Carey, Dimmitt, Hatch, Lapan, & Whiston (2008) stated that the panel "was established to improve the practice of school counseling by helping to develop the research base that is necessary for responsible and effective practice" (p. 197). To accomplish this mission the panel developed an Outcome Research Coding Protocol that consisted of the following seven domains: Measurement, Comparison Groups, Statistical Analysis of Outcome Variables, Implementation Fidelity, Replication, Ecological Validity and Persistence of Effective. "Within each domain, research studies can be categorized as presenting strong evidence, *promising* evidence or *weak* evidence that an intervention causes a change in an important student outcome"(p. 198). Because of its importance the full protocol is published in Appendix B.

A Final Note: Accountability is an Ongoing Responsibility

Why has accountability been a topic of long-standing concern? By this time one might think that this topic no longer requires professional attention because empirical studies have demonstrated that guidance and counseling does make a difference in the lives of students. I believe the topic keeps reappearing because accountability is not a one-time phenomenon. Accountability is an ongoing responsibility of the profession at the national, state and local levels.

If accountability is never over, what can be learned from the extensive literature on accountability of the past 80 plus years that can help school counselors meet their accountability obligations today? Space does not permit a detailed presentation concerning how the specific accountability techniques and methods of the past can be applied to today's world. However there are several dominant themes that have appeared consistently in the accountability literature that speak to necessary prerequisite conditions that must exist if accountability is to be achieved.

The first theme deals with mindset that individuals have about accountability. Some see it as a threat. The literature makes it clear that it is important to rid the mind of the phobia of accountability, of the persistent fear of accountability that often leads to a compelling desire to avoid it. What is required is a mindset that being accountable is simply a part of the guidance and counseling work that is done in schools every day. It is a way this work can be improved and its effectiveness demonstrated. It is important to begin each school year, semester, month, week and day by being results-oriented. When providing guidance and counseling activities and services, always begin by first identifying the results anticipated.

The second theme focuses on the results of guidance and counseling work in the schools. If questions arise concerning which results are important to focus on, review the local school district or local building improvement plan. Those plans contain outcomes that a local district has deemed important. Most plans contain goals to which guidance and counseling programs and/or specific activities and services can contribute. There is extensive language describing possible outcomes for guidance and counseling available in the literature dating back to the 1930s. These outcomes are as applicable to today's work as they were for the work in the past.

The third and final theme is that accountability talk is not enough. It is important to remember that expressing concern about accountability is necessary, but it is not sufficient. It is time for action. Who should take the lead? Sink (2009) clearly stated that school counselors and school counselor educators should become accountability leaders.

"Public scrutiny of school counseling practice will not diminish until members of the profession lead the way, demonstrating the effectiveness of their CSCPs by evaluating their key components, activities, services and interventions. In short, as a principal element of the leadership role, school counselors and school counselor educators must do more than merely acquiesce to the rising accountability tide; rather, they need to be genuinely committed to and engaged in improving student educational outcomes and the profession, rigorously testing and then jettisoning unproven practices and refining those that show positive results" (pp. 72-73).

References

Alstetter, M. L. (1938). Guidance service in two hundred secondary schools. *Occupations 16*, 513-520.

American College Testing Program (1976). *River City high school guidance services: A conceptual model*. Iowa City, IA: author.

Astramovich, R. L., & Coker, J. K. (2007). Program evaluation: the accountability bridge model for counselors. *Journal of Counseling and Development, 85,* 162-172.

Atkinson, D. R., Furlong, M. J., & Janoff, D. S. (1979). A four-component model for proactive accountability in school counseling. *The School Counselor, 26,* 222-228.

Bardo, H. R., & Cody, J. J. (1975). Minimizing measurement concerns in guidance evaluation. *Measurement and Evaluation of Guidance, 8,* 175-179.

Bardo, H. R., & Cody, J. J., & Bryson, S. L. (1978). Evaluation of guidance programs: Call the question. *Personnel and Guidance Journal, 57,* 204-208.

Bauman, S. (2004). School counselors and research revisited. *Professional School Counseling, 7,* 141-148.

Becker, E. G. (1937). How shall guidance be evaluated? *High Points, 19,* 5-10.

Borders, L. D., & Drury, S. M. (1992). Comprehensive school counseling programs: A review for policymakers and practitioners. *Journal of Counseling & Development, 70,* 487-501.

Brott, P. E. (2006). Counselor education accountability: Training the effective professional school counselor. *Professional School Counseling, 10,* 179-187.

Buckner, E. T. (1975). Accountable to whom? The counselor's dilemma. *Measurement and Evaluation of Guidance, 8,* 187-192.

Burck, H. D., & Peterson, G. W. (1975). Needed: More evaluation, not research. *Personnel and Guidance Journal, 53,* 563-569.

California State Department of Education (1981). *Guidelines for developing comprehensive guidance programs in California public schools: Kindergarten through adult school.* Sacramento, CA: Author.

Campbell, C. A., & Dahir, C. A. (1997). *The national standards for school counseling programs.* Alexandria, VA: American School Counselor Association.

Campbell, C. A., & Deck, M. D. (Eds.) (1990). Research and evaluation in school counseling [Special issue]. *Elementary School Guidance & Counseling 25*(1).

Campbell, R. E. (1978). Developing exemplary guidance programs. In G. R. Walz & L. Benjamin (Eds.), *New imperatives for guidance* (pp. 30-62). Ann Arbor, MI: ERIC Counseling and Personnel Services Clearinghouse.

Campbell, R. E., Dworkin, E. P., Jackson, D. P., Hoeltzel, K. E., Parsons, G. E., & Lacey, D. W. (1971). *The systems approach: An emerging behavioral model for career guidance.* Columbus, OH: The Center for Vocational and Technical Education.

Carey, J. C., & Dimmitt, C., (2006). Resources for school counselors and counselor educators: The center for school counseling outcome research. *Professional School Counseling, 9*, 416-420.

Carey, J. C., Dimmitt, C., Hatch, T. A., Lapan, R. T., & Whiston, S. C. (2008). Report of the National panel for evidence-based school counseling: Outcome research coding protocol and evaluation of student success skills and second step. *Professional School Counseling, 11*, 197-206.

Carr, R. (1977). The counselor or the counseling program as the target of evaluation? *Personnel and Guidance Journal, 56*, 112-118.

Christy, E. B., Stewart, F. J., & Rosecrance, F. C. (1930). Guidance in the senior high school. *The Vocational Guidance Magazine, 9*, 51-57.

College Entrance Examination Board (1978). *Implementing the career skills assessment program.* New York: Author.

Cottle, W. C. (1957). The evaluation of guidance services. *Review of Educational Research, 37*, 229-235.

Crabbs, S. K., & Crabbs, M. A. (1977). Accountability: Who does what to whom, when, where, and how? *The School Counselor, 25*, 104-109.

Cramer, S. H., Herr, E. L., Morris, C. N., & Frantz, T. T. (1970). *Research and the school counselor.* Boston, MA: Houghton Mifflin Company.

Dahir, C. A., & Stone, C. B. (2003). Accountability: A M.E.A.S.U.R.E. of the impact school counselors have on student achievement. *Professional School Counseling, 6*, 214-221.

Dayton, C. (n.d.). *Module 3 Assessing desired outcomes.* Palo Alto, CA: American Institute for Research.

Dunn, J. A. (1972). *The guidance program in the plan system of individualized education.* Palo Alto, CA: American Institutes for Research.

Edgerton, A. H. (1929). Evaluating the effectiveness of guidance practices. *The Nation's Schools, 3*, 38-42.

Edgerton, A. H., & Herr, L. A. (1924). Present status of guidance activities in public schools. *The twenty-Third Yearbook, National Society for the Study of Education, Part II, Vocational Guidance and Vocational Education for the Industries.* Bloomington, IL: Public School Publishing Company.

Fairchild, T. N. (1993). Accountability practices of school counselors: 1990 national survey. *The School Counselor, 40*, 363-374.

Fairchild, T. N., & Zins, J. E. (1986). Accountability practices of school counselors: A national survey. *Journal of Counseling and Development, 65,* 196-199.

Foster, L. H., Watson, T. S., Meeks, C., & Scott Young, J. (2002). Single-subject research design for school counselors: Becoming an applied researcher. *Professional School Counseling, 6,* 146-154.

Foster, L. H., Watson, T. S., Meeks, C., & Young, T. S. (2002). Single-subject research design for school counselors: Becoming an applied researcher. *Professional School Counseling, 6,* 146-154.

Froehle, T. C., & Fuqua, D. R. (1981). Systematic inquiry in the school context. *Personnel and Guidance Journal, 59,* 509-514.

Froehlich, C. P. (1949). *Evaluating guidance procedures: A review of the literature.* Washington, D. C.: Federal Security Agency, Office of Education.

Gamsky, N. R. (1970). Action research and the school counselor. *The School Counselor, 18,* 36-42.

Gelatt, H. B. (1969). School guidance programs. *Review of Educational Research, 39,* 141-153.

Gerler, E. R. (1976). New directions for school counseling. *The School Counselor, 23,* 247-251.

Gerler, E. R. (1985). Elementary school counseling research and the classroom learning environment. *Elementary School Guidance & Counseling, 20,* 39-48.

Gubser, M. M. (1974). Performance-based counseling: Accountability or liability? *The School Counselor, 21,* 296-302.

Gysbers, N. C., & Henderson, P. (2006). *Developing and managing your school guidance and counseling program* (4th Ed.). Alexandria, VA: American Counseling Association.

Gysbers, N. C., & Lapan, R. T. (2009). *Strengths-based career development for school guidance and counseling programs.* Ann Arbor, MI: Counseling Outfitters.

Gysbers, N. C., & Moore, E. J. (1974). *Career guidance, counseling and placement: Elements of an illustrative program guide.* Columbia, MO: Career Guidance, Counseling and Placement Project, University of Missouri-Columbia.

Gysbers, N. C., Hughey, K. F., Starr, M., & Lapan, R. T. (1992). Improving school guidance programs: A framework for program personnel and results evaluation. *Journal of Counseling and Development, 70,* 565-570.

Gysbers, N. C., Lapan, R. T., & Stanley, B. (2006). No fear results evaluation: The Missouri story. *ASCA School Counselor, May-June,* 35-37.

Hatch, P. A., Carey, J. C., & Dimmitt, C. L. (2007). *Evidence-based school counseling*. Thousand Oaks, CA: Sage Publications.

Hayden, C., & Pohlmann, N. (1981). Accountability and evaluation: Necessary for the survival of guidance programs? *NASSP Bulletin, 65,* 60-63.

Hayes, D. G. (Ed.). (1970. *Situation, population, treatment, outcome.* Sacramento, CA: California State Department of Education.

Hedge, J. W., & Hutson, P. W. (1931). A technique for evaluating guidance activities. *School Review, 39,* 508-519.

Hedge, J. W., & Hutson, P. W. (1931). A technique for evaluating guidance activities. *School Review, 39,* 508-519.

Helliwell, C. B., & Jones, G. B. (1975). Reality considerations in guidance program evaluation. *Measurement and Evaluation of Guidance, 8,* 155-168.

Herr, E. L. (1978). Research in guidance. In G. R. Walz & L. Benjamin (Eds.), *New imperatives for guidance* (pp. 63-112). Ann Arbor, MI: ERIC Counseling and Personnel Services Clearinghouse.

Hinderman, R. A. (1930). Evaluating and improving guidance services. *Nation's Schools, 5,* 47-52.

Holcomb-McCoy, C., Gonzales, I., & Johnston, G. (2009). School counselor dispositions as predictors of data usage. *Professional School Counseling, 12,* 343-351.

Huber, C. H. (1980). Research and the school counselor. *The School Counselor, 27,* 210-216.

Hughes, D. K., & James, S. H. (2001). Using accountability data to protect a school counseling program: One counselor's experience. *Professional School Counseling, 4,* 306-309.

Humes, C. W. (1972). Accountability: A boon to guidance. *Personnel and Guidance Journal, 51,* 21-26.

Hutson, P. W. (1935). Testing the guidance program. *Nation's Schools, 15,* 21-23.

Jager, H. A. (1948). Trends in counselor training. *Occupations, 26,* 480-482.

Johnson, S., & Johnson, C. D. (2003). Results based guidance: a systems approach to student support programs. *Professional School Counseling, 6,* 180-184.

Johnson, S., Johnson, C., & Downs, L. (2006). *Building a results-based student support program*. Boston, MA: Lahaska Press.

Johnston, S. K., & Whitfield, E. A. (Eds.) (1991). *Evaluating guidance programs: A practitioner's guide*. Iowa City, IA: American College Testing Program and the National Consortium of State Career Guidance Supervisors.

Jones, A. J. (1951). *Principles of guidance* (4th ed.). New York: McGraw-Hill Book Company.

Jones, G. B., Hamilton, J. A., Ganschow, L. H., Helliwell, C. B., & Wolff, J. M. (1972). *Planning, developing, and field testing career guidance programs: A manual and report.* Palo Alto, CA: American Institutes for Research.

Jones, G. B., Helliwell, C. B., & Ganschow, L. H. (1975). A planning model for career guidance. *Vocational Guidance Quarterly, 23,* 220-226.

Jones, G. B., Helliwell, C. B., & Ganschow, L. H., & Hamilton, J. A. (1971). *Development and evaluation of a comprehensive career guidance system.* Palo Alto, CA: American Institutes for Research.

Kefauver, G. N. (1932). Achievements of guidance in secondary schools. *The Vocational Guidance Magazine, 10,* 199-201.

Kefauver, G. N., & Davis, A. M. (1933). Investigations in guidance. *Occupations, 12,* 17-25.

Kefauver, G. N., & Hand, H. C. (1932). Measurement of outcomes of guidance in secondary schools. *Teachers College Record, 33,* 324-334.

Kefauver, G. N., & Hand, H. C. (1934). Evaluation of guidance programs. *Occupations, 12,* 106-114.

Kefauver, G. N., & Hand, H. C. (1937). *Kefauver-Hand guidance tests and inventories.* Yonkers-on-Hudson, NY: World Book Company.

Kefauver, G. N., & Hand, H. C. (1941). *Appraising guidance in secondary schools.* New York: The Macmillan Company.

Kefauver, G. N., & Hand, H. C., & Block, V. L. (1934). Objectives of experimental guidance programs. *Occupations, 13,* 226-227.

Kelley, J. A. (1955). *Guidance and curriculum.* Englewood Cliffs: Prentice-Hall, Inc.

Knapper, E. Q. (1978). Counselor accountability. *Personnel and Guidance Journal, 57,* 27-30.

Krumboltz, J. D. (1974). An accountability model for counselors. *Personnel and Guidance Journal, 52,* 639-646.

Lapan, R. T. (2001). Results-based comprehensive guidance and counseling programs: A framework for planning and evaluation. *Professional School Counseling, 4,* 289-299.

Lapan, R. T., Gysbers, N. C., & Kayson, M. (2006). *How implementing comprehensive guidance programs improves academic achievement for all Missouri students.* Jefferson City, MO: Missouri Department of Elementary and Secondary Education.

Lapan, R. T., Gysbers, N. C., & Petroski, G. (2001). Helping 7th graders be safe and academically successful: A statewide study of the impact of comprehensive guidance programs. *Journal of Counseling & Development, 79,* 320-330.

Lapan, R. T., Gysbers, N. C., & Sun, Y. (1997). The impact of more fully implemented guidance programs on the school experiences of high school students: A statewide evaluation study. *Journal of Counseling & Development, 75*, 292-302.

Lapan, R. T., Gysbers, N. C., Multon, K. D., & Pike, G. R. (1997). Developing guidance competency self-efficacy scales for high school and middle school students. *Measurement and Evaluation in Counseling and Development, 30*, 4-16.

Lasser, B. R. (1975). An outcomes-based approach to counseling evaluation. *Measurement and Evaluation of Guidance, 8*, 169-174.

Lee, C. C., & Workman, D. J. (1992). School counselors and research: Current status and future direction. *The School Counselor, 40*, 15-19.

Lewis, J. D. (1983). Guidance program evaluation: How to do it. *The School Counselor, 31*, 111-119.

Lombana, J. H. (1985). Guidance accountability: a new look at an old problem. *The School Counselor, 32*, 340-346.

Mahoney, H. J. (1950). 10 years of evaluating guidance services. *Occupations, 29*, 194-197.

McDaniel, H. B. (1954). Organization and administration of guidance in elementary and secondary schools. *Review of Educational Research, 34*, 109-112.

McDaniel, H. B. (1970). *Youth guidance systems.* Palo Alto, CA: College Entrance Examination Board.

McKinnon, B. E. (n.d.). *Toward accountability: A report on the Mesa approach to career guidance, counseling, and placement.* Mesa AZ: Mesa Public Schools.

Miller, J. V., & Grisdale, G. A. (1975). Guidance program evaluation: What's out there? *Measurement and Evaluation of Guidance, 8*, 145-154.

Milsom, A. (Ed.) (2009). Action research in school counseling [Special issue]. *Professional School Counseling, 12*(6).

Milstein, B., & Colton, D. (2000). *Defining concepts for the presidential stand on building evaluation capacity.* University of Pennsylvania (CPRE Policy Briefs, RB-32).

Minor, B. J. (Ed.) (1981). Bridging the gap between research and practice [Special issue]. *The Personnel and Guidance Journal, 59*(8).

Mitchell, A. M. (1978). The design, development, and evaluation of systematic guidance programs. In G. R. Walz & L. Benjamin (Eds.), *New imperatives for guidance* (pp. 113-148). Ann Arbor, MI: ERIC Counseling and Personnel Services Clearinghouse.

Myers, C. E. (1926). *Some tentative standards for judging a comprehensive guidance plan.* Pittsburgh, PA: Department of Vocational Guidance, Pittsburgh public Schools.

Myrick, R. D. (2003). Accountability: Counselors count. *Professional School Counseling, 6,* 174-179.

National Defense Education Act of 1958. Pub. L. No. 85-864, 72, Part 1, Stat. 1580 (1958).

Neidt, C. O. (1965). *Relation of guidance practices to student behavioral outcomes* (OE-5-99-222). U.S. Department of Health, Education, and Welfare (Mimeographed).

Nelson, D. E., Fox, D. G., Haslam, M., & Gardner, J. (2007). *An evaluation of Utah's comprehensive counseling and guidance program: The fourth major study of Utah's statewide program.* Salt Lake City, UT: The Institute for Behavioral Research in Creativity.

Nelson, D. E., Gardner, J. L, & Fox D. G. (1998). *An evaluation of the comprehensive guidance program in Utah public schools.* Salt Lake City: Utah State Office of Education.

O'Connor, J. R., & Wigtil, J. V. (1975). Guidance program evaluation: A follow-up of effectiveness and value. *Measurement and Evaluation of Guidance, 8,* 163-168.

O'Hare, R. W., & Lasser, B. (1971). *Evaluating pupil personnel programs.* Fullerton, CA: California Personnel and Guidance Association.

Patterson, C. H. (1963). Program evaluation. *Review of Educational Research, 33,* 214-224.

Payne, A. F. (1924). Problems in vocational guidance. *National Vocational Guidance Association Bulletin 2,* 61-63.

Pine, G. J. (1975). Evaluating school counseling programs: Retrospect and Prospect. *Measurement and Evaluation in Guidance, 8,* 136-144.

Pine, G. J. (1981). Collaborative action research in school counseling: The integration of research and practice. *The Personnel and Guidance Journal, 59,* 495-501.

Poynton, T., A., & Carey, J. C. (2006). An integrative model of data-based decision making for school counseling. *Professional School Counseling, 10,* 121-130.

Proctor, W. M. (1930). Evaluating guidance activities in high schools. *The Vocational Guidance Magazine, 9,* 58-66.

Proff, F. (1965). *Research and counseling.* Contractor's Report, U.S. Office of Education. (Mimeographed)

Remer, R. (Ed.) (1981). The counselor and research, part 1 [Special issue]. *The Personnel and Guidance Journal, 59*(9).

Rosecrance, F. C. (1930). Organizing guidance for the larger school system. *The Vocational Guidance Magazine, 9,* 243-249.

Rothney, J. W. M. (1958). *Guidance practices and results*. New York: Harper & Brothers, Publishers.

Rothney, J. W. M., & Farwell, G. F. (1960). The evaluation of guidance and personnel services. *Review of Educational Research, 30*, 168-175.

Rothney, J. W. M., & Roens, B. A. (1950). *Guidance of American youth: An experimental study*. Cambridge, MA: Harvard University Press.

Schultz, F. G. (1941). A re-check of articles on guidance in five educational magazines. *Occupations, 19*, 492-495.

Shay, M. J. (1981). A zero-sum game: Are today's economics crunching counselor services? *NASSP Bulletin, 65*, 10-16.

Sink, C. A. (2009). School counselors as accountability leaders: Another call to action. *Professional School Counseling, 13*, 68-74.

Sink, C. A. (Ed.) (2006). Research methods in school counseling [Special issue]. *Professional School Counseling, 9*, (5).

Sink, C. A., & Stroh, H. R. (2003). Raising achievement test scores of early elementary school students through comprehensive school counseling programs. *Professional School Counseling, 6*, 350-364.

Sink, C. A., Akos, P., Turnbull, R. J., Mvududu, N. (2008). An investigation of comprehensive school counseling programs and academic achievement in Washington State Middle Schools. *Professional School Counseling, 12*, 43-53.

Smith, F. C. (1931). How guidance should affect the individual. *The Vocational Guidance Magazine, 9*, 291-295.

Stone, C. B., & Dahir, C. A. (2004). *School counselor accountability: A measure of student success*. Upper Saddle River, NJ: Pearson.

Stone, C. B., & Dahir, C. A. (2007). *School counselor accountability: A measure of student success* (2nd Ed.). Upper Saddle River, NJ: Pearson Education.

Strowig, R. W., & Farwell, G. F. (1966). Programmatic research. *Review of Educational Research, 36*, 327-334.

Sullivan, H. J., & O'Hare, R. W. (1971). *Accountability in personnel services: A process guide for the development of objectives*. Fullerton, CA: California Personnel and Guidance Association.

Sullivan, H. J., & O'Hare, R. W. (1971). *Accountability in pupil personnel services: A process guide for the development of objectives*. Fullerton, CA: California Personnel and guidance Association.

Tamminen, A. W. & Miller, G. D. (1968). *Guidance programs and their impact on students, Research Project No. OE-5-85-035*. St. Paul, MN: Department of Education.

Thompson, D. L., & Borsari, L. R. (1978). An overview of management by objectives for guidance and counseling services. *The School Counselor, 25*, 172-177.

Thurow, L. C. (1980, September 27). No progress without pain. *Time*, p. 74.

Travers, R. M. W. (1949). A critical review of techniques for evaluating guidance. *Educational and Psychological Measurement, 9*, 211-225.

Treacy, J. P. (1937). Analyzing a guidance program. *The American School Board Journal, 44*, 29-30.

Trevisan, M. S. (2002). Evaluation capacity in K-12 counseling program. *American Journal of Evaluation, 23*, 291-304.

Trevisan, M. S., & Hubert, M. (2001). Implementing comprehensive guidance program evaluation support: Lessons learned. *Professional School Counseling 4*, 225-228.

Vocational Education Act of 1946, Pub. L. No. 586, 60, Part 1, Stat. 775 (1946).

Wagner, E. E., Arbuckle, D. S., & Carnes, E. F. (1951). Programs of guidance. *Review of Educational Research, 31*, 106-114.

Wellman, F. E., & Gysbers, N. C. (1971). Main Question is: Did the program make a difference? *American Vocational Journal, 46*, 47-50.

Wellman, F. E., & Moore, E. J. (1975). *Pupil personnel services: A handbook for program development and evaluation.* Columbia, MO: Missouri Evaluations Projects, University of Missouri-Columbia.

Wellman, F. E., & Moore, E. J. (1975). *Pupil personnel services: A handbook for program development and evaluation.* Washington, DC: U.S. Department of Health, Education, and Welfare.

Wellman, F. E., & Twiford, D. D. (1961). *Guidance Counseling and Testing Program Evaluation Suggestions for Secondary Schools Title V-A National Defense Education Act of 1958.* Washington DC: United States Government Printing Office.

Wheeler, P. T., & Loesch, L. (1981). Program evaluation and counseling: Yesterday, today, and tomorrow. *The Personnel and Guidance Journal, 59*, 573-577.

Whiston, S. C., & Aricok, O. T. (2008). Development and initial investigation of school counseling program evaluation scale. *Professional School Counseling, 11*, 253-261.

Whiston, S. C., & Quinby, R. F. (2009). Review of school counseling outcome research. *Psychology in the Schools, 46*, 267-272.

Whitson, S. C. (1996). Accountability through action research: Research methods for practitioners. *Journal of Counseling & Development, 74*, 616-623.

Whitson, S. C., & Sexton, T. L. (1998). A review of school counseling outcome research: Implications for practice. *Journal of Counseling & Development, 76*, 412-426.

Wiggins, J. D. (1981). For counselors only: Steps to take in evaluating a school's guidance program. *NASSP Bulletin, 65*, 29-33.

Wilson, F. M. (1945). *Procedures in evaluating a guidance program*. New York: Teachers College, Columbia University.

Wilson, N. H., Rotter, J. C. (1982). School counseling: A look into the future. *The Personnel and Guidance Journal, 60*, 353-357.

Wilson, N. S. (1985). School counselors and research: Obstacles and opportunities. *The School Counselor, 33*, 111-119.

Wilson, N. S. (1985). School counselors and research: Obstacles and opportunities. *The School Counselor, 33*, 111-119.

Wrenn, C. G. (1940). The evaluation of student personnel work: Critique of the "guidance movement". *School and Society, 52*, 409-414.

Wrenn, C. G. (1947). Trends and predictions in vocational guidance. *Occupations, 25*, 503-513.

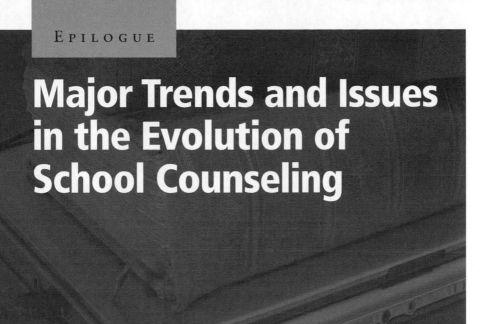

Major Trends and Issues in the Evolution of School Counseling

This book, through its eight chapters, provides a chronology of the evolution of school counseling over 100-plus years. But the book is much more than a chronology of people, places and events because it helps us understand this evolution from sociological, psychological and economic perspectives and contexts. It also helps us see how the forces that grew out of these perspectives and contexts shaped the field of school counseling. Finally the book gives us insights into the minds of the many individuals who were involved in the discussions and debates about the purposes, structures and practices of school counseling and the often-substantial challenges they faced.

Rather than summarize the contents of the book's eight chapters, the intent of this epilogue is to bring into clear focus 10 predominant trends and issues in the evolution of school counseling.

Ten Trends and Issues

One: School counseling was not born in and did not grow up in a vacuum. It was born and grew up in context, affected by many social, economic and educational forces over the past 100-plus years. Many years ago Miller (1961) captured this point when he stated that guidance was a coat of many colors. He said it was woven together over the years from many strands representing different social, economic and educational movements from inside and outside of education.

You will recall that the progressive movement at the turn of the last century had substantial impact, resulting in the birth of vocational guidance. In turn, vocational guidance was shaped by the mental hygiene movement, the psychometric-measure movement, the child development/study movement and great interest in educational guidance. Federal legislation over the years, responding to societal concerns and economic conditions, also shaped school counseling's purposes and direction. By the time we reached the 1950s–1990s, the civil rights movement, multicultural and diversity concerns and sexual orientation issues were also at work shaping school counseling content, organizational structures and practices.

During this same time period and extending into the first decade of the 21st century these forces converged, in part, around a major national priority of academic achievement for all students but particularly for low-income and minority students.

Two: There has been a clear progression in the way school counseling has been structured and organized over the past 100-plus years. It was first structured as a position, occupied by teachers, administrators and individuals called deans, and then by more and more part- and full-time school counselors.

The person occupying the position was given a list of duties, some related to the work of school counseling and some not. The problem of other duties as assigned, present from the beginning of school counseling, continues to be a major problem today. Then the position, a person with a list of duties, was placed in a group of guidance services including information, assessment, counseling, placement and follow-up. In turn, the guidance services were placed in a larger group called pupil personnel services, sometimes called student services today. Finally positions and services were encompassed by the concept of developmental, comprehensive school counseling programs.

Three: Concurrent with the changes in the organizational structure for school counseling and the move over the years to more full-time school counselors came a clearer distinction between the responsibilities of administrators and school counselors. Remember, in the early years, administrators served as counselors as well as the disciplinarians of the school. Debate ensued over the years as to whether or not full-time school counselors should carry discipline responsibilities. Today it is clear that school counselors are not in charge of discipline in the school, although some administrators still see school counselors in this role.

Four: What began as vocational guidance soon became educational guidance and then personal-social guidance. In fact during the 1920s and 1930s it was common to add other forms of guidance such as health guidance, leisure guidance and moral guidance. As the years unfolded three kinds of guidance emerged as predominant, namely, education (academic) guidance, vocational (career) guidance and personal-social guidance. Unfortunately, in some people's minds, these three kinds of guidance were seen as separate programs each with its own personnel. Educational or academic guidance was stressed by academic/college personnel, vocational or career guidance became the focus of career and technical education personnel and labor economists, and personal-social guidance became the territory of mental health workers. Today this false separation continues to be an issue because there are groups who want to add personnel to schools such as college guides, job coaches, career specialists and mental health counselors rather than providing existing school counselors with the time and resources to carry out a holistic program that incorporates all three kinds of guidance.

Five: Content for guidance, the knowledge, skills and dispositions students need for their growth and development was included in early conceptions of school counseling. Then, for a while, discussion of the knowledge, skills and dispositions that students need became a lesser priority. When the program approach to school counseling emerged, content for school counseling once again became a priority, this time in the form of standards and/or competencies. Today, interestingly, the labels used for types of school counseling, academic, career and personal-social, are also the labels for the program content.

Six: The terminology issue is still with us today. Is it guidance, counseling, guidance and counseling, or counseling and guidance? The American School Counselor Association (ASCA) has come down firmly on the side of the term school counseling program although the literature still reflects the usage of various combinations of terms. The terminology issue also is reflected in personnel titles. Again, ASCA has come down firmly on the title school counselor, although the public still uses the title guidance counselor, and some school districts use the title guidance dean, going back to a title used earlier.

The terminology issue is interesting from a historical perspective too. Remember the first term was vocational guidance, and then many modifiers were placed in front of the word guidance. In the 1930s guidance became a service within pupil personnel services with five services: information, assessment, counseling, placement and follow-up. Then the counseling service assumed prominence, so the common labels used were guidance and counseling. Information and assessment continued to be a part of guidance and counseling, but placement and follow-up became less important and have now almost disappeared as active parts of school counseling. Following ASCA's lead, counseling became the label of choice as in school counseling programs. Guidance is still present but is used to label one of the delivery components of the program, namely, the guidance curriculum.

Seven: Concern about the selection, background, education and supervision of school counselors, first expressed many years ago, continues today. The teaching certification and experience debate, heavy at times in years past, seems to have diminished as more and more states have dropped these requirements from their school counselor certification standards. Although some states that dropped them, they still recognize the need for some exposure to schools by requiring education coursework and educational internships. The nature of the education of school counselors has also been heavily influenced by the work of the Association for Counselor Education and Supervision (ACES), the standards for the education of school counselors put forward by CACREP, ASCA, the National Center for Transforming School Counseling, and the Multicultural Counseling Competencies and Standards published by the Association for Multicultural Counseling and Development.

Eight: The purposes of school counseling and how those purposes should be achieved received a great deal of attention in the literature. Some writers suggested that school counseling should consist mainly of direct services to students with school counselors spending the majority of their time (80 percent or more) providing direct services. Other writers recommended that school counseling should focus more on indirect roles such as consultation, advocacy, coordination and collaboration. This direct-indirect discussion played out in the accountability debate too. Again, some writers recommended that school counselors spend more time in consultation and evaluation roles identifying problems and collecting, analyzing and using data to recommend ways to respond to these problems. Brown and Trusty (2005) stated they believe that direct services will end up being the choice of school counselors. "We believe that when they [school counselors] consider their context and its needs they will stay with the direct services model, perhaps with minor modifications" (pp. 420-421).

Even with individuals who favored the direct services approach however, there were differing opinions as to what direct services should be provided. Some felt that too much attention was being given to academic issues and concerns at the expense of providing individual and small group counseling, in light of the increasing mental health needs of students. Others felt the opposite stating that academic achievement of students should be the priority for direct services.

Nine: Leadership for school counseling at the local, state and national levels as well as the supervision of school counselors has been of concern for a long time. Leadership at the federal level has been dependent upon federal legislation. During the 1940, 1950s and early 1960s strong leadership existed at the federal level. The same was true at the state level with many states having large numbers of state supervisors. As federal legislation featuring school counseling such as the National Defense Education Act of 1958 ended, so too did funding for federal and state positions. The only consistent support for state level leadership positions has been Career and Technical Education legislation, but even that legislation has not been used in all states. Local leadership and supervision for school counselors varies greatly depending upon how local school districts organize and administer counseling in their schools. Improving local leadership and supervision have been identified as two major tasks for the future.

Ten: It may come as a surprise to some that accountability in school counseling is not a new phenomenon. Being accountable, or answerable for the work school counselors do and the impact it has on student behavior, has been part of the ongoing discussion in our field since the 1920s. Chapter Eight provides a chronology of the literature highlighting expressions of the need to be accountable as well as actual studies that have shown the impact on student behaviors. Today, there is a renewed sense of urgency concerning accountability. At the same time, recent advances in technology have placed tools in the hands of school counselors to conduct evaluation studies of their work that early leaders probably could not have imagined. The literature makes it clear the evaluation is here to stay and needs to be designed and carried out to not only demonstrate effectiveness but also to improve the work being done by school counselors.

The Future

Over the past 100 years discussion about the purposes, content and practices of school counseling, influenced by interacting social, economic and educational forces, have moved the field from a position to a service to a program. At this point in our history the program concept, as the framework and organizer of choice for school counseling, predominates discussion in the literature. Disagreements continue, however, about what the program purposes, content and practices should be.

The position of school counselor has evolved too from being primarily administrators and teachers filling the role to full-time school counselors. Their selection and training has changed as well so that today there are well-established standards for selection and training. Federal, state and local leadership for school counseling continues to be of concern however, even though the literature presents clearer descriptions of leaders' and supervisors' knowledge, skills and practices.

While accountability for student outcomes is a topic almost as old as the field itself, calls for accountability and descriptions about how to do it continue to fill the pages of the literature. Driven by a national priority on student achievement and the development of new technology and statistical tools, the opportunity to be accountable is available to individual school counselors today as never before. As a result, school counselors are able to present data that demonstrates the impact of their work on student outcomes as well as use the data to help them improve their work with students and parents.

What will the next 100 years be like for school counseling? No one knows for sure. However, if the next 100 years are like the first 100 years, school counseling will continue to evolve. The forces that shaped school counseling so far will continue to do so as the decades of this century continue to unfold. Will the program framework, popular today, be flexible enough to respond to changing and challenging social, economic forces in the future? Will some other framework for school counseling emerge?

No one knows what the future holds, but the current literature suggests that at least for the near future, knowing what we know today, students and their parents in school districts across the country will continue to benefit from having fully implemented school counseling programs.

"When school counseling is organized and implemented as a program, it places school counselors conceptually and structurally in the center of education, making it possible for them to contribute directly and substantially to their local school districts' educational goals. As a result, school counseling becomes an integral and transformative program in the district, not a marginal and supplemental activity."

The program approach not only provides the means and common language across all school district levels for ensuring all students and their parents benefit from guidance and counseling activities and services, but it also provides the foundation for accountability. This approach is results-based, contributing to the achievement of student results, results established by local districts in their school improvement plans. Also, this approach mandates regular review and evaluation of a district's comprehensive school counseling program using program standards; ongoing review and enhancement of the program's content, service and activities; and yearly evaluation of the district's school counselors' performance, using established performance standards.

Being involved in developing and implementing a comprehensive school counseling program may seem overwhelming, but the rewards are substantial. More pride in being a school counselor is evident. More support is generated because school counseling is no longer seen as an ancillary support service. And perhaps most important, students, parents, teachers, administrators and the community are served more effectively. These are the strong messages sent by school counselors and administrators who are using the program approach to guidance and counseling in their school districts" (Gysbers, pp. 4-5).

References

Miller, C. H. (1961). *Foundations of Guidance*. New York: Harper & Brothers.

Brown, D., & Trusty, J. (2005). *Designing and leading comprehensive school counseling programs*. Belmont, CA: Thomson Brooks/Cole.

Gysbers, N. C. (2005). The center of education. In American School Counselor Association *ASCA National Model for school counseling programs* (2nd Ed.) (pp. 4-5). Alexandria, VA: Author.

Appendix A

Pertinent Portions of the National Defense Education Act of 1958 to the Counseling and Guidance Institutes Program

(Reprinted below in the language of the National Defense Education Act of 1958 are the "Findings and Declaration of Policy" of the Congress from Title I and Title V in its entirety.)

TITLE I – GENERAL PROVISIONS
Findings and Declaration of Policy

Sec. 101. The Congress hereby finds and declares that the security of the Nation requires the fullest development of the mental resources and technical skills of its young men and women. The present emergency demands that additional and more adequate educational opportunities made available. The defense of this Nation depends upon the mastery of modern techniques developed from complex scientific principles. It depends as well upon the discovery and development of new principles, new techniques and new knowledge.

We must increase our efforts to identify and educate more of the talent of our Nation. This requires programs that will give assurance that no student of ability will be denied an opportunity to higher education because of financial need; will correct as rapidly as possible the existing imbalances in our educational programs which have led to an insufficient proportion of our population educated in science, mathematics and modern foreign languages and trained in technology.

The Congress reaffirms the principle and declares that the States and local communities have and must retain control over and primary responsibility for public education. The national interest requires, however, that the Federal Government give assistance to education for programs which are important to our defense.

To meet the present educational emergency requires additional effort at all levels of government. It is therefore the purpose of this Act to provide substantial assistance in various forms to individuals, and to States and their subdivisions, in order to insure trained manpower of sufficient quality and quantity to meet the national defense needs of the United States.

TITLE V – GUIDANCE, COUNSELING AND TESTING; IDENTIFICATION AND ENCOURAGEMENT OF ABLE STUDENTS

Part A – State Programs

Appropriations Authorized
Sec. 501. There are hereby authorized to be appropriated $15,000,000 for the fiscal year ending June 30, 1959, and for each of the three succeeding fiscal years, for making grants to State educational agencies under this part to assist them to establish and maintain programs of testing and guidance and counseling.

Allotments to States
Sec. 502. From the sums appropriated pursuant to section 501 for any fiscal year the Commissioner shall reserve such amount, but not in excess of 2 per centum thereof, as he may determine for allotment as provided in section 1008. From the remainder of such sums the Commissioner shall allot to each State an amount which bears the same ratio to the amount of such remainder as the school-age population of such State bears to the total of the school-age populations of all the States. The amount allotted to any State under the preceding sentence for any fiscal year which is less than $20,000 shall be increased to $20,000, the total of increases thereby required being derived by proportionately reducing the amount allotted to each of the remaining States under the preceding sentence, but with such adjustments as may be necessary to prevent the allotment of any such remaining States from being thereby reduced to less than $20,000.

State Plans
Sec. 503 (a) Any State which desires to receive payments under this part shall submit to the Commissioner, through its State educational agency, a State plan which meets the requirements of section 1004(a) and sets forth –

1. a program for testing students in the public secondary schools, and if authorized by law in other secondary schools, of such State to identify students with outstanding aptitudes and ability and the means of testing which will be utilized in carrying out such program; and
2. a program of guidance and counseling in the public secondary schools of such State (A) to advise students of courses of study best suited to their ability, aptitudes and skills and (B) to encourage students with outstanding aptitudes and ability to complete their secondary school education, take the necessary courses for admission to institutions of higher education and enter such institutions.

(b) The Commissioner shall approve any State plan and any modification thereof which complies with the provisions of subsection (a).

Payments to States
Section 504. (a) Payment under this part shall be made to those State educational agencies which administer plans approved under section 503. For the fiscal year ending June 30, 1959, such payments shall equal the amount expended by the State in carrying out its State plan, and for the fiscal year ending June 30, 1960, and for each of the two succeeding fiscal years, such payments shall equal one-half of the amount so expended; except that no State educational agency shall receive payment under this part for any fiscal year in excess of that State's allotment for that fiscal year as determined under section 502.

(b) In any State which has a State plan approved under section 503 and in which the State educational agency is not authorized by law to make payments to cover the cost of testing students in any one or more secondary schools in such State to determine student abilities and aptitudes, the Commissioner shall arrange for the testing of such students and shall pay the cost thereof for the fiscal year ending June 30, 1959, and one-half of the cost thereof for any of the three succeeding fiscal years out of such State's allotment. Testing of students pursuant to this subsection shall, so far as practicable, be comparable to, and be done at the same grade levels and under the same conditions as in the case of, testing of students in public schools under the State plan.

Part B – Counseling and Guidance Training Institutes

Authorization
Sec. 511. There are hereby authorized to be appropriated $6,250,000 for the fiscal year ending June 30, 1959, and $7,250,000 for each of the three succeeding fiscal years, to enable the Commissioner to arrange, by contracts with institutions of higher education, for the operation by them of short-term or regular session institutes for the provision of training to improve the qualifications of personnel engaged in counseling and guidance of students in secondary schools, or teachers in such schools preparing to engage in such counseling and guidance. Each individual engaged or preparing to engage in counseling and guidance, who attends an institute operated under the provisions of this part, shall be eligible (after application therefore) to receive a stipend at the rate of $75 per week for the period of his attendance at such institute, and each such individual with one or more dependents shall receive an additional stipend at the rate of $15 per week for each such dependent for the period of such attendance.

From *The National Defense and Guidance Training Institutes Program: A report of the first 50 institutes* (pp. 81-83) by L.E. Tyler, 1960, Washington, DC: U.S. Government Printing Office.

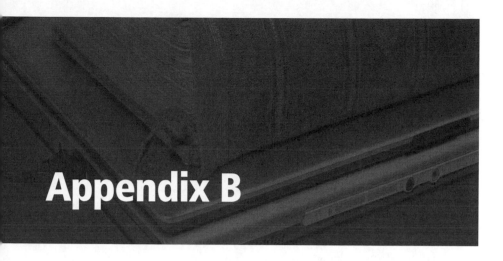

Appendix B

Outcome Research Coding Protocol

CODING STUDIES AND RATING THE LEVEL OF EVIDENCE FOR THE CAUSAL EFFECT OF AN INTERVENTION

School counseling interventions will be evaluated by the Evidence-Based Practice Panel to determine the level of evidence that exists in outcome studies that supports the contention that the intervention causes a change in an important student outcome. The following seven domains will be used in this evaluation. Each domain has threshold criteria for two levels of strength: Strong Evidence and Promising Evidence. To be considered an Evidence-Based Practice, an intervention must exceed the Strong Evidence threshold in all seven areas. To be considered a Promising Practice, an intervention must exceed Promising Evidence threshold in all seven areas.

Three panel members will independently review the outcome research related to a given intervention and independently rate each intervention on all seven criteria. Consensus in ratings will be achieved through consultation. The panel will disseminate its overall rating and, in cases where interventions fail to achieve Evidence-Based Practice or Promising Practice status, an analysis of deficiencies in the evidence base will be offered.

The seven domains and criteria are included below:

Domain 1: Measurement
Principle: Important academic, career and/or personal/social outcomes are measured using reliable and valid instruments.

Strong Evidence:
- Outcome measures have established high reliability and validity characteristics.
- Outcome measures are established to be appropriate for the population under study.

Promising Evidence
- Outcome measures have been used in previous studies.
- Reliability characteristics are evaluated in the study and show adequate reliability.
- Logical argument supports the appropriateness of the measures for the population under study.

Domain 2: Comparison Groups
Principle: Comparison groups with adequate controls are included so that resulting group differences can be attributed to the intervention.

Strong Evidence:
- Active comparison groups (alternative treatment) with adequate controls (attention, placebo) are included in an outcome study.
- Initial group equivalence is assured through random assignment.
- Group equivalence in mortality/attrition is established.

Promising Evidence:
- Groups equated through matching or statistical procedures (e.g. ANCOVA) or strong pre-post-test designs are used with adequate controls.

Domain 3: Statistical Analyses of Outcome Variables
Principle: Statistical analysis documents low probability of type 1 error and potency of intervention.

Strong Evidence:
- Statistically significant finding using appropriate test.
- Control the experiment-wise error rate.
- Adequate N.
- At least a moderate effect size for critical outcome variables.

Promising Evidence:
- Statistically significant finding using appropriate test.
- Control for experiment-wise error rate.

- Adequate N.
- At least a small effect size for critical outcome variables.

Domain 4: Implementation Fidelity
Principle: Intervention can be delivered with fidelity across contexts and is not contaminated by implementer.

Strong Evidence:
- Intervention is extensively documented (manual or protocol) so that it can be reliably replicated.
- Intervention is delivered by multiple people with adequate training and checks for adherence to protocol.

Domain 5: Replication
Principle: The same intervention independently implemented with an equivalent population results in equivalent outcomes.

Strong Evidence:
- Independent evaluators find equivalent outcomes with a similar population.

Promising Evidence:
- Same evaluator finds equivalent outcomes with same population.

Domain 6: Ecological Validity
Principle: The intervention can be implemented effectively in a public school with consistent effects across all student subgroups or with known differences between student subgroups. Limitations of the generalizability of results are clearly explicated.

Strong Evidence:
- Study conducted in a diverse public school.
- Outcomes are assessed across different subgroups of students or clearly specified as valid for a specific subgroup.

Promising Evidence:
- Study conducted in a private, laboratory or charter school or in a public school with limited diversity.

Domain 7: Persistence of Effect

Principle: The intervention results in a lasting effect on an important outcome measure.

Strong Evidence:
- Treatment-comparison group differences are demonstrated to persist for a practically significant time period.

Promising Evidence:
- Treatment-comparison group differences are demonstrated to persist beyond the immediate implementation.

From "Report of the national panel for evidence-based school counseling: Outcome research coding protocol and evaluation of student success skills and second step: by Carey, J.C., Dimmitt, C., Hatch, T.A., Lapan, R.T., & Whitson, S.C. (2008). *Professional School Counseling, 11*, pp. 205-206. 2008. American School Counselor Association. Reprinted with permission.

ABOUT THE AUTHOR

Norman C. Gysbers, Ph.D., is a curators' professor in the Department of Educational, School and Counseling Psychology at the University of Missouri. He received his B.A. degree from Hope College, Holland, Mich., in 1954. He was a teacher in the Muskegon Heights Michigan School District (1954-1956) and served in the U.S. Army Artillery (1956-1958). He received his master's degree (1959) and doctoral degree(1963) from the University of Michigan. He joined the faculty of the College of Education, University of Missouri in 1963 as an assistant professor. In addition to his duties as an assistant professor he also served as the licensed school counselor at the University Laboratory School until 1970.

He was awarded a Franqui Professorship from the Universite Libre de Bruxelles, Belgium and lectured there in February 1984. He was a visiting scholar at the University of Hong Kong in May 2000, 2002 and 2004, the Chinese University of Hong Kong in January 2001 and a Scholar in Residence at the University of British Columbia July-August, 2000. Gysbers' research and teaching interests are in career development, career counseling and school guidance and counseling program development, management and evaluation. He is author of 88 articles, 36 chapters in published books, 15 monographs and 19 books, one of which has been translated into Italian, Korean, Japanese and Chinese.

He has received many awards, most notably the National Career Development Association's National Merit Award in 1983, the American Counseling Association's Eminent Career Award in 1989, the American School Counselor Association's Mary Gehrke Lifetime Achievement Award in 2004, the William T. Kemper Award for Excellence in Teaching in 2002, the Governor's Award for Excellence in Teaching in 2004, the Faculty/Alumni Award from the University of Missouri-Columbia in 1997, and the Distinguished Faculty Award from the University of Missouri Alumni Association in 2008.

Gysbers was editor of the *Career Development Quarterly*, 1962-1970; president of the National Career Development Association, 1972-73; president of the American Counseling Association, 1977-78; and vice president of the Association of Career and Technical Education, 1979-1982. He was also the Editor of *The Journal of Career Development* from 1978 until 2006.